D1188459

JOURNAL FOR THE STUDY OF THE OLD TESTAMENT SUPPLEMENT SERIES
72

Editors
David J.A. Clines
Philip R. Davies

BIBLE AND LITERATURE SERIES
20

General Editor
David M. Gunn

Assistant General Editor
Danna Nolan Fewell

Consultant Editors
Elizabeth Struthers Malbon
James G. Williams

Almond Press
Sheffield

In memory of

John Wesley Rast

teacher
friend
a light eclipsed

CIRCLE OF SOVEREIGNTY

A Story of Stories in Daniel 1–6

DANNA NOLAN FEWELL

The Almond Press · 1988

Bible and Literature Series, 20

General Editor: David M. Gunn
(Columbia Theological Seminary, Decatur, Georgia)
Assistant General Editor: Danna Nolan Fewell
(Perkins School of Theology, Dallas, Texas)
Consultant Editors: Elizabeth Struthers Malbon
(Virginia Polytechnic Institute & State University, Blacksburg, Virginia)
James G. Williams
(Syracuse University, Syracuse, New York)

Copyright © 1988 Sheffield Academic Press

Published by Almond Press
Editorial direction: David M. Gunn
Columbia Theological Seminary
P.O. Box 520, Decatur
GA 30031, U.S.A.
Almond Press is an imprint of
Sheffield Academic Press Ltd
The University of Sheffield
343 Fulwood Road
Sheffield S10 3BP
England

Typeset by Sheffield Academic Press
and
printed in Great Britain
by Billing & Sons Ltd
Worcester

British Library Cataloguing in Publication Data

Fewell, Danna Nolan
    Circle of Sovereignty
    1. Bible. O.T. Daniel-Critical Studies
    I. Title   II. Series
    III. Series
    224'.506

ISSN 0206-4493
ISSN 0309-0787
ISBN 1-85075-158-7

CONTENTS

ACKNOWLEDGMENTS

Several people deserve a word of thanks for the interest they have shown in my work and the energy they have invested in this project in particular.

Robert Detweiler has guided me, with remarkable skill and patience (and sometimes a much-needed sense of humor), in the field of literary criticism and theory. Eager to see the courtship between literary criticism and biblical studies develop further, he has instilled in me an excitement for the possibilities that both fields, when combined, can offer.

Martin Buss has consistently encouraged creativity and the exploration of new approaches to biblical studies. He has shown me that the balance of academic discipline and creative freedom is precarious but rewarding.

Gene Tucker showed me years ago just how much fun exegesis could be. Though a close reader in a more traditional vein, he is a close reader nonetheless. His appreciation for detail and his enthusiasm for new discovery have been contagious. He supported my interest in literary criticism during a time when it was not popular to do so. For that and for his friendship, I convey my thanks.

I thank Carol Newsom not only for the inordinate amount of time and energy she has spent in reading, critiquing and reflecting upon this project, but also for her fine teaching ability, an ability which drew me, as an MTS student, to the graduate program in Old Testament studies. It was her vision of ancient texts and their theological relevance that made me recognize that the Hebrew Bible still has much to say to the modern world. Her fascination with the book of Daniel has inspired my own. Because of her familiarity with the text, her responses to my readings have been of immeasurable value.

Finally, my gratitude goes to David Gunn who, before I ever met him, gave me many hours of pleasure with his readings of other Old Testament narratives, the stories of David and Saul in particular, and who, since I have come to know him, has engaged this project as enthusiastically as if it were his own. His skills and perceptions as a literary critic of the Bible are an undeniable and much appreciated influence upon my approach to the text. Our conversations, ranging from debate to banter, have been a crucial sustenance for me, never failing to renew my energy and bolster my excitement about the text and the task that I have undertaken.

To my friends and family, I also extend my love and my gratitude. Without their continuous support and their words of encouragement, I might never have been able to complete this project. A special family contribution to this book is that of a much-loved and talented uncle, Van Ross Nolan, who designed the cover.

I express my deepest appreciation to my dearest friend and companion David Fewell, whose confidence in me, even in the most trying of times, has never once wavered.

INTRODUCTION

This study brings together elements both old and new: an old collection of even older stories—Daniel 1-6; an ancient activity—reading; and some relatively new theories about narrative poetics[1] and the reading process.[2] The offspring of this somewhat polygamous union is a new reading, for better or worse, of the story of stories in Daniel 1-6.

Text and Translation

The literary selection under scrutiny here is the particular arrangement of the particular words as preserved in the Massoretic Text of Daniel 1-6.[3] The Greek and Latin versions of the Daniel narratives not only include narrative sequels (Susanna and Bel and the Dragon), but also insertions into the earlier stories, causing emphases to fall on characters, events, points of view, etc., other than those elevated in the Massoretic stories. In short, these versions are different texts: different arrangements of different words. A comparison and contrast of these different texts and their subsequent different meanings would be an interesting and helpful study; however, I will not be including such an examination here.

The selection of chapters 1-6 from the book of Daniel has been made on form critical grounds. Daniel 1-6 is narrative material; the remainder of the book falls into the genre of apocalyptic.[4] I am concerned not only with the poetics of the individual stories, but also with the poetics of the narrative unit Daniel 1-6.[5]

A translation introduces each of the chapters in this work. The translations are not intended to raise or solve text critical issues in Daniel 1-6; they simply provide the opportunity to retell the stories. I present them as a convenience to my readers, as a memory aid and as a standard by which my subsequent readings can be measured. Of course, just as stories remembered are stories re-membered, so translations, as retellings, are interpretations. Consequently, I encourage my readers to follow their Massoretic text, and I invite them, if they are so inclined, to see my translations as foreshadowers of the readings that follow.

Readers will probably notice that the translations are not always as smooth as they might be. As often as possible, they attempt to recapture the wordplays, the repetitions, the images that can so delight the reader of Hebrew and Aramaic. In many instances, however, this has not been possible and I have been forced to use notes and discussion to recreate associations.

Reading Strategy

Form Critical Influences

Form criticism, more than any other traditional discipline of Old Testament study, furnishes an important aspect of the study of biblical poetics. Consequently, I begin my discussion, not with a history of interpretation or a survey of all the problems of Daniel 1–6 or the secondary sources that have attended to these problems;[6] rather, I begin with a discussion of recent form critical studies that have provided the starting point for my subsequent work on the poetics and the reading of Daniel 1–6.

According to recent form critical study of biblical narative, the stories in Daniel can most appropriately be classified as either 'tale'[7] or 'short story'.[8] Granted, short story is a broad classification, but it might also be as specific a label as can be applied to the narratives in Daniel.

Other, less applicable, genres have been proposed for these stories.[9] H.-P. Müller has argued that the stories in Daniel originated as *Märchen*,[10] 'traditional narrative set in a mysterious world of fantasy, provoking sympathy for the principal figure'.[11] Obviously, the stories do contain fantastic elements, but, for the most part, the story world of Daniel is realistic.[12] Furthermore, Müller's proposal is based upon the presupposition that Daniel and his Hebrew friends are the principal figures in the stories. A close reading of characterization and point of view in Daniel 1–6 reveals, however, that the principal characters in the Daniel stories (with the exception of Daniel 1) are not the Judean sages, but the foreign sovereigns. Audiences have traditionally responded more sympathetically to the secondary figures, the Jewish courtiers, than to the primary characters, Nebuchadnezzar, Belshazzar, and Darius.

Other scholars[13] have designated the stories as *midrashim*. A midrash is 'a work that attempts to make a text of Scripture understandable, useful and relevant for a later generation. It is the text of Scripture which is the point of departure and it is for the sake of the text that the midrash exists'.[14] The contribution that this classification makes to our understanding of Daniel 1-6 (and indeed of the Hebrew canon in general) is its recognition of the inter-relatedness of scripture.[15] The Daniel stories do contain many allusions to, and analogies with, other parts of the Hebrew Bible; nevertheless, one can hardly say that the Daniel stories exist primarily to illuminate these external texts. If the stories were midrashic then they, being dependent upon and subordinate to other texts, would be incoherent, or at least incomplete, in and of themselves, which is certainly not the case. A more appropriate way to read texts analogous to parts of Daniel 1-6 is simply to read looking for comparisons and contrasts. Parallels (e.g. of plot, theme, characterization, language) initiate dialogue; differences clarify the stance of each text. The goal of this kind of reading is much less ambitious than attempting to show how one text exists mainly to serve another; the goal of exploring *intertextuality*[16] is to enrich the reading of both part and whole.[17]

Another, and recently more popular, classification of the Daniel stories is that of *legend*.[18] A legend is 'a narrative primarily concerned with the wonderful and aimed at edification'.[19] The legend focuses on character rather than plot[20] and has been distinguished from story (or tale) by its 'specific practical aim' and 'its consequent relative indifference to narrative art'.[21] A close reading of Daniel 1-6 shows the description of these stories as singularly 'aimed at edification' and 'indifferent to narrative art' to be a drastic underreading of the text. In the first place, the stories do more than edify. In the second place, if the stories are indeed designed to edify, then an examination of exactly how the stories edify is in order. I suspect that, in the case of Daniel 1-6, edification involves something much more complicated than simply providing an example of how one should live. In the third place, to say that the stories are 'indifferent to narrative art' implies not only a preconceived notion of what 'narrative art' is, but also a premature judgment (that is, a judgment made before a study of the poetics of Daniel 1-6) concerning whether or not Daniel 1-6 meets the requirements of 'narrative art'. It would be better, I think, to take the stories on their own terms, to study how these particular stories work as stories, before judging whether or not their construction can be deemed artistry.

The classification of the Daniel stories as short stories requires further consideration. Lee Humphreys, in presenting the novella as a genre falling between short story and novel, gives a helpful list of the characteristics of the short story (and the novel).[22] According to Humphreys, short stories can be characterized accordingly:

1. Short stories (and novels) are fiction. They are true to life in various ways, but they are not attempts at historical record. 'This does not, of course, preclude the appearance in them of personages and events from the area of history; what is reported in them is not designed, however, to meet any tests of historical accuracy'.[23]

2. Short stories (and novels) are narratives constructed around a plot that begins with a general description of the situation (exposition)[24] that continues with the creation of complication and tension, and moves to a resolution.

3. Short stories (and novels) are prose although they may contain poetic pieces within them.

4. Short stories (and novels) are 'the conscious creative work of generally a single author. They are not folk products that evolve over time' although they 'may use motifs, themes, plot structures, and characters drawn from the realm of folklore and popular oral and written traditions'.[25] Unfortunately, the presence of elements from other literature has too often been used as evidence for literary dependence or the evolution of tradition. Authors, however, borrow much material from other places in their acts of literary creation, fully expecting (at least part of) the audience to recognize the borrowed material—structures, motifs, or whatever— and to incorporate the borrowed elements into their understanding of what the author is saying.[26]

5. Short stories (and novels) are measured by 'aesthetic success' and by the quality of their mimetic portrayal of the world. They are designed to entertain[27] and their success depends in part upon their presentation of a world and a situation to which the audience can relate.[28]

A short story is to be distinguished from either a novel or novella by its limitations. Short stories are limited in the length of narration (biblical short stories range from a few verses to a chapter or two). They have a limited succession of events and, consequently, limited complication. The action in a short story takes place in a limited period of time. Along with having a limited number of characters, the characterization itself is limited: '... the short story *reveals* the nature of a character or a situation while a novel *develops* characters or situations'.[29] Through the course of a short story the audience may gradually learn more about a character or situation, but normally the story world does not provide the kind of expanse needed for a character to undergo any extensive change.

For the most part, this revelatory quality is an accurate description of the individual stories of Daniel 1-6, though one could make a case for ch. 4 as an exception. However, when one reads the entire collection—and it is edited to be read as continuing story—one can see characters and situations changing through the duration of the time narrated. The whole narrative of 1-6 is not, in a strict sense, a novella.[30] It is not structured around a continuing, complex plot line; instead, it is paratactically constructed—one plot line is linked with another plot line which is linked with another and so forth. Nevertheless, 1-6 does display continuity on other levels—characters, setting, theme, etc.—and does show development of character and situation as the narrative progresses.

A few scholars have classified the individual narratives in Daniel 1-6 as 'tales' or 'stories' and then endeavored to find a narrower, more precise designation. Humphreys[31] used the setting of the story world, a foreign court, to qualify the genre of all the stories; thus, they are court tales, court stories, or stories about courtiers.[32] He uses the motifs of 'conflict' and 'contest' to narrow further the categorization of the stories. Chapters 3 and 6 are *tales of court conflict* in which one faction of the court seeks to bring about the ruin of another faction; chs. 2, 4, and 5 are *tales of court contest* in which one courtier succeeds at some endeavor where all the others fail.[33] According to Humphreys, all of the stories have common functions (that are to be distinguished from those of the visions in the latter half of the book): The stories are designed to entertain[34] and to 'present a style of life for the diaspora Jew which affirms most strongly that at one and the same time the Jew can remain loyal to his heritage and God and yet can live a creative, rewarding, and fulfilled life precisely within a foreign setting, and in interaction with it. . .'[35]

Susan Niditch and Robert Doran[36] have focused more narrowly on one particular type of (what would be in Humphrey's schema) tale of court contest. By studying not simply motifs but the structure of motifs, Niditch and Doran found that Daniel 2 fits a particular type of folktale,[37] that has to do with a hero's wisdom.[38] Briefly, the motif pattern of type 922 is that a lower-class hero solves a difficult problem posed by a higher-class character and is subsequently rewarded.[39]

Both of the studies of Humphreys and Niditch and Doran find typical elements in the literature of Daniel 1-6. However, both also admit to unusual elements present in the material that do not fit easily with the proposed genres. The unusual elements noted in these two studies have to do with the role of the divine.[40] Philip Davies has observed the prominence of God in the Daniel stories and has redescribed the genres accordingly. He separates the stories into *interpretation stories* (chs. 2, 4, 5) and *deliverance stories* (chs. 3, 6).[41] In Davies's outline, the stories' resolutions contain an additional common motif: 'the king learns that the hero's god is all-powerful'.[42]

If these studies of form have found typical elements in Daniel 1-6, they have also pointed to non-typical elements as well. And this, too, (perhaps especially) is part of form criticism's contribution to literary study.

> Genre study depends on finding the typical in a piece of literature. But it can also facilitate identification of the unique, simply by enabling the critic to discover what elements of a piece do not correspond to the class. And the unique would serve the task of interpretation by setting the context for the intention of an individual piece of art.[43]

The following reading of Daniel 1-6 explores each story as a unique mixture of typical elements and the narrative complex of 1-6 as a text which assimilates the individual stories into its larger system.

Literary Critical Influences

The strategy employed in the close reading that follows is informed by several different ideas and methodologies.[44] From the legacy of New Criticism has come the close attention to textual detail in terms of the work's language and structure and, in the case of narrative, the work's plot, characterization, thematic development, point of view, and so forth. Whatever one's quarrel with New Criticism's attempt to divorce the text from its historical backgrounds (the authorial intention, the historical and social situation of production) and its affective foregrounds (the impact of the work on the reader),[45] one cannot deny that New Criticism's emphasis on the close reading of texts has made a lasting and positive impact on biblical literary criticism.

To my strategy of reading, structuralism has also made contributions, particularly in terms of its theory of meaning production.[46] According to structuralist ideology, meaning is produced in discourse through relations between or among (i.e. structures of) terms. The terms themselves, *signs* according to Saussurean linguistics,[47] are also the products of relation: A linguistic sign (i.e. a word) is the union of a form which signifies (i.e. 'the signifier') and an idea that is signified (i.e. 'the signified'). The two parts of the sign (the signifier and the signified) come into existence simultaneously. Their union is a cultural construct, not a product of nature.[48] How this informs my understanding of a literary text has to do with the problem of *reference*. According to structuralist theory, the referent of a text is not something out there in the real world, but the text itself.[49] What this means for the reading of Daniel 1–6 is this: Although the narrative may use historical events, personages, settings to construct the story world, the frame of reference is still only the story world itself. Daniel 1–6 does not tell us what court life was actually like during the reign of Nebuchadnezzar, the historical Babylonian king; Daniel 1–6 only describes the court life in the story world.

At the heart of signification is differentiation. Elementary concepts of thought are defined in relation to one another by their mutual opposition to each other: day and night, wet and dry, male and female, good and evil, human and divine, etc. Binary oppositions, when embodied in characters, events, and situations, create stories. The tension of narrative is, most basically understood, the result of differentiation.[50] In the stories of Daniel 1–6, the most basic opposition, and indeed the differentiation that creates the complication, is that of divine sovereignty and human sovereignty.

Deconstruction[51] is yet another influence on my strategy of reading. Deconstruction acknowledges textual differentiation, opposition, and self-reference; however, deconstructive criticism reaches beyond structuralism in an exploration of how these elements render the text *unstable*.[52] A deconstructionist mode of reading recognizes that binary oppositions do not simply coexist in a balanced equitable relationship. Binary oppositions are in fact hierarchical: one element takes priority over the other. In the case of Daniel 1-6, divine sovereignty takes priority over human sovereignty. The hierarchical relation between oppositions, however, is a slippery one.[53] The secondary element subtly but constantly undermines the primary one. So, for example, Daniel 1-6 makes point after point about God's sovereignty over human beings, but God's sovereignty is undercut by the way in which human sovereignty keeps pushing to the fore: God's power and presence is constantly being screened through human characters' points of view; God's identity is expressed in terms of human identity; God's wisdom is translated by a human mediator and so forth. And, because a text's 'production of meaning cannot be arrested through a relationship with absolute referents. . ., textuality will always be in progress and unfinished and thus undecidable'.[54] In other words, the meaning of a text cannot be exhaustively determined by an appeal to anything in the real world, an historical event, for example. With every rereading of it, a text has the potential to produce new meaning.

When the idea of differentiation within a text is pushed to its ultimate conclusion, then the text (or its meaning) can differ from and within itself. The text does not produce one meaning; the text does not even produce a range of meanings that are all compatible: The text produces meanings that are in tension with one another.

> It is this type of textual difference that informs the process of deconstructive criticism. *Deconstruction* is not synonymous with *destruction*, however. It is in fact much closer to the original meaning of the word *analysis*, which etymologically means 'to undo'—a virtual synonym for 'to de-construct'. The de-construction of a text does not proceed by random doubt or arbitrary subversion, but by the careful teasing out of warring forces of signification within the text itself. If anything is destroyed in a deconstructive reading, it is not the text, but the claim to unequivocal domination of one mode of signifying over another. . .[55]

Within a text, undercurrent meanings repeatedly disturb, if not displace, surface meanings. Because of this textual instability, because textual meaning is undecidable, and, because we as readers, in the interest of coherence, re-present texts as consonant communications, then every reading is fated to be a misreading. In actuality, there is no 'definitive reading' of anything; some readings' 'misses' simply go longer unrecognized than do the 'misses' of other readings.[56]

Reader response criticism acknowledges that the reader contributes to the instability of the text. The reader, in fact, in the very act of reading the literary work, helps to *create the text*. Because all texts contain indeterminable elements, gaps in information, the reader must, in order to make sense of the work, fill the gaps.[57] How the reader fills gaps helps to determine meanings in the text.

My reading of Daniel 1-6 is a coloring between the lines. The Massoretic text provides the lines and I paint the gaps. The paint used is a mixture of pigments from a number of different sources. The reading tools, skills, and influences, those that are implicit and those that are made explicit in this work, have been provided by the Academy, particularly the fields of Old Testament study and of literary criticism. Nevertheless, one cannot suppose that this represents the total constraint of my reading. As Terry Eagleton has so aptly put it, all criticism is political.[58] What I see in the text, the judgments that I make, the values that I elevate, the attitudes that I critique, are as much influenced by my nationality, race, gender, religious tradition, locality, temporality, and a multitude of experiences resisting simple classification, as they are guided by academic agenda. No reader escapes ideology.

My reading of Daniel 1-6 is, of course, neither final nor exhaustive. It is inspired by and parasitic on, what I think are, the misreadings of others.[59] It is, itself, doomed to be a misreading—one that, I hope, will prompt yet other readings. Such is the way we pay tribute to the power of the biblical text.

The discussion contained in chs. 1-6 is one long exercise in filling gaps. While I may not be constantly making this activity explicit, I *am* constantly doing it. While my language, in places, may sound assertive, it functions as invitation: Consider this reading. Try it on. See if it fits.

Narrative Poetics and the Mechanics of Reading
My basic presuppositions about biblical narrative concern the narrative itself, the narrator, and the audience. In spite of its unique trappings of plot, characters, themes and such, narrative is basically discourse,[60] a piece of writing designed to communicate certain

knowledge to its audience. However, the communication is not direct but indirect. Consequently, the reader is not the passive receiver of a message; rather, the reader, because of incomplete knowledge, must actively participate in the transmission. Much like putting together a puzzle, the reader must piece together small bits of information before the larger picture is visible.

Another presupposition is that the narrator is reliable in the sense that, if the reader follows what the narrator says, even uncritically, the reader will, in most cases, be able to make some sense of what is going on in the story, who the characters are, and what they are doing.[61] What the narrator tells is lucid enough; what draws the reader in, however, is the fact that the narrator does not tell all.[62] In terms of reading and piecing together meaning in a story, the most volatile narratorial omission has to do with the *significance* of what is being told.[63] Questions about significance (what is important, why is it important, how is it important?) present themselves on small scale and large, from the significance of minute detail to that of entire stories.

The close reading of biblical narrative involves not only assimilating explicit information, but also teasing out what is implicit, the information that falls into the gaps. Because any narrative leaves informational gaps in the story world, the reader proceeds by inference. The reading procedure involves asking and answering basic questions about the story world: What is happening? Who are the characters involved? Why are they involved? How do they relate to each other? What is the social world of the story like? Do the characters behave according to any particular social expectations? And the list of questions, of course, goes on. The text itself explicitly answers very few of these questions. The reader supplies the answers. Some answers are tentative, temporary, and partial; some are complete and final.[64]

The gaps left in a story might be anything—an event, a motive, a causal link, a character trait. The omitted information might be told later explicitly, implicitly, or not at all. In the meantime, the reader formulates an hypothesis that makes sense of, or tentatively 'closes', the gap. We may discover, in the course of reading, that our hypothesis was correct or incorrect or we may be left uncertain.

The gaps that leave the reader uncertain are usually ambiguous in either one of two ways. On the one hand, several compatible explanations may fill the gap. For example, if the gap is character motivation, the reader might conclude that a character's act of violence is motivated by anger, revenge, and ambition. In such an instance, one motivation does not necessarily preclude other motivations. On the other hand, two or more mutually exclusive hypotheses might make sense of the text. A character might act out of ignorance or out of a certain knowledge. A fine example is Meir Sternberg's study of Uriah the Hittite.[65] Uriah might be read as a character totally unaware of what David has done and is planning to do to him. Or Uriah might be read as a character who suspects what has transpired between his wife and his king. In the first reading, Uriah is an innocent pawn whose ideals bring about his downfall; in the second, Uriah is a man 'torn between his sense of betrayal and his sense of duty' who takes silent revenge upon David.[66]

Close reading involves orienting oneself within the poetics of the narrative. The following discussion outlines narrative poetics and suggests ways of working with the poetics toward the goal of interpretation. The immediate general outline categorizes the poetic aspects and thereby reflects the procedure of 'picking apart', of 'undoing' the text in attention to detail. In actuality, however, the categories overlap: One cannot have plot without actors; point of view is integral to characterization, and so forth. In the reading of Daniel 1-6 that follows, I discuss poetic elements not categorically but contextually—as I encounter them in the text—in an attempt to preserve the flow of the narrative as well as the flow of the reading process.

Plot Structure

Plot structure simply refers to the pattern of the events that take place in the story world.[67] In a well-constructed plot, every event is integral to the story; there are no extraneous elements. The events in a short story are connected to one another either chronologically or causally or both.[68] Furthermore, story events are arranged dramatically, i.e. in a manner that allows tension to rise and fall.

There are three basic parts of a narrative plot. The *exposition* or the introduction sets forth the beginning of the story. The exposition usually provides the general setting and situation, introduces (all or some of) the major characters, and often includes an event that initiates the chain of events to follow. The story itself revolves around a *conflict* or a complication that moves to a climax. (Of course, there may be more than one conflict and more than one

climax.) The *denouement* (literally 'unknotting') resolves or presents
the outcome of the conflict.[69]

Plot evokes narrative interest through indeterminacy or gapping.
The most common kind of plot indeterminacy is the question of what
will happen in the future of the story world. When the reader
knows'... enough to expect a struggle but not to predict its course,
and above all its outcome...', the narrative has generated interest in
the form of *suspense*.[70] The sharpest form of suspense arises when
story clues point to two (or more) possible, but incompatible
outcomes of the conflict, one that plays upon the reader's hope (what
the reader wants to happen) and one that plays upon the reader's fear
(what the reader is afraid might happen).[71]

The technique of foreshadowing in biblical narrative[72] rarely
involves explicitness on the part of the narrator.[73] Foreshadowing in
biblical narrative is done in various ways with varying degrees of
subtlety. The success of some foreshadowing devices depends upon
the reader's familiarity with other Hebrew literature. A narrative
might point to a (supposedly) known literary precedent, by staging a
similar situation, by establishing a similar system of character
relationships, or by using similar language. The conflict between
Absalom and Amnon that follows Amnon's rape of Tamar (2 Samuel
13) is foreshadowed by analogy to the story of Dinah in Genesis 34, a
story which also involves siblings, rape, deceit, and murder. The
stories alluded to do not exist to foreshadow other stories (they have
independent integrity); it is the narrator's suggested comparison that
provides the foreshadowing potential. It is left to the reader,
however, to recognize the connection and its function.

Another foreshadowing technique that also depends upon the
reader's associative skills is the allusion to paradigm. Narrative
patterns become paradigms through frequency of expression.[74]
(Frequency, of course, breeds familiarity; consequently this kind of
allusion is easier to recognize.) The established paradigm involving
conflict between older and younger siblings, the favoritism toward
the younger and the success over the older (Cain and Abel, Jacob and
Esau, Rachel and Leah) influences our expectations concerning the
conflict of the Joseph story. The paradigm of barren women
appealing to surrogacy (Sarah and Hagar, Rachel, Bilhah, Leah,
Zilpah) casts an unsettling shadow on the complications that arise in
the story of Ruth and Naomi.

The least subtle foreshadowing device is what Sternberg calls a 'dramatic forecast'.[75] Lest the reader miss this kind of foreshadowing, it is consciously accentuated as part of the narrative structure. Lest the reader fail to take it seriously, the dramatic forecast is usually couched as a message from God (see e.g. 2 Sam. 12.11). Dreams, visions, and oracles fall into this category. Such pointed foretelling often functions to underscore a particular theological worldview: God is in control of the events of the story; the reader is left to make the analogy that God is likewise in control of history.[76]

Another way in which the narrator holds the reader's interest in the plot is by inducing *curiosity*. Whereas suspense arises from a lack of information about the future, curiosity hinges on ambiguity concerning the past. When the reader enters a story in the narrative present without fully knowing the background of the scene unfolding, then the reader becomes curious about what is going on, why characters are acting and speaking the way they are, what events have led up to the present situation, and so forth. The narrator produces curiosity by arranging the events in some order other than the order in which they occur. By twisting the story's time line, the narrator makes the reader wait for the desired information about the past.[77]

Another way the narrator holds the reader's interest is through *surprise*.[78] When our attention is held by suspense or curiosity, we are aware of what we do not know and we act accordingly. Surprise, however, depends upon the reader's being lured into false certitude of knowledge. Discontinuities in chronology must appear to be continuities. Old information must look settled for new information to be unsettling, i.e. surprising.[79]

Understanding the Characters

As a pattern of events taking place in a particular period of time, plot is inextricably bound to characters on at least two accounts. Characters initiate, endure, and are affected by events, and characters, like real people, are shaped by their temporality. The experience of their present becomes their past and informs how they anticipate the future.

Story characters can be presented in varying degrees of complexity.[80] The most simple kind of character is the *agent*. Agents are not usually given any distinguishing features. Their function on the mechanical level of the narrative is to keep the plot moving. The importance of their presence in the story world lies in the effect they have on the plot and the other characters. The most common kind of agent found in biblical narrative is the messenger who rarely has personality but who, by transferring knowledge from one character to another, is integral to the ongoing plot. *Type* characters are flat characters, characters built around one particular trait. They are not portrayed with depth or individuality. They are sometimes collective characters, i.e. a group of people in the story world who act and speak as one. The most complex characters are round characters or *full-fledged* characters who reveal many personality traits. Full-fledged characters manifest qualities that 'real people' have. Characters often change their levels of complexity as the story progresses. A character who is an agent in one scene may be a full-fledged character in the next.

Characterization is dependent upon the narrator's construction and the reader's reconstruction. The narrator constructs character by providing information; the reader reconstructs character by observing, assessing, combining and interpreting the information that is given as well as by speculating about information that is not given. While, in the past, biblical critics have resisted discussions of characters' motivations, attitudes, emotions, for fear of reading too much into the text, now more critics are of the opinion that economy of characterization invites and encourages such speculation. Seymour Chatman writes

> ... should we restrain what seems a God-given right to infer and even to speculate about characters if we like? Any such restraint strikes me as an impoverishment of aesthetic experience. Implication and inference belong to the interpretation of character as they do to that of plot, theme, and other narrative elements...
> ... A viable theory of character should preserve openness and treat characters as autonomous being, not as mere plot functions. It should argue that character is reconstructed by the audience from evidence announced or implicit in an original construction and communicated by the discourse, through whatever medium.[81]

In constructing a character, the biblical narrator sometimes speaks directly to the reader.[82] The narrator's explicit information rarely includes physical description. When a character's appearance or physical ability is noted, it is done in very general terms—fat, tall, beautiful, strong—and not in terms that would allow the reader to visualize in any kind of detail how the person looks. More often, the kind of information that a narrator will relate directly to the reader has to do with the character's status in society, for example, vocation or family background.[83]

The most prevalent techniques of characterization in biblical narrative have to do with *showing* rather than *telling*. We learn less about characters from the narrator's direct description of them, than we do from the characters themselves. We get to know story characters much the same way we get to know people in real life—by watching and listening to them as well as by watching and listening to how other characters respond to them. Sometimes we are privy to a character's inner thoughts, and this is where the narrator's telling merges with showing. The omniscient narrator may describe or present interior perception or monologue that helps the reader to understand what kind of person the character is.[84]

One helpful way of reconstructing a character is through comparison and contrast. If one presupposes that meaning is produced through differentiation, then one recognizes that the narrative offers an open, though usually implicit, invitation to compare and contrast. This kind of reconstructive activity can include: (1) comparing and contrasting one character with another; (2) comparing and contrasting a character's action with his or her earlier action; (3) comparing and contrasting a character's behavior with expected norms.[85]

Point of View

What is implicit in this discussion of showing characters versus telling about characters, the narrator's construction of characters and the reader's reconstruction of characters, is the idea that narrative is a network of communication, an interplay of relations involving the narrator and the reader, the narrator and the characters, and the characters and the reader.[86] The position or perspective from which story information is given, whether it be information concerning character or otherwise, is, broadly speaking, called *point of view*.[87]

The author who has fashioned the story (that is, the real flesh and blood person who actually wrote the story and who, as a historical person, is inaccessible to the reader) manipulates point of view by allowing story information to be given sometimes by the narrator who tells the story (and who is a literary construct) and sometimes by the characters who enact the story. While most recent literary critics of the Bible have affirmed that biblical narrators are omniscient and reliable[88] (and, indeed, this certainly seems to be the case in many biblical narratives), until an exhaustive study of point of view in biblical narrative is done, such general affirmation should be held suspect. An omniscient narrator expresses knowledge of the thoughts as well as of the deeds of any of the characters. A biblical narrator often claims knowledge of the thoughts and deeds of God as well as of human characters, and, therefore, could reasonably be labeled omniscient. Sometimes, however, the narrator's knowledge appears to be limited to the minds of a few or only one of the characters, in which case, the narrator is better described as being partially or selectively omniscient.[89]

Point of view in biblical narrative is multi-faceted. The voice that communicates story information shifts from being that of the narrator to being that of one or more of the characters. The narrator's voice is heard in narration, summary, description, comment, even the simple 's/he said'. This voice is the background (or unobtrusive), necessary voice of mediation. From time to time, however, the narrator, in attempting to orient the reader, resorts to giving direct information to the reader with, for example, etiologies, geographical notes, and similar explanations. This kind of communication brings the narrator's presence to the fore, bringing attention to the mediating process, and thereby 'breaking the frame'.[90] The narrator's point of view reflects the narrator's relation to the story: The narrator can be internal or external to the story world, close or distant (temporally, socially, emotionally) to the situation being recounted, neutral or biased (ethically, theologically) toward the characters and events.

An internal narrator, that is, a narrator who is also a character in the story, implies the presence of an additional external narrator (what might be called an implied narrator[91] or implied author)[92], a controlling figure who allows the perspective of the internal character-narrator to be elevated.

A common mistake in the interpretation of biblical texts is the confusion of the narrator's and the characters' points of view. Too often have readers assumed that the thoughts, values, etc., of a character are also the thoughts, values, etc., of the narrator, and are, consequently, the opinions and values that the narrator is urging the reader to adopt. The perspectives of characters and narrator are to be distinguished; they are different angles from which the story is seen. In fact, the plurality of perspectives is precisely what the text employs to resist the simplistic idea that a narrative pushes only one kind of rhetoric, that it offers only one basic message, one model of living, one meaning.

In examining point of view in terms of the characters, one must recognize further complexity. On one level, a character's point of view is, put simply, what the character perceives. A character's perception may be conveyed through the character's own speech or through words of the narrator. A character's inner life, if it is presented, can reveal what that character thinks or feels, how the character perceives events and how he or she is affected by the perception. The other side of point of view in terms of characterization is how a character is perceived by others—the narrator and other characters. Here again, the reader must rely upon what the narrator and the other characters say (or think) about the particular character in question, and what the other characters do in response to that character. An important indicator of how a character is perceived is how that character is *named* by others. Occasionally a narrator will play with proper names in order to communicate something of a character's personality, for example, the name Jacob establishes the child and the man as one who grabs the heel, who supplants (Gen. 25.26; 27.36). Proper names can also reflect someone else's perception of the person's character and lifestyle. 'The man's' renaming of Jacob as Israel by the Jabbok reveals God's perception of Jacob as someone 'who struggles with God and men and prevails' (Gen. 32.22-32). The use of particular titles that designate familial relationships or societal status also reveal how a person is perceived. The constant reference (on the part of narrator and characters) to Ruth as 'the Moabite woman' reflects the community's perception of her as an outsider (e.g. Ruth 1.22; 2.2, 6, 21; 4.5, 10). The reference to Bathsheba as 'the wife of Uriah' (2 Sam. 11.26; 12.15; and see also Mt. 1.6) comments not only on her place in society but also on David's lust, and, in a sense, summarizes the crux of the conflict: The limits established by society have not been respected.[93]

In order to distinguish between the narrator's and the characters' points of view, one must examine direct discourse (the showing) in relation to narration (the telling). Often narration repeats or summarizes direct discourse, either adopting the same point of view or presenting a different one. Alternative expressions (e.g. synonyms, slightly different wording) in narration and discourse can indicate a difference in point of view.[94]

℗ The third point of view to be considered is that of the reader. Essentially, the reader's or audience's point of view has to do with how the reader relates to the story.[95] The story teller, by focusing the reader's attention on particular incidents or people by arousing the reader's sympathies toward certain characters, manipulates the reader's point of view through choice of language, story structuring, and presupposing ethical and social norms.

The biblical text, then, speaks to an implied reader, a reader who has some kind of investment in the story. In the case of Daniel 1–6, the implied reader is one who knows and is interested in the larger story of Israel (and hence, whose attention is naturally drawn to Daniel and his friends). The implied reader is one who resonates with the theological issues that arise in Israel's religious experience (and consequently, who is concerned with things like the temple vessels from Jerusalem, religious fidelity, and the nature of divine revelations). The implied reader is one who can appreciate the power of politics, the politics of power, and the delicate balance between 'chuch and state'. Admittedly, these are broad characteristics of the implied reader of Daniel 1–6, but a more specific portrait is not, I think, possible. The text assumes a particular kind of reader, but the implied reader has a myriad variations.[96]

Just as sometimes there is an internal as well as an external narrator who participates in the telling of the story, likewise, there is, on occasion, an internal as well as an external audience, a *narratee* who is inside the story world as well as a(n implied) reader who is outside the story world.[97] While such an occurrence is rare in biblical narrative, an instance can be found in Daniel 4. In terms of point of view, one must remember that what the internal narrator says to the internal audience, or narratee, may not be what the external narrator (the implied narrator or author) is saying to the reader. Furthermore, while the narratee 'willingly suspends disbelief' and accepts unquestioningly what the internal narrator says, the reader's way of assessing what is being said is more complex. In determining the meaning(s) of a story, the reader is free to compare the story world—its presentation of reality—with the reality experienced by the reader in the world external to the story. (An internal audience, on the other hand, has no such freedom; the story world offers the only reality they know.) Knowledge of a larger 'text' or 'con-text', for example, a knowledge of history or culture or the natural world order, informs the reader's understanding of what a story means. If there are obvious incongruities between what happens in the story world and what happens in the real world, such incongruities figure into the creation of meaning.

The Language Medium

Underlying the narrative elements discussed thus far is the language itself. The story world—with its setting, its events, its characters—is a verbal construct, a world made of words. In narrative, life is language. Thus, at the heart of close reading is the scrutiny of words.

Words create the narrative world and words hold the key to the significance of that world. The search for narrative significance is one that, on a mechanical level, sorts out likenesses and differences and pays attention to arrangement.

The most obvious type of likeness and difference used in narrative is repetition and variation. The repetition of a word, phrase, sentence or set of sentences can function to structure the story, to build theme, to emphasize a certain point to the reader, to create suspense. A repetition might exaggerate and thus be a humorous ploy or a means of ridicule.[98] Repetition and then a variation on the repetition can first lull the reader into false expectations and then, through sudden variance, introduce an element of suprise.[99] Repetition in conjunction with variation can equate and contrast events or characters through association, inviting the reader to consider similarities and dissimilarities. When repetitions and variations come from different sources in the story, the narrator versus one of the characters, for example, then repetition and variation can be understood as means of revealing character and indicating point of view.[100]

Another kind of repetition that does not necessarily involve verbatim reiteration is the occurrence in the story of words and phrases that fall into the same semantic range. A narrator can use words that are related in meaning to stress or to clarify some matter in the story, for example, a particular character trait. A system of related words can create a certain atmosphere or mood. Related words can also build theme. The words can be any part of speech. They may stand close together in the story for an obvious emphasis or they may be sprinkled throughout for a subtle effect.[101]

Language produces meaning through relation and association, on both small scale and large. Association on the small scale, the level of detail, involves verbal ambiguity—words, phrases, and grammatical constructions that associate several meanings at once.[102] The plurality of meaning (in relation to a single signifier) can express itself in several ways. There may be two or more meanings that are balanced in terms of importance and plausibility. For example, when Naomi says to Ruth, 'Blessed be he (Boaz) by Yahweh whose kindness has not forsaken the living or the dead!' (Ruth 2.20), the grammatical construction has produced a balanced ambiguity. The phrase 'whose kindness has not forsaken the living or the dead' may refer to Yahweh or it may refer to Boaz. The undecidability of the referent underscores a major theological point of the book of Ruth, that the kindness of God and the kindness of human beings are not to be separated.

In some cases of ambiguity, one meaning is elevated over another, yet both meanings contribute to the overall effect. In Ruth 1, for example, words like 'cleave to', 'forsaken', 'go after' are used by the narrator and by Ruth. The primary meaning reflects the context of the physical and verbal interchange between characters: Ruth 'cleaves' to Naomi. She promises not to 'forsake' her or to return from 'going after' her. On the surface of the narrative, the words point to Ruth's physical commitment to Naomi: she is determined to accompany her back to Bethlehem. The words, however, have secondary connotations as well. They are words that carry theological impact because they are words often used to describe the relationship between Israel and Yahweh: Israel is to 'cleave' to Yahweh, and not to 'forsake' Yahweh by 'going after' other gods. Consequently, the secondary connotations of these words invite the reader to view Ruth's commitment to Naomi as a kind of theological commitment.

The hierarchy of potential meanings in a word or phrase can, of course, be more pronounced. The primary meaning may be strongly pushed to the fore while the secondary meaning may merely be a nuance that many readers miss. When Boaz speaks to Ruth on the harvest field about the '*kenāphîm* of Yahweh', his primary concern is to convey the message that refuge can be found under the 'wings' of Yahweh. *Kānāph*, however, is also sexually euphemistic (cf. Deut. 22.30; 27.30) and, while the sexual nuance may not at first viewing be obvious to the reader, the nuance certainly does not escape Ruth's notice, as we can see by her use of the term on the threshing floor.

The associative function of language on a large scale can be seen in the use of literary allusion. Allusion can be effected through the choice of identical or similar words, similar grammatical arrangement, or similarly constructed narrative situations. Allusion to other literature can enrich a narrative in several ways: Allusions can foreshadow;[103] they can help the reader fill gaps in terms of character motivation, for example, or of social expectation. Allusions invite textual dialogue—sometimes amiable conversation, sometimes debate. Allusions reflect the larger text or context of literary expression and give the reader another means by which to decipher the commonality and the uniqueness of the work in question.

Likeness and difference, similarity and dissimilarity, commonality and uniqueness are terms that I have employed thus far to describe the basic dynamic of literary expression and the main focus of close reading. Consistency and inconsistency are an important dynamic in the grammar of the text as well.[104] If a common sentence pattern is continuously repeated in the telling of a story (as it often is in Hebrew narrative), then any disruption of this pattern usually functions either to accent the meaning being communicated in the distinctive sentence or to make some sort of transition, either to another phase of the plot or to another point of view, for example. Simple, straight-forward sentences allow the reader to absorb the story quickly. Convoluted sentence structures force the reader to linger upon the arrangement of words. Any kind of unusually constructed phrase or sentence inherently brings attention to itself and can be a potential signal to the reader to be more attentive to what is being said at that particular point.

Another significant aspect of language, which is rather difficult to articulate, but which is important to recognize in the reading of Daniel 1–6, is the difference between what language *says* and what it *does*. Wolfgang Iser writes:

> As far as literature is concerned, the meaning of the literary work is not the same as the formulated aspects, but can only be built up in the imagination through continual shifting and reciprocal qualification of those aspects. What the language *says* is transcended by what it *uncovers*, and what it *uncovers* represents its true meaning.[105]

Not only do speeches of individual characters in Daniel 1–6 uncover more than they say, but the literary corpus as a whole uncovers more about sovereignty than its words say.

Narrative Tempo
Reading tempo leads us to the issue of how time is handled in general

in narrative texts. The relationship between the time of the action narrated in the story (measured in minutes, hours, days, weeks, months, years, etc.) and the length of text used to relate the action (measured in lines, pages, etc.), or alternatively the duration of the story and the length of the narrative work, might be thought of as narrative tempo.[106] The ratio between the duration of the story and the length of narrative is never equal and seldom steady. Narrative tempo constantly changes, producing a kind of rhythm. In *scenes*, where the narrator *shows* the action rather than *tells* it, the duration of the story and the length of narrative is most closely balanced though still not equal.[107] Summaries (where the narrator tells rather than shows) accelerate the tempo, giving overviews of action that may last days, months, or years, in one or two sentences.[108] Occasionally, there are pauses in the tempo, when the narrator stops narrating action long enough to offer a description, explanation, or exhortation.[109] (The exhortations in Deuteronomy are an example of a rather extensive pause in narrative tempo.) Finally, the narrative can also employ ellipses, temporal jumps, in which time passes but there is no narrated action to fill it.[110]

The slowing of narrative tempo, like convoluted sentences, forces the attention of the reader to the material being presented. When the narrator invests time in narrating, the reader must invest time in the reading. Ellipses, because they are gaps, hold narrative interest by producing curiosity. Pauses can generate suspense. Narrative tempo, then, not only holds the reader's interest; it also serves to accent portions of narrative.

The consideration of narrative tempo in the book of Daniel is particularly appropriate because Daniel is, in many respects, a book about time. It is about a few days in the lives of Daniel and his friends. It is about the period of time of the exile. It is about a larger period of foreign domination. It is about the end of this time, when judgment is passed and a new temporality instated. But in all of these linear periods there is also repetition, transformations of the same scenario—the same kinds of conflict, the same kinds of lessons to be learned, the same kinds of characters, and even, some would argue, the same kinds of narrative (or in the case of the latter half of the book, apocalyptic) form.

Narrative tempo in the book of Daniel helps to construct this preoccupation with time. The narrative tempo is the slowest and most deliberate during the recounting of the dreams and visions (in both halves of the book). The dreams and visions image a potential future, another time, another world, another reality. Thus, the narrative tempo, by accenting the vision of the future, underscores one of the thematic, temporally linear currents of the book, that the future looms larger than the past. On the other hand, by repeating the rhythm of brief exposition, prolonged conflict, and brief resolution, the narrative tempo also creates a cyclical pattern of time and, consequently, uncovers the irony of the vision of the future: The structure of power in this future, and thus the potential for conflict, is hauntingly similar to that of the story world's past. As a further complication, the narrative tempo, by moving back and forth between the average duration of the story world's reality and the retarded duration of the world of dreams and visions, narrative tempo shows the pendulum quality of time, how the future invades the present. I think we will find that Daniel's vision of the future has a marked effect upon his dealings in the present. Perhaps this is true for all of us.

Visions of the future characterize the end of the story; let us start now at the beginning.

Chapter 1

DANIEL 1

The Story

(1) In the third year of the reign of Jehoiakim king of Judah, Nebuchadnezzar king of Babylon came to Jerusalem and besieged it. (2) Adonai gave Jehoiakim king of Judah into his hand along with some of the vessels of the house of God. He brought them to the land of Shinar, to the house of his god, and he placed the vessels in the treasury of his god.

(3) The king commanded Ashpenaz his chief eunuch to bring some of the Israelites who were from the royal family and from the nobility —(4) young men who were without blemish, pleasing in appearance, skilful in all wisdom, knowledgable, perceptive in thought, and who were capable of serving in the king's palace—and to teach them the letters and language of the Chaldeans. (5) The king appointed for them a daily allowance of the king's special food and of the wine which he himself drank. He allowed the chief eunuch[1] three years to make something of them,[2] at the end of which time they would stand before the king.

(6) It so happened that among the Judeans were Daniel, Hananiah, Mishael, and Azariah. (7) The chief eunuch assigned them names: He assigned to Daniel the name Belteshazzar, to Hananiah the name Shadrach, to Mishael the name Meshach, and to Azariah the name Abednego.

(8) Daniel resolved that he would not defile himself[3] with the king's special food or with the wine which he drank. And so he requested of the chief eunuch that he not have to defile himself. (9) (Now Elohim gave Daniel favor and compassion before the chief eunuch). (10) The chief eunuch said to Daniel, 'I fear my lord the king who appointed your food and drink. If he should view your faces to be discontent in comparison to the young men around you, you would endanger my head with the king'.

(11) So Daniel said to the guardian whom the chief eunuch had appointed over Daniel, Hananiah, Mishael and Azariah, 'Please test your servants for ten days. Let us be given vegetables to eat and water to drink. (13) Then observe[4] our appearances and the appearance of the young men who have eaten the king's special food and, according to what you observe, so deal with your servants'. (14) He listened to them concerning this matter and he tested them for ten days.

(15) At the end of ten days, it was seen that their appearances were better and healthier than those of all the young men who had been eating the king's

special food. (16) So it was that the guardian took their special food and the wine which was their drink and he gave them vegetables.

(17) As for these four young men, Elohim gave them knowledge and made them skilful in all letters and wisdom and, as for Daniel, he understood all dreams and visions.[5]

(18) At the end of the time, when the king had commanded that they be brought in, the chief eunuch brought them before Nebuchadnezzar. (19) The king spoke with them and among them no one was found like Daniel, Hananiah, Mishael, and Azariah; and so they stood in attendance before the king. (20) In every matter of wisdom and understanding[6] about which the king sought answer from them, he found them ten times better than all the magicians and enchanters who were in all his kingdom.

(21) So it was with Daniel until the first year of Cyrus the king.

The Reading

The narrator of Daniel 1 ends a story to begin a story. Nebuchadnezzar's capture of Jerusalem, the royal family, and the vessels from the house of God ends a story of life in the Judean homeland. The ending of the old story provides the setting for the new and, though the new story takes over, it is curiously subordinated to the old. By using the time line of the old story, 'In the third year of the reign of Jehoiakim[7] king of Judah', rather than using a temporal designation more suitable to the structures of the new story world, 'In the such-and-such year of Nebuchadnezzar, king of Babylon', the narrator suggests that, in order to appreciate fully the story that follows, one must know something of the story that precedes.

The old story world sets the new story world in relief. Homeland gives way to alien land. At least a similitude of political autonomy turns into political captivity. A native, though weak, king is harshly succeeded by a strong, but foreign, one.

Daniel 1 is both a story and an exposition to a larger story, that found in the narrative corpus of Daniel 1–6 or, if one thinks in broader terms, the entire book of Daniel. Consequently, the ending that begins Daniel 1 (1.1-2) is strategic not only for the first short story, but also for the story that continues beyond ch. 1. Besides establishing the general temporal and locational setting of small and large story alike, it introduces a dramatic irony that permeates the first story and the conflict that is to develop through the ensuing chapters.

The dramatic irony results from disparate points of view. Two points of view are represented in this introduction. First, there is the perspective of Nebuchadnezzar, king of Babylon. As far as he is concerned, the conflict reported in vv. 1-2 primarily involves himself and Jehoiakim king of Judah. He perceives that his conquest of Jerusalem is the result of his own action. He *comes* (*bô'*), he *besieges*, he *takes* (*bô'*), he *places* (*bô*). After the defeat he acknowledges the help of his god. As we can see from his transferral of the temple vessels from Jerusalem to the treasury of his god in Shinar, the human conflict, in Nebuchadnezzar's point of view, mirrors a divine conflict. His god has defeated the god of Jerusalem. In summary, Nebuchadnezzar views himself and the god of Babylon as victors over Jehoiakim and the god of Jerusalem.

Though for the narrator the outcome of the events is the same, the cause is quite a different matter. According to the narrator, Nebuchadnezzar does not defeat Jehoiakim through his own skill or power. Nebuchadnezzar's self-image of aggressor is overshadowed by the narrator's view that the Babylonian king is but a passive recipient: *Adonai gives* Jehoiakim into Nebuchadnezzar's hand. Thus, the narrator and the reader know something that Nebuchadnezzar does not.

Furthermore, the narrator's point of view realigns the characters, creating a dynamic that is present in the first story but becomes even more prominent in the episodes that follow. According to the narrator, the issue is not between Nebuchadnezzar and his god and Jehoiakim and his god. Two of these four parties, Jehoiakim and Nebuchadnezzar's god, quickly fade into the background and, essentially, die to the story. Nebuchadnezzar and the narrator's god —and I use the term narrator's god because, through the choice of *Adonai*, my lord, the narrator confesses allegiance—emerge as the only two characters to survive the exposition. Adonai and Nebuchadnezzar have sought to accomplish the same thing—the defeat of Jerusalem—and thus are allies. On the other hand, Nebuchadnezzar does not recognize Adonai as the source of his victory. He does not know this god; he offers this god no credit and thus the potential conflict is born.

By pairing Adonai's will with Nebuchadnezzar's activity, the narrator braces the story with a certain theological worldview. First of all, the narrator's appeal to Adonai's will explains the theological difficulty of the conquest of Jerusalem and the destruction of the temple. Secondly, by attributing the exile to Adonai, the narrator constructs a world in which Adonai is in control of world events and is capable of manipulating foreign rulers even though they are not believers. Thirdly, with the idea that Adonai has turned against Judah, the narrator implies that the people have done something to cause the anger of their god. The reason for the deity's anger is not specified, but its justification is not questioned. As a common motif in Israelite literature, i.e. the older story mentioned above, God's anger against the Israelites is usually caused by their religious or political apostasy. Consequently, the filling of this gap, that is, Adonai's motivation to move against the Israelites, relies upon the reader's familiarity with the larger context. Finally, Adonai may be a punisher in the worldview of this story, but Adonai is also a protector. God's participation in the fall of Jerusalem, the end of the old story, foreshadows the possibility of God's participation in the story about to be told and thereby lends an air of hope.

The story continues with Nebuchadnezzar's perceived control. He wastes no time in making the most of his victory. He commands his chief eunuch, Ashpenaz, to select (*bô'*, hiphil) some of the captives for royal service. A convoluted description of requirements stresses that the ones to be chosen can be nothing but the very best—the best by blood, the best of appearance, the best in intelligence. Nebuchadnezzar insists that the captive young nobles be 'without blemish'. To be without blemish in service of sovereignty—can the reader not hear an echo from the older story? Yahweh requires sacrifices and those in divine service to be without blemish (Lev. 22.17-25; 21.16-24).[8] Allusion subliminally pairs the two sovereigns, pitting them against one another to vie for the allegiance of their subjects.

The selected captives are to undergo a period of training in which they are 'to learn the letters and language of the Chaldeans' and so ready themselves for service in the Babylonian court. The stage is set for a success story like that of Joseph or Esther:[9] Jewish captive makes good, or something of the sort. The reader might even be tempted to consider Nebuchadnezzar a generous, tolerant monarch with worthy aesthetic and intellectual values.

However, while our expectations for a success story may yet be fulfilled, our reading of Daniel 1 could use some subtle shading. The scenario surrounding the captives and the king's plans for them is one that is highly ambiguous and loaded with tension. The reader need only backtrack a moment and recall which captives the king singles out: young men from the 'royal seed' and from the nobility. The royalty and the nobility are the ones who have the most stake in political autonomy. Is it not a tricky business to transform former enemies into trustworthy courtiers?

What, exactly, is involved in this training process? First, the young men are to 'learn the letters and language of the Chaldeans'. The term Chaldeans is an ambiguous one in the story world of Daniel. It is, on the one hand, the (anachronistic) designation of a class of professional sages (cf. Dan. 2.2-10; 3.8-12; 4.7; 5.7).[10] Thus, 'the letters and language of the Chaldeans' could refer to a field of knowledge. On the other hand, Chaldean is also used as an ethnic label (cf. Dan. 5.30; also 9.1) and thus allows the reader to associate the learning of Chaldean language and literature with instruction in Chaldean culture. Consequently, the choice of the term 'Chaldean' rather than 'sage' or 'magician' suggests that the training involves national (and thus political) as well as professional indoctrination.

Besides, providing guidelines for the captives' education, the king also stipulates their diet, assigning them food and wine from his own table. This assigned diet not only is related to his insistence upon physical perfection (v. 4), but this particular diet also has political connotations. The rebellion against the king of the south in Dan. 11.26 is unexpected and extreme because the rebels eat the king's *patbag*; they eat from the king's table.[11] We know from the older story, the story of life in the land, that eating from the king's table is symbolic of political covenant and compromise. When David stops eating at Saul's table, Saul surmises that David has rebelled against him (1 Sam. 20.30-34). Perhaps to keep his claim to the throne secure, King David demands that the last remaining member of Saul's family, Mephiboseth, eat (always) at the king's table (2 Sam. 9.9-13). Jehoiachin, after the fall of Judah, spends his last days in exile, eating from the Babylonian king's table (2 Kgs 25.27-29). Consequently, by assigning such a diet, Nebuchadnezzar imposes political allegiance. The captives are to be dependent upon him and indebted to him for their very existence, not to mention their social success. The king gives them three years to complete their development before they are to stand in attendance at court. Their development is to be both physical and mental,[12] as the diet and education make clear. To stand in attendance before the king, they are to be physically perfect, mentally astute, culturally sophisticated, and, as advisors, politically loyal.

After relating the king's intentions, the narrator narrows the reader's vision from the general group to four specific captives. Among the Judeans, the narrator tells us, are Daniel, Hananiah, Mishael, and Azariah. When the chief eunuch takes charge of the young men, he assigns them Babylonian names: Belteshazzar, Shadrach, Meshach, and Abednego.[13]

At this point in the narrative, it becomes apparent that what is being forced upon the young men fits the classic model of a *rite of passage*, a ritual designed to facilitate a person's passing from one phase of life into another.[14] Initiates participating in a rite of passage go through three basic stages in the ritual process. First, they are separated from their community and put in seclusion (so Nebuchadnezzar's first command in v. 3). Once they are secluded from normal society, they endure a temporary 'betwixt and between' or liminal existence in which they are taught special knowledge that will enable them to function in the new roles they will be assuming ('the letters and language of the Chaldeans'). They are fed special food (the king's *patbag* and wine). Instructors encourage the initiates to suppress their former allegiances (e.g. attachments to mother or father, but in the case of Daniel 1, political allegiance to Judah's royal house) and elevate their new allegiances (e.g. to husband or wife, but here, to Nebuchadnezzar, king of Babylon). The initiates are expected to be completely submissive to their instructors. These induced experiences in the liminal stage are designed to bring about a change of being, a change of identity (and thus, the symbolic renaming). The third stage of the passage is the reintegration into society. (Our narrator alludes to such a reintegration in v. 5 and reports it explicitly in v. 18.)

The analogy between this model and Nebuchadnezzar's plans for the captives is further support of the fact that the training is not intended to be simply professional education. They are to learn the Babylonian way of life, adopt a Babylonian profession, and confess Babylonian allegiance. Such a transformation benefits the king; the captives must be made to see that such a transformation benefits them as well. The narrator, however, leaves the reader two options for judging what is becoming of the young Judeans. In one sense their rite of passage is a promotion from prisoners to professionals. But in another sense, the passage is a descension from 'royal seed' to servanthood.

Throughout the narration thus far, the prisoners make no response to what is happening to them. Their point of view is not reported. They are as faceless and voiceless as Jehoiakim the defeated king. In v. 8, however, as the narrator narrows our vision further to one character and his subsequent conversations, at least that character, Daniel, begins to awaken to the story. It is at the point of the renaming that the pace of the narration slows and we see the situation's effect and Daniel's response. After the chief eunuch 'fixes upon' or 'sets for' them (*yāśem*) Babylonian names, Daniel 'fixes' or 'sets' (*yāśem*) upon his heart that he will not defile himself with the king's food or drink.

The selectively omniscient narrator gives us an internal view of Daniel's silent decision; yet the narrator does not clarify what prompts such resolve or what it is about the king's food and drink that Daniel thinks defiling. By making the shift of perspective pivot on the verb 'to set or fix', the narrator suggests that the assignment of new identity may be part of what spurs Daniel to show resistance. In other words, Daniel is making an attempt to limit in some way the all-consuming indoctrination process.

The term *gā'al*, to defile, also offers a clue to Daniel's motivation. Since (at least in this late spelling) *gā'al* is normally used to refer to cultic pollution, the word invites the reader to understand Daniel's aversion to the food to be motivated by religious piety. By introducing the idea of defilement, the narrator permits the speculation that the assigned food and drink are not in accordance with Israel's dietary laws and are, consequently, ritually polluting.[15]

As Daniel's motivation, however, cultic defilement is not explicit and stands rather uneasily by itself. In the first place, the narrator implies that Daniel makes his decision concerning the food before it is ever actually presented to him. He does not know what the king's *patbag* includes; he only knows that the king has assigned it. An aversion to the food on ritual grounds might be feasible in terms of meat, either kind (Lev. 3.17; 11.1-47) or method of preparation (Lev. 17.10-14), but his refusal of the wine makes no sense at all if Levitical law is the assumed dietary guide. If the reader is allowed to appeal to a final form reading of the book, then Dan. 10.3 implies either that Daniel does not view meat and wine (also labeled desirable or delightful food) *per se* to be a problem of cultic defilement or that Daniel, in his later years, drastically relaxes his religious principles concerning diet. Furthermore, one might argue that the defiling nature of food eaten in exile is unavoidable (cf. Ezek. 4.13; Hos. 9.3,

4). In other words, choosing not to be ritually defiled by food substance is not an option for captives.[16]

Thus, the defilement, so clearly put in religious terms, is difficult to relate specifically to the *substance* of the food and wine. I propose, rather, that Daniel's rejection of the diet has not so much to do with the food and wine itself as it has to do with its source. It is the *king's* special food and the wine which the *king* himself drinks.[17] It is, in other words, the symbol of political patronage, the eating of which would be tantamount to declaring complete political allegiance. This reading does not deny that Daniel's decision is religiously motivated; it simply suggests that Daniel's religiosity is of a more complex nature. His piety extends beyond cultic or ritual concerns. We are given no indication that Daniel is aware that Adonai has given Jerusalem's royalty and holy things to Nebuchadnezzar. How can he in good conscience confess unqualified allegiance to the man who has destroyed and plundered the temple of his god? Daniel's mixture of religious and political interests is understandable. Daniel is, after all, at least a Judean noble if not a member of Judah's royal family.[18] Though his gesture of discreet resistance may not amount to much in the course of political history (i.e. the political history of the story world), it is an attempt to express some kind of personal control in a seemingly uncontrollable situation.[19]

When Daniel asks the chief eunuch not to make him defile himself, the narrator tells us that Elohim gives Daniel favor and compassion before the officer. The request is voiced as a religious concern and, through Elohim's manipulation, the chief eunuch is sympathetic, but realistic. The gist of his response to Daniel is a refusal, but his actual words continue to color the story with the blend of religion and politics.

His first words are, 'I fear my lord the king who appointed your food and drink. . . ' (v. 10). The apellative 'my lord', *adoni*, echoes the narrator's use of Adonai earlier in the story. Each occurrence reflects the speaker's sense of hierarchy and allegiance. For the chief eunuch, lordship belongs to the king; for the narrator, lordship belongs to God. The use of *adoni/Adonai*, then, reflects the crux of Daniel's dilemma—the acknowledgment of sovereignty.

The chief eunuch's speech continues with curious ambiguity: 'if he [the king] should view *penâkem zō'aphîm* in comparison to the young men around you, you would bring guilt upon my head before the king'. The phrase *penîkem zō'aphîm* can be translated to reflect the chief eunuch's view of the relationship between the food and a healthy appearance, thus: 'if he should view your appearance to be inferior' or 'your condition to be poorer in comparison to the other young men. . . ' on the other hand, 'face' can refer to one's expression as well as one's appearance,[20] and *zā'aph* literally means to be displeased, even angry.[21] Consequently, the chief eunuch's response, while giving Daniel's request the benefit of the doubt, takes into account the political ramifications of the situation: 'I fear my lord the king. . . should view your expressions to be discontent [or even malcontent?] in comparison with the young men around you and you would bring guilt upon my head before the king'. The eunuch's language mixes the issue of healthy appearance with the issue of attitude. Refusing the king's food symbolizes political dissent and, in the eunuch's opinion, such an attitude will eventually be manifested in more obvious ways. The chief eunuch will take no responsibility for nonconformity.

After this initial interchange, Daniel, nevertheless, refuses to give up. Inspired by the chief eunuch's play on healthy appearance, he goes behind the eunuch's back to his appointed guardian with a new tactic.[22] He solicits the guardian's help with a conditional program: 'Please test your servants[23] for ten days. Let us be given vegetables to eat and water to drink. Then observe our appearance and the appearances of the young men who have eaten the king's *patbag* and, according to what you observe, so deal with your servants' (vv. 12-13). This request of the guardian is quite different from his previous appeal to the chief eunuch. In this speech Daniel says nothing about defilement; in fact, he gives the guardian no reason at all why the change of menu should take place. He proposes the idea simply is a 'test', stipulates a limited period of time, and so minimizes any risk on the part of the guardian. His most clever strategy, however, is to portray the situation exclusively in physical terms. He carefully uses the term 'appearance' (*mar'êh*) rather than the ambiguous 'face' (*penî*) which could also connote expression or demeanor. He omits the chief eunuch's concern about *zā'aph*, discontent. He allows the guardian to think that the only thing he need worry about is whether or not the four captives look healthy. The proposal is sweetened also by what is unspoken—the guardian is left to dispose of the king's food and wine (surely much better fare than that to which the guardian is accustomed) as he sees fit! Small wonder that the guardian heeds the request.

After ten days, Daniel and his friends look better and healthier than the other young men (though the narrator never explains the exact relationship between the different food and their superior appearances) and so the situation continues, with everyone involved all the happier with the agreement. Daniel and his friends can discreetly confess allegiance to a higher authority and so preserve themselves from being completely consumed into Babylonian life. And as for the guardian, he is quite content to 'take' (*nōśê'*, v. 16) their food and wine.

At this point the narrative tempo picks up considerably. The remainder of the three years of training is covered in the narrator's description of the success of Daniel and his friends. All of them excel in wisdom and knowledge, but Daniel, we are told, has an additional talent for understanding dreams and visions. This singling out of Daniel prepares the reader for Daniel's prominence in the remainder of the book, and the mention of his special ability foreshadows his distinctive role as interpreter of mysteries.

According to the narrator, the superior skills of these four young men are due, not to their fine Babylonian education, but to Elohim's graciousness. Indeed, the only verb associated with God in Daniel 1 is the verb 'give'. Adonai gives Jehoiakim and the temple vessels to Nebuchadnezzar (v. 2). Elohim gives Daniel *ḥesed* and compassion during his interview with the chief eunuch (v. 9). Elohim gives the four young men unsurpassed wisdom and knowledge (v. 17). By revealing God's participation in the story, the narrator lets the reader in on a secret concealed from some if not from all of the characters. What the Babylonian characters think to be the result of their own effort is, in actuality, the result of God's intervention. As far as the four young Judeans are concerned, the narrator leaves us uncertain as to the extent to which they recognize their skills to be gifts from God.

At the end of the training, the young men are brought before the king. The narrator reports 'none among them were found to be like Daniel, Hananiah, Mishael, and Azariah. They stood in attendance before the king'. Irony of ironies—the four who disobey the king's orders are the four who show themselves to be exceptional. The four who refuse to align themselves politically with the king are the ones chosen for royal service. Moreover, the independence of the four is underscored by the narrator's use of their Hebrew names rather than their assigned Babylonian names. Thus, though they stand in royal service, they are not what they seem, in the king's eyes, to be. The illusion of political unanimity covers the reality of compromise and raises a question for the reader: What will happen later, in the larger story, if these men are called upon to prove their political fidelity?

With an indefinite temporal ellipsis, the story ends with a coda[24] that closes the story's temporal frame and brings the reader out of the story's time: 'In every matter of wisdom and understanding about which the king questioned them, he found them ten times better than all the magicians and enchanters who were in all his kingdom. So it was with Daniel until the first year of Cyrus the king'. For the remainder of their service at court, the four Judeans continue to surpass their peers with an excellence that, in later chapters, makes them targets of conspiracy. As for Daniel in particular, his career spans the exile itself. He is the link between the beginning and the end, between Nebuchadnezzar and Cyrus, between destruction and restoration. The narrator jumps to the end of the exilic story to tell us of Daniel's success and thereby captures our curiosity: What happens to Daniel in the meantime, between here and there, between now and then?

Chapter 2

DANIEL 2

The Story

(1) In the second year of the reign of Nebuchadnezzar, Nebuchadnezzar dreamed dreams. His spirit was troubled and his sleep left him.[1]

(2) The king commanded that the magicians and the conjurers and the sorcerers and the Chaldeans be summoned[2] in order to tell the king his dreams. So they came and stood before the king. (3) The king said to them, 'I have dreamed a dream and my spirit is troubled to know the dream'. (4) The Chaldeans spoke to the king,[3] 'Oh, King, may you live forever! Tell the dream to your servants and we will disclose the interpretation'. (5) The king answered and said to the Chaldeans, 'My word is firm; if you do not make the dream and its interpretation known to me, you will be dismembered and your houses will be laid in ruins.[4] (6) But, if you can disclose the dream and its interpretation, you will receive gifts, rewards, and great honor from me. Therefore, disclose to me the dream and its interpretation!' (7) They answered a second time, 'Let the king tell the dream to his servants and we will make its interpretation known'. (8) The king answered saying, 'I know that, undoubtedly, you are buying time because you see that my word is firm—(9) that if you cannot make the dream known to me, there is one sentence for all of you. You have agreed with each other to speak a false and corrupt word before me until the present situation is changed.[5] Therefore, tell me the dream and I will know that you are able to disclose its interpretation to me'. (10) The Chaldeans answered the king, 'There is not a person upon the earth who would be able to disclose the matter of the king. Never before has any great and masterful king asked such a thing as this of any conjurer, sorcerer, or Chaldean. (11) The thing that the king asks is too difficult.[6] There is no other who could disclose it—except the gods who do not dwell with the flesh'.

(12) As a result of this, the king grew angry and was quite enraged and he commanded that all the sages of Babylon be destroyed.[7] (13) So the sentence went forth and the sages were to be executed. Daniel and his companions were also sought out[8] for execution.

(14) When this happened,[9] Daniel cautiously and tactfully responded[10] to Arioch, the captain of the royal guard, who had come forth to execute the sages of Babylon. (15) He said to Arioch, the king's captain, 'What is the reason for the king's severe[11] sentence?' Thereupon Arioch explained the

matter to Daniel. (16) And Daniel went and made a request of the king, that he might give him time to disclose the interpretation to the king.

(17) After that[12] Daniel went to his house and made the matter known to Hananiah, Mishael, and Azariah, his companions (18) and sought[13] compassion from before the God of heaven concerning this mystery so that Daniel and his companions would not be destroyed along with the rest of the sages of Babylon. (19) Then, in a vision of the night, the mystery was revealed to Daniel. Thereupon Daniel blessed the God of heaven. (20) Daniel responded, saying:

> 'May the name of God be blessed forever and ever
>   for wisdom and strength are his!
> (21) He changes the times and the seasons;
>   He deposes kings and sets up kings;
> He gives wisdom to the wise
>   and knowledge to those who have understanding.
> (22) He reveals the deep and hidden things;
>   He knows what is in the darkness
>   and the light abides with him.
> (23) To you, God of my fathers, I give thanks and praise
>   for you have given me wisdom and strength,
> and now you have made known to me what we have asked of
>   you,
>   for you have made known to us the matter of the king'.

(24) As a result of this, Daniel went into Arioch whom the king had appointed to destroy the sages of Babylon. He went and thus he said to him, 'Do not destroy the sages of Babylon. Bring me before the king and I will disclose the interpretation to the king'.

(25) Then Arioch hastily brought Daniel before the king and thus said to him, 'I have found a man from among the Judean exiles who can make the interpretation known to the king'. (26) The king answered and said to Daniel (whose name was Belteshazzar), 'Are you able to make known to me the dream that I have seen and its interpretation? (27) Daniel answered the king, 'No sages, conjurers, magicians, or astrologers would be able to disclose to the king the mystery that the king has asked. (28) However, there is a God in heaven who reveals mysteries and he has made known to King Nebuchadnezzar what is to be in the days to follow. This is your dream and the mental vision that you had while upon your bed. (29) While you were upon your bed, Oh king, your thoughts arose of what is to be after this. He who reveals mysteries has made known to you what is to be. (30) But as for me, it is not because there is more wisdom in me than in all else living that this mystery was revealed to me, but it was in order that the interpretation could be made known to the king and you could know your innermost thoughts.

(31) You, Oh King, were looking and lo—a great image! This image, large and of exceeding brightness, was standing before you and its appearance was frightening. (32) The head of the image was of fine gold. Its chest and its arms were of silver. Its belly and its hips were of bronze. (33) Its lower legs were iron. Its feet were partly of iron and partly of pottery.[14] (34) You continued seeing until a stone was cut, but without human hands, and it struck the image upon its feet of iron and pottery and it broke them in pieces. (35) Then, as one, the iron, the pottery, the bronze, the silver, and the gold were broken in pieces and they were like chaff from summer threshing floors—the wind carried them away and nothing of them could be found anywhere. And the stone, which struck the image, became a great mountain and filled all the earth. (36) This was the dream and we will tell its interpretation before the king.

(37) 'You, Oh King, king of kings, to whom the God of heaven has given the kingdom, the power, the might, and the honor, (38) and into whose hand he has given all that dwell—human beings, beasts of the field, birds of the heaven—and he has caused you to rule over all of them: You are the head of gold. (39) In your place, another kingdom, inferior to you,[15] will arise and then a third kingdom of bronze which will rule over all the earth. (40) The fourth kingdom will be as strong as iron because iron breaks and shatters all things and, like iron which crushes, it will break up and crush all of these. (41) And, according to that which you saw—the feet and the toes partly of potter's ware and partly of iron—the kingdom will be diverse.[16] Some of the firmness of iron will be in it just as you saw in the iron mixed with the clay pottery. (42) As the toes of the feet were partly iron and partly pottery, the kingdom will be strong in part and partly, it will be brittle.[17] (43) As you saw iron mixed with clay pottery, the people will mix their seed, but they will not be able to hold together just as iron cannot mix with pottery. (44) In the days of those kings, the God of heaven will raise up a kingdom which will never be destroyed and its reign will not be left to another people. It will break up and put an end to all of these kingdoms and it will stand forever, (45) just as you saw that, from the mountain, a stone was cut but not by human hands and it broke apart the iron, the bronze, the pottery, the silver, and the gold. A great God has made known to the king what is to be after this. The dream is certain and its interpretation sure'.

(46) Then King Nebuchadnezzar fell upon his face and worshipped Daniel and he commanded that an offering and incense offerings be poured out[18] to him. (47) The king responded to Daniel by saying, 'Truly your god is god of gods and Lord of kings and a revealer of mysteries that you are able to reveal this mystery'.

(48) Then the king gave Daniel prominence and gave him many great gifts. He made him ruler over the whole province of Babylon and he became chief-prefect over all the sages of Babylon. (49) Daniel made a request of the

king and, over the administration of the province of Babylon, he appointed Shadrach, Meshach, and Abednego. Daniel remained at the king's court.

Excursus I: Formal Characteristics of Daniel 2

In a recent study,[19] Susan Niditch and Robert Doran have shown that Daniel 2 has many of the formal characteristics of a particular type of folktale,[20] most of which are shared with stories of Joseph (Genesis 41) and Ahiqar (Ahiqar 5-7). The basic plot of this folktale type is as follows: A person of lower status is called before a person of higher status to answer a question that seems unanswerable or to solve a problem that appears to be unsolvable. The question or problem may be a genuine dilemma or it may be concocted as a test. Frequently, in stories of this type, the person of higher status will threaten the person of lower status with punishment for failure. The person of lower status solves the problem and is rewarded for this accomplishment.[21]

According to Niditch and Doran, the theme of this type of narrative is '. . . the wise man wins in the end, no matter how lowly his origins; wisdom is the road to success'.[22] The tale is a traditional tale, i.e. its primary function is to preserve a traditional plot which expresses a traditional theme concerning the success of the wise. Although some versions may contain certain biases, the purpose of such a tale is not usually polemical. The presence of polemics marks a departure from traditional usage. Consequently, this kind of variation is the key to understanding the distinctive message of a particular version of the tale.[23]

In the case of Daniel 2, the traditional theme—wisdom brings success—becomes a frame for a more prominent theme about the revelation of divine will. Daniel 2 contains three motifs that are foreign to the traditional type. The employment of these motifs shapes the theme of divine revelation. There are two new action motifs—(1) the act of prayer and (2) the answer to prayer—and one new character motif—(3) the presence of the divine helper.[24]

The study by Niditch and Doran provides a springboard for a literary critical reading of Daniel 2 because of its meticulous attention to both the typicalities and the distinctive elements in Daniel 2. As these authors suggest, once generic affinities have been established, the peculiarities of the story will provide insight into the purpose of the story. If the typical skeletal plot outlined above represents the reader's expectation, then one must conclude that the narrator lures the audience into the story with typicality but actually gives them much more than they anticipate.

The Reading

The exposition, or introduction, to Daniel 2 (v. 1) establishes the time and the initial situation of the story: In the second year of his reign, Nebuchadnezzar has a dream that leaves him troubled. This event sets the story in motion and is the essential concern of the story.

The temporal designation, the second year of Nebuchadnezzar, both orients and disorients the reader of Daniel 1-6. On the one hand, it informs us that Nebuchadnezzar is relatively new to the throne and thus allows the reader to consider that the king's restless and troubled sleep might be the result of political insecurity.[25] On the other hand, when read in the context of Daniel 1, which spanned three years, the temporal designation suggests that we are dealing with a flashback. The reader must suppose that, in the chronology of the story world of Daniel 1-6, Nebuchadnezzar captures Jerusalem in his first year and dreams unsettling dreams in his second.[26]

This opening sentence then shows another side of Nebuchadnezzar. The self-confident military aggressor (Nebuchadnezzar's self-perception in ch. 1) is, in fact, a less confident administrator, now that the days of military glory are over. Could it be that Nebuchadnezzar finds *retaining* control decidedly more difficult than *taking* control?

The exposition focuses our immediate attention upon the king, but it also carries over from ch. 1 what the reader found to be of interest there, namely Daniel. With the mention of the dream, we are reminded of Daniel's special talent, understanding in all dreams and visions. If the conflict is going to revolve around a problematic dream, we expect that Daniel will have something to do with the conflict's resolution.

As a result of his troubling dream, the king summons his professional sages, and thus we enter the first major scene in the story. The list of specialized personnel—magicians, conjurers, sorcerers, and Chaldeans—suggests that the brightest and best Babylonian scholars are represented. (If one reads ch. 2 as a flashback, the absence of Daniel from this interview can be explained by the fact that he is still undergoing initiation.)

The narrator makes a point of explaining to the audience that the sages are called before the king 'in order to tell the king his dreams'. This seemingly innocent statement appears to be ambiguous. Led by expectation (cf. Genesis 41), the reader easily interprets this phrase to mean something like 'in order to help the king understand his dream(s)'. But, in reality, the statement is not innocent, nor is it ambiguous. It is quite literal and it functions to foreshadow the coming complication. The *telling* of the dream itself, and not simply the interpreting of the dream, is a critical part of the king's agenda.

The scene involving the sages before their sovereign (vv. 2-12) is structured by the popular storytelling device of trebling.[27] Three times the king makes his request to the sages; three times they answer. With each interchange, the tension mounts.

In his first speech the king tells the sages of the event that the narrator reported to the reader in v. 1. He makes his request implicitly with the statement, 'my spirit is troubled to know the dream'. The sages misunderstand this request, thinking that the king merely wants them to interpret his dream. As a collective character, they respond in unison and with confidence, 'Tell [imperative] the dream to your servants and we will disclose the interpretation'. The king's troubled spirit quickly becomes irritation. It is clear in his next speech that he, in turn, misunderstands the sages' response. He seems to think that they understand the request, but are avoiding it. Consequently, he issues an ultimatum: 'If you do not make known to me the dream and its interpretation, you will be destroyed; but if you do disclose the dream and its interpretation, you will be rewarded'. He finishes the speech with a command: 'Therefore, disclose [imperative] to me the dream and its interpretation!' At this point perhaps it begins to dawn on the sages that the king is actually commanding them to recount the dream itself. They are caught off guard and cannot think of anything else to say. They feebly repeat their first response (though without the earlier confidence) as if to give the king the benefit of the doubt, 'Let the king tell [jussive rather than imperative][28] the dream to his servants that we might disclose the interpretation'. With the king's third speech, however, their worst fears are confirmed. The king accuses them of evading the issue and of conspiring to deceive him and he throws their first imperative (v. 4) back in their faces, 'Tell me the dream so that I will know that you can disclose to me its interpretation'. The sages explain to the king that they cannot do what the king has asked because the task does not fall within the range of human capabilities. Such a request has no historical precedent. Only a deity could do such a thing. Here the dialogue ends. The king loses his temper completely and orders that all the sages of Babylon are to be executed. The scene is over. The sages have been dismissed—ultimately.

In this first scene the narrator shows us *what* happens but does not explain *why* it happens. Why the king wants the dream told is indeterminate. Two mutually exclusive explanations can answer the question of why the king behaves the way he does. He could have forgotten the dream and thus the reader might understand the situation to be a classic case of suppressed unpleasantry. On this reading, which understands 'I am troubled to know the dream' to be a literal confession, the king's irrational demand results from his inability to remember and his subsequent frustration. A sense of foreboding that cannot be articulated leads to his unmitigated anger.[29] The alternative explanation is that the king has not forgotten the dream, but for some reason feels the need to test the ability of his sages.[30] If they can tell the dream, then he can trust their interpretation of it. Perhaps political anxiety has produced warranted or unwarranted suspicion of the royal advisors. Thus, the king's accusation 'You have conspired to speak a false and corrupt word before me until the present situation is changed', can be read as an expression of the king's insecurity, his paranoia that his courtiers are awaiting the downfall of his reign.[31] Or perhaps Nebuchadnezzar's decision to test the sages is arbitrary and we are being led to interpret his unreasonable demand as a sign of a dangerous, unpredictable, even sadistic character.

By not reporting the content of the dream at the point in which Nebuchadnezzar dreams it, the narrator steers the reader's sympathy toward the group of sages. Like the sages, we have no idea what the king has dreamed. Our lack of knowledge aligns our view with the sages' view that, indeed, the king's request is absurd.

Verse 13 makes a transition into the next movement of the story. In this verse we are told that the sentence of execution is official and that Daniel and his friends are among those to be executed. It is clear from the way in which this latter information is presented that the reader who is being addressed, i.e. the implied reader,[32] is one who is familiar with Daniel and his friends. These characters are given no introduction; they are not described or identified. The purpose of the narrator's statement here is to inform the audience of the involvement of these men in the story.[33] This information reinforces the interest point of view[34] that was stirred with the subject of the dream. We are correct to expect that Daniel might be participating in this story. The narrator's manipulation of our interest in Daniel, the Judean exile, suggests that the implied reader of this story, too, is one who, at the least, has knowledge of and, at the most, has a stake in the larger story of Israel. In other words, the identity of the implied reader is to be located somewhere in the matrix of Judeo-Christian traditions. Up until this point, the reader might only be mildly concerned with the fate of Babylonian sages. But once Daniel and his friends are included in the crisis, the reader's involvement in (and enjoyment of) the story is now intensified.

The inclusion of Daniel and his friends in the order of execution, when read in the context of ch. 1, portrays the king's sentence to be all the more monstrous. Not only is he willing to kill all the sages for the failure of a few to accomplish the impossible, but his order extends even to those who are preparing to become his future advisors. If we continue to read his character as one motivated by political insecurity, then his move to purge his advisory staff (even those in training), though an extreme gesture, makes sense. After all, those in training are from the royal and noble seed of a conquered nation. Perhaps his present courtiers are from similar stock. Any of them could have political designs of their own.

In the second movement of the story, vv. 14-24, the narrator shifts our attention to a different location and to different characters. The executioner is the transitional figure who takes us from the presence of the king to an encounter with Daniel in an unidentified location. The executioner, who has both name, Arioch, and title, captain of the royal guard, is the one who is to mediate the king's sentence against the sages. On the mechanical level of the plot, he is an agent who mediates knowledge as well. If Daniel is to resolve the conflict, and thus fulfill our expectations, then Daniel must find out what has transpired. Arioch is the informant who insures the continuation of the plot.[35]

In terms of the story's mechanics, Arioch is, like the chief eunuch and the guardian in ch. 1, basically a functional character. But, in terms of the social world of the story, he is, also like the eunuch and the guardian, a character who has power and authority. Daniel, whose wisdom obviously includes the art of diplomacy, wins Arioch's confidence. He tactfully questions Arioch concerning the sentence of execution. Arioch, who perhaps has not yet begun the massacre and who does not seem to be overly eager to fulfill his task, explains the matter to Daniel and allows him to ask for royal reprieve.[36] Somewhat surprisingly, the reprieve is implicitly granted. It seems that, for whatever reason, Daniel is allowed to 'buy time' that was not afforded to the earlier group of sages, even though he, at this point, has no answer either. The execution is postponed.

In the next scene (vv. 17-23), Daniel leaves the company of Arioch and returns to his house. He makes the matter known to his companions and seeks compassion from the God of heaven. According to the narrator, Daniel seeks divine compassion 'so that Daniel and his friends would not be destroyed with the rest of the sages of Babylon'. Notice that the wording is not 'so that Daniel, his friends, and the rest of the sages of Babylon would not be destroyed'. Daniel's primary motivation is self-preservation and the preservation of his friends. Only secondarily is he concerned with his professional colleagues who are, in the scheme of things, also Daniel's potential rivals.

The mystery is revealed to Daniel in a vision during the night. Here, as in the introduction to the story, is a prime opportunity to present the content of the dream, but again, the narrator refrains from disclosure. When the narrator reports that Daniel now has the answer, the reader's sense of suspense decreases substantially. Although we do not know precisely how the resolution will work itself out, we are confident that Daniel will indeed be capable of fulfilling the king's demand. Nevertheless, our interest now remains captive to the story by our curiosity[37] concerning what is now past. We wait to learn the content of Daniel's vision, which is, for the most part, the content of Nebuchadnezzar's dream. Of course, some degree of suspense is retained through what we have seen of Nebuchadnezzar's volatile character. The dream, after all, was a troubling dream. The revelation of its meaning has the potential for disaster.

The episode that takes place during this night at Daniel's house (vv. 17-23) contains the critical elements that, according to Niditch and Doran, make the story unique. The act of prayer, the answer to prayer, and the presence of the divine helper are the motifs that turn the focus of the story from human wisdom to divine revelation.[38]

Indeed, in this pivotal scene, divine revelation emerges as a prominent theme, but not without ambiguity. It is, as its image portrays, a vision that comes in darkness.

This scene makes the point foreshadowed earlier by the sages (v. 11) that only a god has the ability to do what the king has asked. But as we examine the scene more closely, we soon discover that divine ability is rather difficult to distinguish from human ability. Daniel does 'seek compassion from *before the God of heaven*' and he does learn the mystery that he later reports *before the king*. But, rather than stating, as we might have expected, that '*God* revealed the mystery to Daniel', the narrator reports the event in passive voice, 'the mystery was revealed to Daniel'. The narrator does not allow the 'divine helper' to be a character. God does nothing that we can see. God says nothing that we can hear.

We are forced to depend upon human revelation to learn anything of divine revelation. We must trust Daniel's song of thanksgiving for information concerning God's participation in the story.[39] In his song of thanksgiving, Daniel praises God for being the source of wisdom and for being the controller of natural and political history. His praise of God's wisdom is a response to the revelation event that has taken place in his vision. Daniel's words verify that God is the source of the vision. On the one hand, his affirmation is like that of the sages: The divine can reveal what human beings cannot. On the other hand, his affirmation stands in contrast to the sages' view that gods 'do not dwell with the flesh'. Not only does he portray God to be involved in human affairs, but he also claims that divine wisdom and strength[40] (v. 20) can be given to humans, and in fact, has been given to him (v. 23). Divine wisdom can only be recognized and praised when it is revealed to human beings and, once human beings have divine wisdom, it loses its quality of 'otherness'. The pious language that elevates divine transcendence also, ironically, minimizes divine transcendence. Divine wisdom is 'knowable'. By the end of his response, the 'God of heaven' has become the 'God of my fathers'.

After Daniel learns the mystery, he goes to Arioch and instructs him, 'Do not destroy the sages of Babylon. Bring me before the king and I will disclose the interpretation...' He does not say 'I will disclose what God has revealed to me'. At least to Arioch, Daniel makes no distinction between his ability and God's revelation.

The brief scene with Arioch (v. 24) mirrors the earlier scene involving these two characters (vv. 14-15) and closes the frame surrounding the nocturnal vision. In the earlier scene with Arioch, the execution procedures are instigated; in the latter the execution procedures are halted. In the earlier scene Arioch informs Daniel of the problem; in the latter scene Daniel informs Arioch that he has the solution.

Though v. 24 is essentially a scene in itself (the location and situation changes in the next verse), v. 24 initiates a transition into the final major movement of the story. The instrumental nature of Arioch's role makes the transition work. Just as he brings the problem of the story to Daniel's attention in v. 15, an action which is necessary for the development of the plot, likewise he brings Daniel to the attention of the king, thereby facilitating the resolution of the story.

In v. 25 Arioch 'hastily' takes Daniel before the king and introduces him. The motivation for Arioch's haste is left to speculation. Is he motivated by a concern for the king's dilemma? Is he concerned for the lives of the sages? Is he anxious to gain personal recognition? In his announcement to the king, he echoes Daniel's use of the first person pronoun and takes credit for himself: 'I have found a man among the Judean exiles who can make the interpretation known to the king'.[41] However, if reward is what he seeks, he is to be disappointed. The king immediately turns his attention to Daniel and Arioch is not mentioned again in the story.

This scene at the king's court is built around the king's point of view and, to some extent, the reader's point of view is channeled through that of the king. Daniel is introduced to Nebuchadnezzar, not by his Hebrew name, but as the king perceives him, 'a man from among the Judean exiles'. As far as the king is concerned, Daniel's name is Belteshazzar (v. 26). (The use of the name Belteshazzar gives further support to reading Daniel 2 as a flashback. Daniel has been in training long enough to receive a new name, but he has not been formally introduced to the king's court.) The king's address to Belteshazzar qualifies Arioch's exclusive mention of the interpretation; he is concerned that the young sage before him be able 'to make known *the dream*' as well as its interpretation.

As Daniel responds, the reader hears what Nebuchadnezzar hears. Like the king, we wait to hear the dream come from Daniel's lips, but like the king, we must first listen to Daniel's rather verbose explanation of how he came to know the dream and of the significance of the king's having such a dream to begin with.[42]

Daniel's introduction remarks are packed with irony. Daniel first, indirectly and perhaps unintentionally, defends the sages who have failed to fulfill the king's demand. He reiterates what the sages themselves have said earlier (vv. 10-11), that no one, not even a professional sage, is capable of making such a mystery known. Having said this, he goes on to talk about a god in heaven who reveals mysteries, and Daniel purports to know that this god in heaven has revealed to Nebuchadnezzar, through the dream, the mystery of the future (v. 28). Daniel begins to tell about the dream by describing the circumstances of the dream: 'While you were upon your bed, O King, your thoughts arose of what is to be after this' (v. 29). Then, as if realizing that he has not clarified how he himself knows the dream—especially since he has so boldly claimed that no human could know such a thing—he interrupts his narration with a rather awkward disclaimer: 'But as for me, it is not because there is more wisdom in me than in all else living that this mystery was revealed to me, but it was in order that the interpretation could be made known to the king and you could know your innermost thoughts' (v. 30).

This reason is certainly designed to appease the king: Revelation takes place for the sake of the king. But does Daniel really know God's reason for revealing the mystery to him? Or do we, for that matter? (We were never allowed to hear God speak.) All we know is Daniel's reason for asking that the mystery be revealed and, at the time, the reason had nothing to do with the king's knowing his innermost thoughts: He 'sought compassion before the God of heaven concerning this mystery so that Daniel and his friends *would not be destroyed*...' Furthermore, does Daniel really believe that his wisdom has nothing to do with God's revelation? In his song he had said, 'He [God] gives wisdom to the wise and knowledge to those who have understanding', which might be read as a simple affirmation of the divine source of human wisdom and knowledge or as an assertion that God gives divine wisdom and knowledge (only) to those who are capable of dealing with it. On this reading, in other words, it is Daniel's exceptional wisdom and, in the words of ch. 1, 'understanding in all visions and dreams', that makes him a fit recipient for this additional knowledge from God.

But Daniel, with typical diplomacy (cf. v. 14), says nothing to the king of needing to save his own skin and takes care to elevate the king's reception of knowledge and not his own. What Daniel's speech *says* and what it *does*, however, are two different things. Daniel's speech *says* that Nebuchadnezzar is wrong to rely on his (human) sages when the only one who can help him is a god. But what Daniel's speech *does* is to point out to Nebuchadnezzar that he has merely relied on the wrong sages. If he had, from the beginning, depended upon someone like Daniel, his problem would have been solved long ago without the distasteful threats.

The dream that Daniel recounts to Nebuchadnezzar is a narrative within a narrative. Daniel takes us back to the moment of Nebuchadnezzar's dreaming by telling the dream from the king's point of view. Daniel begins the account by addressing the king in the second person, 'You, O King, were looking...' but immediately shifts to seeing the dream through the king's eyes: '...and, lo!—a great image!'[43] Though Daniel verbalizes the dream, we see the dream as Nebuchadnezzar had seen it on that restless night.

The dream opens with a great and frightening image standing before Nebuchadnezzar. The image is a human form with a head of gold, chest and arms of silver, belly and thighs of bronze, legs of iron, and feet partly of iron and partly of clay. The image remains visible until a stone is cut, but not with human hands, and it strikes the image upon its feet and breaks them in pieces. Then, the entire image breaks into pieces and the wind carries the refuse away until nothing of the image remains. At this point, the stone becomes a great mountain and fills the whole earth.

Daniel shifts out of the dream and back into the context of its telling by saying, 'This is the dream and we will tell its interpretation before the king'. The interpretation draws connections both between the dream and the surrounding narrative and between the dream and events that will supposedly occur beyond the time narrated in the story. In other words, the dream both reflects the story world and temporally transcends it: The dream has both synchronic and diachronic significance.

Daniel's first explanatory comment associates the dream image with Nebuchadnezzar's present reign: 'You, O king, king of kings, to whom the God of heaven has given the kingdom, the power, the might, and the honor, and into whose hand he has given all that dwell—human beings, beasts of the field, birds of the heaven—and he has caused you to rule over all of them: You are the head of gold'. Daniel's words correlate the vast rulership of Nebuchadnezzar with the golden head of the dream image. Daniel's explanation, like the image itself, employs height and hierarchy to communicate the extent of power. As the head sits at the top of the body, so Nebuchadnezzar rules over the natural ('all that dwell—human beings, beasts of the field, birds of the heaven. . . ') and the political ('king of kings' having 'kingdom, power, might, and honor') world. Daniel's words, however, also point out a part of the hierarchy that Nebuchadnezzar has not seen, either in his dream or in his life:[44] The 'God' of heaven' stands over the 'head of gold'. The God of heaven 'gives' control and 'causes rule'.

The remainder of Daniel's interpretation is an exclusively temporal reading. Daniel connects the various elements of the dream to events that will occur after the present story has ended, indeed, after Nebuchadnezzar's reign has ended. The remaining anatomical parts of the image, presented from the shoulders to the feet and made from a series of different (mostly metallic) elements, represent a succession of kingdoms that will arise after Nebuchadnezzar's reign. Superiority is conveyed through hierarchy and the relative values of the metals: Each kingdom is inferior to the one preceding, although it is not made clear in what way this inferiority manifests itself except in the case of the last kingdom. The last kingdom, which begins with legs of iron and ends in feet of iron and pottery, starts with strength, but in the end becomes too diverse and loses the strength that comes with unity. The stone is an indestructible kingdom established by the God of heaven. It puts an end to these other kingdoms and it stands forever.

After interpreting the dream, Daniel says, 'A great God has made known to the king what is to be after this. . . ' (v. 45) and thus condenses the dream to its diachronic dimensions. The dream is the future that the God of heaven wants Nebuchadnezzar to see. The future contains a confrontation between human power and divine power in which divine power will be victorious. The God of heaven wants Nebuchadnezzar to recognize the supremacy of divine power.

The problem with this exclusively temporal reading, however, is that the supremacy of divine power is an *eventual* supremacy, not a supremacy that is easily recognized in the present structure of things. By reading the dream primarily as a vision of the future, Daniel has minimized its judgmental nature. If the stone that crushes is, to Nebuchadnezzar, a disturbing image, then upon Daniel's temporal reading, he, like Hezekiah, can comfort himself with the thought

'Why not, if there will be peace and security in my days?' (2 Kgs 20.19). Small wonder, then, that his response to Daniel's interpretation is so benign. Daniel's somewhat one-sided view of the dream's content suggests to him that he need not be concerned with the destructive element of the dream: This will not happen in his lifetime. Thus, he easily turns his attention from the content of the dream to Daniel's remarkable ability to recount and interpret it.

Daniel is, in my reading of the text, like Meir Sternberg's biblical narrator:[45] one who tells the truth but not the whole truth. Daniel's reading of the dream is an underreading. There are elements in the dream for which he has not given account to the king. The image, though built of multiple components, is still a singular entity, a unified structure that stands as one and falls as one. As a singular construct, its temporality is marked, not by succession, but by synchrony.[46]

Furthermore, Daniel never explains the significance of the image's human form or the contrast between the giant human figure and the stone which is cut, pointedly, without human hands. When Daniel speaks of the stone, he describes it as another kingdom raised up by the God of heaven, its distinction being that it will not be taken over by another people (v. 44). The difference between the kingdom represented by the stone and those represented by the various metals is not noted as a difference in kind. It is not, according to Daniel's interpretation, a divine kingdom as opposed to a human one, for instance[47]—the God of heaven has also raised up the 'head of gold' and we know that, in Daniel's view, the God of heaven raises up all kings (v. 21). Rather, the difference is its longevity, which is implicitly the result of its immense power.

The contrast between the gigantic human form and the stone uncontaminated by human chisel is more striking in the dream itself than it is in Daniel's interpretation. In a more synchronic reading of the dream, the accent falls more readily on the inherent tension created by the distinction. The image is shaped like a human body. It is composed of elements usually worked by human hands and valued by human society—gold and silver that adorn and give economic power, bronze and iron that make tools and weapons, and even pottery so necessary for literary and domestic purposes. The image is an idol, not of a divine being,[48] but of humanity. The top-heavy image is a symbol of a humanity that has over-reached itself. Juxtaposed to the human image is a power completely devoid of

human characteristics, a force that is completely 'other'. The stone is
a natural element that does rather unnatural things. It divorces itself
from its surroundings, it propels itself against the image, it grows as if
an organic entity, into a mountain that fills the entire earth. The
mountain, in contrast to the image, is raw and undomesticated. It
represents something that cannot be tamed by human power.[49]

The dream, of course, has a personal dimension as well. Daniel
touches upon this when he identifies Nebuchadnezzar as the head of
gold. The unstable image, with its glory and its commonality, its
strength and its weakness, also represents the rule of Nebuchadnezzar.
It is an awe-inspiring rule with a fragile foundation. If we see the
dream as a product of Nebuchadnezzar's head (which Daniel himself
encourages us to do when he identifies the dream as 'the thoughts of
your heart' [v. 30]) as well as a communication from God, a reading
that understands the king's character to be plagued by political
uncertainty is given further support.[50] The dream reflects worry. Is
his control truly secure? Are those beneath him really dependable?
Might they not make unexpected alliances (v. 43)? Might they not
rise up and crush authority (v. 40)?[51]

The revealed content of the dream invites the reader to recall the
initial scene involving the king and his sages. Now that we know the
dream, we better understand his conversation. Why test his sages?
Why the paranoid accusation 'Undoubtedly you are buying *time*. . . You
have agreed with one another to speak a false and corrupt word
before me *until the time has changed*' (v. 8)? Perhaps political
suspicion. The dream suggests a fear that time will not be kind to his
reign. Why threaten dismemberment and destroyed house? Perhaps
that is what he fears for himself and his kingdom—the image in his
dream is certainly 'dismembered'. Why the wording 'there is but one
sentence for all of you'? Perhaps he echoes what he saw in his dream,
that there was but one sentence for all the components of the image.
Could the ominous vision of what might be his own end now make
him wield his power with an even heavier hand? If so, he is fulfilling
the dream's symbolism, deifying his own power, claiming autonomy
over life and death.

If, as a product of Nebuchadnezzar's head, the dream represents
both his hope and his fear—his hope of a magnificent, golden rule,
but his fear of failure—and if, as a message from the God of heaven,
the dream passes judgment upon his hubris, then Daniel's explanation
of the dream has fallen short of the dream itself. By interpreting the

dream as a vision of the future, by conveying the judgment as a judgment against the whole of political history, Daniel minimizes Nebuchadnezzar's culpability.

Daniel's version of the dream is the version of diplomacy. Perhaps he is keeping in mind the king's volatile nature as he consistently elevates the king's importance. The king is the head of gold. He is the recipient of a special gift, the divine gift of the kingdom. He is the one chosen by the God of heaven. Even the dream marks his favored status: The God of heaven wants to impart to him this knowledge concerning the future. Daniel's very presence and ability to interpret are signs of God's interest in the king.

In this public encounter Daniel verbally expresses complete allegiance to the king. Yet, the reader remembers the prayer that Daniel sings in the privacy of his home. Daniel's prayer responds not simply to the fact that God has made the dream known to him; his prayer responds to the content of the king's dream. He gleefully thanks God for 'changing the times and the seasons' and not only for 'setting up kings' but for 'allowing kings to pass away'. Perhaps Daniel is, as Nebuchadnezzar views the sages earlier, looking forward to a day when the 'situation is changed'. Daniel's private political hopes are more complex than those he is willing to express in public.

Since, throughout Daniel's speech, the reader has not been allowed to see the king's face, the moment of Nebuchadnezzar's reaction is rather climactic. If he were to suspect the synchronic as well as the diachronic significance of the dream, his response could easily be anger. It appears, however, that he has been mesmerized by Daniel's ability to recount the dream and convinced by Daniel's diplomatically temporal account of its meaning. His response is a mixture of relief and wonder. Perhaps Daniel's interpretation has been more favorable than he thought he could expect. Certainly, Daniel's ability to do what only a god can do fills him with awe, not to mention confusion. If only a god can recount the dream of another, then Daniel must, somehow, be divine. Thus, he falls upon his face before Daniel, worships (cf. the usage of *sgd* in Isa. 44.15, 17, 19; 46.6 and throughout Daniel 3) him, and commands that an offering (*minḥāh*) and incense offering (*nîḥōḥîn*) be poured out (*nsk*) as a libation to him.[52]

At this point we might expect Daniel to clarify the situation to the king, to explain that he is not divine, but simply a human agent.

Daniel, however, does no such thing. His ability to tell the dream has completely drowned out his disclaimer that God has revealed the mystery to him. Moreover, his acceptance of religious homage undercuts the dream's messages about human limitation, the need to recognize human limitation, and the distinction between human and divine power.

Nebuchadnezzar's ambiguous confession, 'Truly your god is god of gods and lord of kings and a revealer of mysteries that you are able to reveal this mystery', is further evidence of his theological confusion. In the first place, 'god' is subordinated to Daniel: The deity in question is not the 'God of heaven' but 'your god'. Secondly, Nebuchadnezzar's grammar leaves us wondering about his understanding. Is it *because* Daniel's god is god of gods that Daniel is able to reveal the mystery or is his god now god of gods *because* Daniel is able to reveal the mystery? Can divinity and humanity be distinguished? Judging from Nebuchadnezzar's reaction, obviously not.

The story's denouement is brief. Nebuchadnezzar puts Daniel in charge of the entire province of Babylon and appoints him to be chief prefect over all the sages of Babylon. Daniel, in turn, requests that the service of the province be passed to his friends, Shadrach, Meshach, and Abednego. He keeps the role of leadership over the sages, however, and remains at the royal court.

It is at this point that the reader becomes disoriented. It seems that here we have a different version from that in ch. 1 of how Daniel and his friends become successful in Nebuchadnezzar's administration. If Daniel 2 is to be read as a flashback, the narrator has been rather careless in the reestablishment of chronology. We might have expected Daniel and his friends to return and finish their training; instead, they are immediately incorporated into court life and promoted to high position. Thus, the two versions stand in tension with one another and raise the question of the narrator's reliability.[53] Does Daniel become successful because his special wisdom and ability are of constant, but general assistance to Nebuchadnezzar, as the narrator tells us in ch. 1? Or does Daniel become successful because, on this particular occasion, he so impresses the king with his ability and diplomacy that the king mistakes him for divine and his partial truth for the whole truth?

Chapter 3

DANIEL 3.1-30

(1) Nebuchadnezzar the king made an image of gold. Its height was sixty cubits; its width six cubits. He erected it in the plain of Dura in the province of Babylon. (2) Nebuchadnezzar the king sent to assemble the satraps, the prefects and the governors, the counselors, the treasurers, the judges, the officials and all the authorities of the province[1] to come to the dedication of the image which Nebuchadnezzar the king had erected. (3) Then the satraps, the prefects and the governors, the counselors, the treasurers, the judges, the officials and all the authorities of the province assembled themselves for the dedication of the image which Nebuchadnezzar the king had erected. They stood before the image that Nebuchadnezzar had erected (4) and the herald called loudly to them, saying, 'Peoples, nations and languages! (5) When you hear the sound of the horn, the pipe, the lyre, the trigon, the harps, the bagpipes, and every kind of music[2] you will fall down and pay homage to the gold image that Nebuchadnezzar the king has erected. (6) Whoever does not fall down and pay homage will immediately be cast into the midst of a blazing fiery furnace'. (7) Consequently, as soon as all the people heard the sound of the horn, the pipe, the lyre, the trigon, the harp, the bagpipes[3] and every kind of music, all the peoples, nations and languages fell down and paid homage to the gold image that Nebuchadnezzar the king had erected.

(8) It was in relation to this, that, at that time, certain Chaldeans came forward and maliciously accused[4] the Jews. (9) They answered and said to Nebuchadnezzar the king, 'O King, live forever! (10) You, O King, have given a command that everyone who hears the sound of the horn, the pipe, the lyre, the trigon, the harp, the bagpipes, and every kind of music must fall down and pay homage to the gold image (11) and whoever does not fall down and pay homage will be cast into the midst of a blazing fiery furnace. (12) There are certain Jews whom you have appointed over the administration of the province of Babylon: Shadrach, Meshach, and Abednego. These men, O King, show no deference to you. They do not serve your gods and they do not pay homage to the gold image that you have erected'.

(13) Then Nebuchadnezzar in rage and anger commanded that Shadrach, Meshach, and Abednego be brought. Then these men were brought before the king, (14) Nebuchadnezzar said to them, 'Is it true,[5] Shadrach, Meshach, and Abednego, that you do not serve my gods nor do you pay homage to the

gold image that I have erected? (15) Now, if you are ready, when you hear
the sound of the horn, the pipe, the lyre, the trigon, the harp, the bagpipes
and every kind of music, you will fall down and pay homage to the image
that I have made. If you do not pay homage, you will promptly be cast into
the midst of a blazing fiery furnace—and who is the god who will deliver
your from my hands'? (16) Shadrach, Meshach, and Abednego answered and
said to the king, 'O Nebuchadnezzar,[6] we have no need to respond to you[7]
concerning this matter. (17) If our God, whom we serve, is able to deliver us[8]
from a blazing fiery furnace and from your hands, O King, then he will
deliver. (18) But if not, be it known to you, O King, that we do not serve your
gods nor will we pay homage to the gold image that you have erected'.

(19) Then Nebuchadnezzar became filled with anger and the expression
on his face changed toward Shadrach, Meshach, and Abednego. He
responded, commanding the furnace to be heated seven times over what was
customary to heat it. (20) He commanded certain strong men who were in
his army to bind Shadrach, Meshach, and Abednego in order to cast [them]
into the blazing fiery furnace. (21) Then these men were bound in their
mantles, their robes, their headcoverings and their garments[9] and they were
cast into the midst of the blazing fiery furnace. (22) Because the king's order
was severe and the furnace was made exceedingly hot, those men who
brought up Shadrach, Meshach, and Abednego were themselves killed by the
flame of the fire. (23) These three men, Shadrach, Meshach, and Abednigo,
fell, bound, into the midst of the blazing fiery furnace.

(24) Then Nebuchadnezzar the king was startled and arose in alarm. He
said to his counselors, 'Did we not cast three bound men into the midst of the
fire'? They answered the king, 'It is true, O King'. (25) He said 'Lo, I see four
men, unbound, walking around in the midst of the fire and no harm has
come to them! And the appearance of the fourth is like that of a son of the
gods'.

(26) Then Nebuchadnezzar approached the door of the blazing fiery
furnace. He said, 'Shadrach, Meshach, and Abednego, servants of the highest
god, step forward and come out'! Thereupon Shadrach, Meshach, and
Abednego stepped forth from the midst of the fire. (27) Those assembled—
the satraps, the prefects and the governors and the king's counselors saw that
the fire had had no power over the bodies of these men. The hair of their
heads was not singed; their mantles were not changed; and the smell of fire
had not passed onto them. (28) Nebuchadnezzar said, 'Blessed be the god of
Shadrach, Meshach, and Abednego who sent his angel and delivered his
servants who set their trust upon him and who violated the king's order and
gave their bodies because they would not serve nor would they pay homage
to any god except their god. (29) I make a decree that any people, nation or
language that says anything amiss against[10] the god of Shadrach, Meshach
and Abednego will be dismembered and his house will be laid in ruins

because there is no other god who is able to deliver like this'. (30) Then the king made Shadrach, Meshach, and Abednego prosperous in the province of Babylon.

The Reading

Unlike the stories in Daniel 1 and 2 which ease the reader into their worlds with temporal and situational orientations, Daniel 3 begins abruptly with catalytic action:[11] Nebuchadnezzar the king made an image of gold...' This first sentence signals that we are to read the story as a continuation of what has preceded. The narrator assumes that we know who Nebuchadnezzar is and, consequently, does not introduce him. Furthermore, as the narrator links our interest in Daniel 1 and Daniel 2 with the subject of dreams, so the narrator links Daniel 3 to Daniel 2 with the image of gold.

The narrator only describes the image in terms of its size and location. We are not told what the image symbolizes or why the king builds it. The association of this construction with the image in 'Nebuchadnezzar's dream, however, is pointed and invites the reader to fill these informational gaps with inferences from Daniel 2.[12] The identical word (slm), the comparable size, and the matching component of gold prompt the understanding that Nebuchadnezzar is duplicating, though with some variation, the image he has seen in his dream. Taken by Daniel's interpretation that he is the head of gold, Nebuchadnezzar builds a corresponding image of gold. His created image remedies the weaknesses inherent in his dream-image: His is made of a unified substance; his has no feet of clay. If, according to Daniel's temporal reading of his dream, his rule is to be remembered as the golden age, then perhaps one is to interpret Nebuchadnezzar's structure as a visual symbol of the way in which he wants himself and his reign to be perceived, both now and in the years to come.[13]

That the king is preoccupied with public perception is verified in his next action. 'And Nebuchadnezzar the king sent to assemble the satraps, the prefects and the governors, the counselors, the treasurers, the judges, the officials and all the authorities of the province to come to the dedication of the image which Nebuchadnezzar the king had erected' (v. 2). No sooner is the long-winded list uttered than it is repeated in the narrator's report of the officials' arrival: 'Then the satraps, the prefects and the governors, the counselors, the treasurers, the judges, the officials and all the authorities of the province assembled themselves for the dedication of the image which Nebuchadnezzar the king had erected' (v. 3).

On the surface, this (almost) verbatim repetition of the list tells us precisely who is summoned and who appears at the dedication of the image. The repetition, however, also presents the power structure of the story world and, by doing so, provides the reader with a clue to the nature of the gathering. All the people involved are identified by political status. This is not an occasion for the general populace; it is an administrative assembly. The extensive list suggests a rather sophisticated political network, but the repetition of the list shows the king's control of this network. Precisely what the king wills is precisely what takes place. The precise people that he summons are the precise people who assemble. Thus, through repetition, the narrator creates a scenario in which conformity is normative, disobedience is unthinkable.

On a mechanical level, the repetition slows the pace of narration and the content of the list itself broadens our range of vision. We began with a view limited to the king and his tremendous image; now our vision is broadened to include not only the king and his image, but also the assembled multitude.

While we look upon the crowd with our wide-angle vision, we hear the herald announce:

> Oh, peoples, nations, and languages! When you hear the sound of the horn, the pipe, the lyre, the trigon, the harps, the bagpipes, and every kind of music, you will fall down and pay homage to the gold image that Nebuchadnezzar the king has erected. Whoever does not fall down and pay homage will immediately be cast into the midst of a blazing fiery furnace (vv. 4-6).

The dedication, it seems, involves more than gathering to admire the king's handiwork. The people are required to swear an allegiance to this image that is akin to worship.[14] If they refuse, they are sentenced to death by burning. By threatening death (cf. Dan. 2.5, 9, 12), Nebuchadnezzar attempts to control. But why is it so important that everyone present worship the image? Is it a god? We are not expressly told so. In fact, the only statement that qualifies the image is the phrase 'that Nebuchadnezzar the king erected'. The recurrence of this phrase (vv. 2, 3, 3, 5, 7, 12, 14, 15, 18) suggests that the significance of the image lies in the fact that Nebuchadnezzar has made it. It is his accomplishment.[15]

The reader might also find the herald's address to be of help in deciphering the import of the situation. When the herald addresses the congregation, we might have expected: 'O satraps, prefects and govenors, etc.' Instead, he makes a substitution:[16] 'O peoples, nations, and languages!, When reporting the congregation's obedience to the order (v. 7), the narrator also employs the herald's terminology: 'all the peoples, nations, and languages fell down and paid homage...' While the list of political offices identifies the people with the Babylonian administration, and thus signals affinity, the variation 'peoples, nations and languages' acknowledges a broad national spectrum and thus signals difference. The people may be part of the Babylonian political structure, but they are also from a variety of national backgrounds. They represent nations who have been conquered and subjugated. To worship the image is to swear allegiance to Nebuchadnezzar. The dedication is a maneuver on Nebuchadnezzar's part to rally political solidarity.[17] Even the religious nuances of the dedication fit well into the promotion of political unity. One need only recall the reforms of Hezekiah and Josiah to understand that religious homogeneity and political autonomy go hand in hand.

The construction of the great image for the purpose of political control accords with the preceding reading of Daniel 2 in which Nebuchadnezzar is a king plagued by political insecurity. His dream, while reflecting his anxiety, has also given him an idea as to how to relieve his anxiety. The image will be a standard of allegiance; the image will be the measure of his control. Thus, when he builds the image of gold, the reader knows that he has not understood the dream at all. He seems to see the need to make himself the head of gold, to show himself superior to all other rulers; he does not see himself as part of the history of political hubris that stands condemned. His lack of understanding legitimates the judgmental message of the dream. By erecting the image that represents his sovereignty, and by requiring that his officials worship the image, he has raised himself to the divine status for which the dream has condemned him.

The narrator's tone ridicules Nebuchadnezzar's misunderstanding of the dream and this attempt to reassure himself of his powerful control. The tedious repetitions (of which we have not heard the last) undermine the solemnity of the occasion and leave the reader wondering about the hierarchy of significance in the story world.

Rather than explaining what the image represents, the narrator spends time repeatedly listing officials and musical instruments. The pomp of the event is given more emphasis than the meaning of the event. The narrator constantly reminds us, as if we could forget at any moment, that the image is something 'Nebuchadnezzar the king has erected (vv. 2, 3, 5, 6, and see also vv. 12, 14, 15, 18)', and thereby mocks the king's attempt to be remembered as the head of gold.[18]

When reporting the crowd's response to the command, the narrator includes the seemingly redundant catalogue of musical instruments and echoes the herald's use of the nomenclature 'peoples, nations, and languages'. The narrator, however, adds the word *all*—'all the peoples, nations, and languages bowed down and worshipped the gold image...' The addition of 'all' produces several effects. 'All' emphasizes the wholesale compliance of the assembly and thus accentuates the point made by the earlier repeated list of the officials: Precisely what the king commands is precisely what happens. The wholesale compliance of the assembly can put the king's political worry to rest.

Or can it? Does the word 'all' represent the narrator's point of view? Might it not represent only Nebuchadnezzar's perspective? And might the narrator, by using the absurd repetition, be ridiculing the king's perspective that he has now attained the unanimous allegiance of his subjects?

The word 'all' unsettles the reader and raises the question of point of view because the reader's interest thus far has been focused on Daniel and his friends. On last report, Daniel, and subsequently, Shadrach, Meshach, and Abednego, had been appointed as officials over the province of Babylon. The narrator tells us that all the officials of the province are present at this dedication (v. 3). If Daniel and his friends would not even eat food from the king's table for fear of compromising authority, would they indeed now bow down and worship an image as a gesture of political allegiance?

Suddenly, the scene shifts and the scope of our vision narrows. We are made to focus on 'certain Chaldeans' who come forth and accuse 'certain Jews' of disobeying the royal order. Since the behavior of 'certain Jews' is on our minds, we are not terribly surprised by this turn in the plot. As they speak, we realize that, if their testimony is reliable, our vantage point in the first scene (vv. 2-7) has been so distant that we have missed some of what must have taken place. Our view of the crowds has been so broad that we have not been able to see individuals. Furthermore, if the Chaldeans are telling the truth, our suspicion that the report of wholesale compliance (v. 7) represents the king's point of view (and not the narrator's) gains credence.

The scene in which Nebuchadnezzar learns of the disobedience of the three Jews could have been handled in several ways. The story could have read at this point, 'And it was told to King Nebuchadnezzar that the Jews he had appointed over the affairs of the province of Babylon, Shadrach, Meshach, and Abednego, had refused to pay homage to the image which he had erected'. Or the king, while officiating at the dedication, could have simply witnessed the disobedience himself.

Instead, our narrator, who never seems to miss a chance to use another verbose repetition in the telling of the story, introduces another party to give the report to the king. However, though they mimic the herald (vv. 4-6) and the narrator (v. 7) before them, their report differs somewhat from what we have heard before. Their version reads:

> You, O King, have given a command that everyone who hears the sound of the horn, the pipe, the lyre, the trigon, the harp, the bagpipes, and every kind of music must fall down and pay homage to the gold image, and whoever does not fall down and pay homage will be cast into the midst of a blazing fiery furnace. There are certain Jews whom you appointed over the service of the province of Babylon—Shadrach, Meshach, and Abednego—these men, O King, show no deference to you. They do not serve your gods and they do not pay homage to the gold image that you have erected.

The Chaldeans' account is what may be termed a *deliberate* variation of the original material. Regarding this type of variation. Sternberg writes:

> The deliberately variant retrospect often plays an... active part in biblical dialogue, one that subsumes 'tactful' reference as a gambit, softening-up flattery, or snare for the addressee. The speaker's deviations then make sense in terms of his endeavor to move, persuade or impose his will on his interlocutor by contriving an ad hominem version of an antecedent speech or event.[19]

In the case of the Chaldeans, they expand and, to a certain extent, reorganize the material in order to move the king to take action against the three Jews. As they reiterate the king's order, they carefully include the condition of disobedience (which the narrator, in reporting compliance in v. 7, logically omitted). Since their purpose is to inform on Shadrach, Meshach, and Abednego, the pointed reminder of the fiery furnace serves as a subtle challenge to the king to act upon his word.

In their first mention of the gold image, the Chaldeans leave out the accompanying phrase, 'that you have erected'. This omission stands out because in every other occurrence of 'the gold image', this phrase, or a variation of it, is present. The Chaldeans do not omit the phrase entirely, however, but they move it to the end of their speech, leaving the king to linger on the personal affront involved in the Jews' disobedience and reminding the king that it is this affront that provides grounds for execution according to the royal decree.

The main addition that the Chaldeans make in their speech is, of course, the information about Shadrach, Meshach, and Abednego.[20] The Chaldeans do not simply say 'these men did not pay homage to the gold image'. They first mention the political position that these three hold: They are the king's personal appointees over the administration of the province of Babylon. As the Chaldeans continue, they craftily vocalize the affront as a personal one. Notice that they do not say 'These men show no deference to the royal decree' or 'to Babylonian law'. They do not refer to the divine as 'Babylonian gods' or 'our gods'. They pointedly make the king the target of the affront by employing the second person singular: 'to *you*', '*Your* gods', 'the image *you* have erected'. Their speech turns political betrayal into personal betrayal. In other words, the king himself appointed them to office and now they blatantly disregard his authority.

The Chaldeans attempt to discredit Shadrach, Meshach, and Abednego further by stressing their national and religious difference. They are Jews and 'they do not serve your gods. . . ' (Thus, they echo with force the religious issue that was but a nuance in the exposition. They have made explicit Nebuchadnezzar's implicit presupposition regarding the dedication: Religious affinity is political affinity and, conversely, religious difference is political difference.) The Chaldeans' tacit equation is: Different is suspect.

The final evidence for the Jews' personal and political betrayal is their disobedience: 'and they do not pay homage to the gold image that you have erected'. Thus, the Chaldeans plant the idea that the failure of the three to pay homage is the manifestation of their *complete* untrustworthiness—they show *no deference* the the king.[21] Consequently, if the king has had any inclination to make an exception for these three, this portrayal functions to make him think twice.

In their rhetoric before the king, the Chaldeans implicitly contrast themselves to the three Jews. By informing the king of the Jews' disobedience, they imply their own obedience. By reporting that Shadrach, Meshach, and Abednego do not serve the king's gods or the image he has erected, they suggest that they themselves are of the same religious persuasion as the king. Through this rhetorical maneuver they align themselves with the king. They present themselves as dutiful subjects who have only the king's interests in mind.

The Chaldeans' presentation of themselves raises, in the reader's mind, the question of their motive(s). Why do they deem it necessary to inform on the Jews? Do they truly come forth out of religious piety and concern for the king as the surface of the narrative suggests? Court 'tattling' appears to be a popular motif in later Jewish literature. Often the informants are involved in framing the victim and misleading the king out of political jealousy or personal hatred (cf. Daniel 6, Esther 3). The Chaldeans appear to be merely acting upon what they have seen. Lest the audience be carried away by the Chaldeans' presentation of themselves as dutiful subjects, however, the narrator warns against such simplistic interpretation with the phrase 'ate the pieces of', i.e. 'maliciously accused' the Jews. Thus, the narrator leaves no doubt of the Chaldeans' hostility toward the Jews.

The shape of the scene itself also provides a clue to the motivations of the Chaldeans. Recall for a moment another court story that involves someone informing an unknowing king of a situation of rebellion: In 1 Kings 1 when David's son Adonijah begins to prepare himself for kingship, Bathsheba (encouraged by Nathan the prophet) goes before the aged and ailing King David and speaks to him in terms not unlike those of the Chaldeans to Nebuchadnezzar. She begins her speech by reminding[22] the king that he has sworn an oath and by repeating that oath: 'My lord, you swore to your maidservant by Yahweh your God saying, "Solomon your son shall reign after me, and he shall sit upon my throne"'. The Chaldeans in Daniel 3 begin in much the same way with a reminder and a repetition: 'You, O King, have given a command that everyone who hears the sound of the horn, the pipe, the lyre, the trigon, the harp, the bagpipes, and every kind of music must fall down and pay homage to the gold image and whoever does not fall down and pay homage will be cast into the midst of a blazing fiery furnace'.

In 1 Kgs 1.18, Bathsheba continues with the actual information that she came to impart to the king: 'And now, behold, Adonijah is king, although you, my lord the king, do not know it'. She then elaborates on this statement: 'He has sacrificed oxen, fatlings, and sheep in abundance, and has invited all the sons of the king, . . . but Solomon your servant he has not invited'. At the same structural point, the Chaldeans also share their critical information: 'There are certain Jews whom you appointed over the administration of the province of Babylon—Shadrach, Meshach, and Abednego—These men, O King show no deference to you'. They also offer elaboration: 'They do not serve your gods and they do not pay homage to the gold image that you have erected'.

Bathsheba's words make it clear that the reason for such a speech is to move the king to action: 'And now, my lord the king, the eyes of all Israel are upon you, to tell them who shall sit on the throne of my lord the king after him . . .' The Chaldeans, however, leave their speech open, leading the king to recognize for himself that 'the eyes of all Babylon' are upon him to see if he will carry out his threat or not. The analogy between the two scenes is further reinforced by the same protocol formula. The Chaldeans preface their speech with 'O King, live forever!' Bathsheba responds to David's promise to make her son king with 'May my lord King David live forever!'

In 1 Kings 1 Bathsheba clearly does not come forward with her information just because she feels obligated to be the eyes and ears of the king. She does not even do so out of hatred for Adonijah: Her feelings about him are never made explicit. She has a personal and political motive: Adonijah occupies the position that she desires for her son. She portrays Adonijah, whether truthfully or not we cannot be sure, as a usurper and thus discredits him. In contrast, the character of Solomon emerges from her speech as the patient son, loyal to the end, the true servant of the king and, consequently, the more attractive candidate for kingship.

Although the corresponding scene in Daniel 3 is not as explicit as that of 1 Kings 1, the Chaldeans present their case in much the same way with a similar goal in mind. The Chaldeans are not interested in simply turning in some disobedient Jews; they are interested in turning in particular Jews, Jews that the king himself has appointed over the administration of the province of Babylon. The implied argument is that, if Shadrach, Meshach, and Abednego show no deference to the king in this matter, they are probably delinquent in other matters as well and thus, they are unsuitable for their present political position. The Chaldeans themselves, on the other hand, are loyal in the matter at hand, loyal enough to report dissent and would certainly make suitable adminstrators over the province of Babylon.

From what we know of Shadrach, Meshach, and Abednego from ch. 1, the reader suspects that the three are indeed guilty of disobeying the king's order. Following Daniel's lead, the three refused the indenturing royal food; it seems most likely that they have also refused to worship the image. What they might do when publicly challenged on this issue is another matter, however. After all, Daniel is not around to take charge. Besides, discrete disobedience is remarkably easier than overt defiance.

What the king believes about Shadrach, Meshach, and Abednego is unclear, but he does not accept the Chaldeans' report unquestioningly. He calls the three before him and questions them concerning the truth of the accusation, but because he does not pause for an answer at this point, the reader is left in suspense as to their reaction. The king continues on, offering them the opportunity to prove the Chaldeans incorrect. He recreates the situation to see their response for himself.

Here, the fourth repetition of the order occurs in yet another context of communication with yet another set of characters. Each repetition has brought us a step closer to the central confrontation of the story. With this fourth and final repetition there are no mediators—no herald speaking on the king's behalf, no narrator reporting obedience, no Chaldeans reporting disobedience. The king and the Jews are face to face.

Having just listened to the Chaldeans' rhetoric and facing the suspected dissidents, the king varies his version of the order accordingly:

> Is it true, Shadrach, Meshach, and Abednego, that you do not serve my gods nor do you pay homage to the gold image that I have erected? Now, if you are ready, when you hear the sound of the horn, the pipe, the lyre, the trigon, the harp, the bagpipes and every kind of music, you will fall down and pay homage to the image that I have made. If you do not pay homage, you will promptly be cast

into the midst of a blazing fiery furnace. And who is the god who
will deliver you from my hands?

Nebuchadnezzar changes the order of the material and also makes
an addition. Rather than giving the order straight away, he first
echoes, in a question to the three, the last statements of the
Chaldeans. Rather than waiting for an answer, he hurries on with the
order. By doing this he seems to be communicating that what it all
boils down to is their performing the act of paying homage. He is less
concerned with their belief than he is with their conduct. They may
not believe in his gods; they may put no stock in the image that he
has made, but they should at least bow down out of respect for and
fear of the king. He deserves their homage because he has the power
to put them to death. He challenges what he correctly perceives to be
their loyalty to their own god: 'Who is the god who will deliver you
from my hands?' The object of such loyalty should be powerful. He
himself is ultimately powerful because he can have them killed; their
god cannot possibly compare. Thus, he attempts to persuade them by
pointing out their misplaced loyalty and by playing upon their
fear.

Shadrach, Meshach, and Abednego are no longer three faceless
people in the obscurity of a multitude. They stand alone, front and
center. Whatever they do now determines what becomes of them.
Suspense builds as we wait through the king's listing of musical
instruments, his threat for disobedience, his gibe at the folly of their
position should they indeed prove to be recalcitrant: 'And who is the
god who will deliver your from my hands?'

Where the tension is highest, our vision is the narrowest. There is
nothing in the scene to distract us (e.g. no account of the Chaldeans'
smug reaction, no mention of other characters who are spectators of
this incident). We are not even allowed to see all four characters at
once, except in v. 13. We see and hear Nebuchadnezzar first with
blinders toward Shadrach, Meshach, and Abednego. Then our sight
and hearing are limited exclusively to the three whom we could not
even spot in the first scene. Not until they finish are we allowed to
learn Nebuchadnezzar's reaction to them.

The speech of Shadrach, Meshach, and Abednego in vv. 17-18
(and it is their only one) marks the first and the major climactic point
in the story. Their speech breaks the verbal rules, so to speak. Their
speech is apart from all the others heard thus far in that they refuse
to answer with the extensive repetition that has become so common

in the story. Not only do they fail to use the full-scale repetition themselves, they speak without waiting for the musical signal and thus deprive the narrator of the final chance to relist the instruments.

The response of Shadrach, Meshach, and Abednego does echo smaller segments of the earlier material. Their selectivity allows the three to answer concisely; they do not attempt to buy time. They offer no self-defense. Instead, they direct their response to the king's closing question, using many of his same terms. Though the king himself intended the question to be rhetorical, to which the implied answer is 'There is no god who can deliver from your hand', Shadrach, Meshach, and Abednego refuse to interpret it as rhetorical. They address the question by affirming loyalty, not to Nebuchadnezzar, but to their god: 'If our god, whom we serve, is able to deliver us from a blazing fiery furnace and from your hand, O King, then he will deliver. But if not, be it known to you, O King that we would not serve your gods nor would we pay homage to the gold image that you have erected'.

Their words overpower the words of the king. By refusing to acknowledge his rhetoric, they render his speech impotent. By assuming his prescribed punishment (they do not beg for mercy), they emasculate his threat.

Furthermore, their response separates all the issues that have been fused together by the king and the Chaldeans before him. The issues of deliverance and divine ability are distinguished from the decision between loyalty and idolatry. Whether or not their god is able to deliver, they will not succumb to idolatry or tyranny. Their action is independent of the action of their god. Their loyalty is not contingent upon his power.[23]

Thus Shadrach, Meshach, and Abednego repeat the verbal elements 'deliver', 'fiery furnace', 'your hand', '[we] do not serve your gods', '[we] do not pay homage to the gold image that you have erected' in such a way as to reexpress the issues in their own terms. For Nebuchadnezzar there is no viable alternative to serving his gods and worshipping his image. For Shadrach, Meshach, and Abednego, there is no viable alternative to 'our god whom we serve'.

Consequently, the words of Shadrach, Meshach, and Abednego put the king in his place, his human place, and they are a judgment upon his hubris. Though the three Jews may be uncertain about their god's *ability* to deliver them, they are confident that their god is *willing* to deliver them[24] and their confidence in divine willingness to deliver communicates something about the nature of their god: Whether or not their god is omnipotent, their god still has a sense of fidelity, justice, righteousness. These are qualities that, obviously, the king does not have. Their confidence in divine willingness is a confession of faith that, if their god is able to right this evil, unjust situation, then indeed their god will.

The scene in which Shadrach, Meshach, and Abednego stand before the king parallels the preceding scene involving the Chaldeans before their sovereign.[25] In both cases the visual picture is the same: subjects standing before their king. Both parties are given similar designations. The informers are called 'certain Chaldeans' (*gūbrîn kaśdā'în*). In their speech they refer to Shadrach, Meshach, and Abednego as 'certain Jews' (*gūbrîn yehûdā'în*).

Comparison, however, invites contrast. The Chaldeans stand before the king, portraying loyalty to his highness. Shadrach, Meshach, and Abednego stand before the king confessing loyalty to a higher authority. The Chaldeans adopt the king's religious practices in order to advance themselves personally and politically. Shadrach, Meshach, and Abednego refuse to adopt the king's religious practices even though it means sacrificing not just political station, but life itself. The Chaldeans appear to have nothing to lose (after all, they have only reported the truth) and everything to gain. The Jews appear to have everything to lose and nothing to gain.

The religious language exchanged between the king and three Jews ('you do not serve my gods'/'our god whom we serve') also provides a common ground for comparing the three subjects to their sovereign. In this case, the piety of the politically powerful stands in ironic contrast to the piety of the politically unprotected. For one, the object of devotion is subordinated—'the image that I have made'. For the other, the object of devotion is absolute—'the god whom we serve'. For one, religion involves personal elevation and political control. For the other, religion demands personal sacrifice and the forfeit of control. Both take a rigid stance. It takes less courage, however, to exercise power than to resist it.

As we have listened to the defiant speech of Shadrach, Meshach, and Abednego, the narrator has given us no glimpse of Nebuchadnezzar. We are made to wait for his reaction. In v. 19 the narrator turns our attention to the king and observes that, at this point, the 'image', i.e. the expression, of Nebuchadnezzar's face changes toward the three men. By employing the same word, *ṣlm*, that has been used to refer to the image of gold, the narrator playfully connects the image of gold with the image of Nebuchadnezzar's face. The word play satirizes Nebuchadnezzar's audacity through allusion: In Genesis 1 Elohim creates humanity in the divine image (*ṣlm*); in Daniel 3 Nebuchadnezzar creates, in his own (very human) image, an object to be worshipped (and note in v. 28 that Nebuchadnezzar substitutes the word 'god' for 'image').[26]

The changing of Nebuchadnezzar's 'image', or expression, marks a turning point in the story. As the plot moves toward the seemingly certain execution, the narrator moves us away from the action. As the preparations are made for the men to be burned, we watch from a more distant position. Our perspective is broader, encompassing more space and more characters.

We anticipate the execution because the story has promised it: The king has threatened it, the Chaldeans have forced it, the Jews have accepted it.[27] The reader is familiar with the theme 'The king's fury is a messenger of death' (Prov. 16.14), not only from our experience of the world, but also from stories like 2 Samuel 12 and Daniel 2 that mimic our human experience of power structures. The reader is also aware that, in the larger story of Israel, people have been known to die by fire for any number of reasons (e.g. Joshua 7; Judges 11; Jer. 29.22).

Although prepared for the execution, the reader also recognizes certain literary allusions in the story that allow for other possibilities. The question, 'Who is the god who will deliver you from my hands'? that the king maniplulatively employs in v. 15 not only echoes Deut. 32.39, in which Yahweh himself says, 'there is no one who can deliver from my hand', but it also brings to mind the story of Sennacherib's attempt to take Jerusalem in 2 Kgs 18.13-19.37.[28] Through the voice of his messenger, Sennacherib sends a similar taunt to the people of the city: 'Has any of the gods of the nations ever delivered his land out of the hand of the king of Assyria?. . . Who among all the gods of the lands have delivered their land from my hand, that Yahweh should deliver Jerusalem from my hand?'

Both of these references aid the reader in seeing the king's audacity and in relating that, though the king does not view himself so, the narrator is portraying him to be blasphemous. The 2 Kings passage, because it, too, is narrative, is particularly suggestive concerning the plot of Daniel 3. In 2 Kgs 18.13-19.37 Sennacherib threatens to take Jerusalem, but a miracle occurs that keeps him from doing so. The

allusion suggests an analogy, and thereby foreshadows what is to
come in Daniel 3. A deliverance miracle is a possible plot alternative.
Based on the analogy, we might expect one that prevents the
threatened punishment from taking place.

This expectation is supported by another possible allusion. In vv.
19-21a the three men are bound in preparation for the burning. The
binding and the fire are reminiscent of another binding for another
fire, the binding of Isaac for a holocaust on Mount Moriah in Genesis
22.[29] In that story, too, divine intervention prevents the destruction.

The Genesis 22 story also invites us to see the sacrificial nature of
the execution. The three Jews are bound to be burned as sacrifices, a
turn of events foreshadowed in Daniel 1 by the king's command to
select for royal service young Judean captives who were 'without
blemish'.[30]

Standing in tension with the narrative elements that point to
certain death, the allusions to miraculous deliverance work on the
consciousness of an alert reader, creating, if not an expectation, at
least a hope that something will happen to prevent the three from
being thrown into the furnace. We look for something to happen to
the king to cause him to change his mind, a divine voice, perhaps, or
for an angel to appear and extinguish the flames.[31]

We are pulled between that for which we are prepared, but which
we fear, and that for which we hope. The narrator holds us in
suspense, teetering between the two possibilities, unsure of what is to
come.[32] The preparations for the execution proceed with a meticulous
cadence similar to that in the Genesis 22 story. The furnace is heated
beyond customary proportion. Strong men are selected from the
army to conduct the execution. The three men are bound. Their state
of dress is described to the last detail. And then, in the moment most
likely for divine intervention to take place, the three are cast into the
furnace. Suddenly the matter is closed, the men are gone, and with a
stroke of finality, the narrator informs us that the men who threw
them in are killed by the intensity of the flame. If those outside the
furnace are slain, those cast in stand no chance.

It appears that the 'certain strong men' (v. 20) and the 'certain
Jews' (v. 12) are linked by more than the narrator's designation.[33]
They (appear at this point to) suffer the same fate and so enact the
hazards of loyalty.

The deaths of the executioners is an ironic twist on the motif of
retribution. The evil accuser coming to the same punishment that

was intended for the heroes may be a typical feature of legends, e.g. Esther, Daniel 6,[34] but this variation deserves closer attention. Why does the narrator have relatively innocent figures suffer the punishment rather than the more logical choices, the Chaldeans or even the king?

Simple retribution is not the issue here. These 'certain strong men', like all the assembled officials in v. 7, are unquestioningly obedient to the king. Their obedience is contrasted to Shadrach, Meshach, and Abednego's calculated disobedience to the king and, at the same time, compared with the three's obedience to their god. The executioners die meaningless deaths[35] in obedience to an unconcerned sovereign with limited power. Nebuchadnezzar cannot control the killing. Even if he wanted to, Nebuchadnezzar is not able to deliver his loyal subjects from his own 'hand', i.e. the blazing fiery furnace.

After this second climactic moment, there is a pause in which we are left to ponder the monstrosity that we have just witnessed.[36] The story could easily end at this point; the plot is complete for a martyr story.[37] The nature of the climactic event, however, is stirring rather than settling. Although we had been prepared for this possibility, we hunger for justice.[38]

When the narrative resumes, our thoughts are on the three men in the fire, but the narrator forces our attention to Nebuchadnezzar. Although something is happening in the furnace, we are only allowed to watch Nebuchadnezzar's response to it.[39] We see his alarm, but not its source. We wait with wonder as he questions his counselors, 'Did we not cast three bound men into the midst of the fire'? and they give answer, 'It is true, O King'. In v. 25 Nebuchadnezzar announces what he sees, and the reader, too, is taken by surprise,[40] 'Lo, I see four men, unbound, walking around in the midst of the fire and no harm has come to them! And the appearance of the fourth is like that of a son of the gods'. What we thought had been settled has not been settled at all. Execution is not the last word.

We had hoped for deliverance *from* the fire; we had not expected deliverance *within* the fire. But perhaps we should have considered the option. Since fire often accompanies theophany in the Hebrew Bible (e.g. Exod. 3; 13.21-22; Num. 16.35), we should have recognized earlier the irony involved in the choice of fire as a means of execution.[41] We now can see that the often repeated phrase, 'blazing fiery furnace', has been foreshadowing this outcome all along. Not only does a divine representative appear in the flames, but, like the burning bush, the men are not consumed.

This turn in the plot requires that the reader backtrack to the moment in which the three are cast into the furnace and in which the executioners are killed. The death of the executioners must now be reinterpreted. On the first reading, the deaths of the executioners appeared to dramatize the certain deaths of Shadrach, Meshach, and Abednego. But on second reading, the executioners' deaths render the subsequent miracle more impressive.

The images of the heroes surviving the fiery furnace and of one 'like a son of the gods' joining them in the flames are so vivid that they are, for the most part, the key images that make the story memorable. These intense images, however, do not function simply to impress the reader: Their central purpose is to make an impact on the story world and on Nebuchadnezzar in particular. These images are not allowed to overpower the reader because our point of view is immediately directed elsewhere.

In v. 26 Nebuchadnezzar summons the three men from the furnace, calling them 'servants of the highest god'. They step forth from the fire, but rather than our attention being focused on them, our attention is directed to the perceptions of those gathered around. The assembled officials—'the satraps, the prefects and the governors and the king's counselors'—witness that the men are completely untouched by the flames. Although not every group of officials is mentioned by name,[42] enough of the list is here to indicate that the same people who were called to worship the image are the very ones who witness the miraculous survival of the three Jews. Hence an irony—the assembly is called for one purpose, but an entirely different purpose is served. Nebuchadnezzar's intention for the dedication, like his intention to kill the three Jews, is thwarted. The gold image is forgotten.

Shadrach, Meshach, and Abednego say nothing else throughout the remainder of the story. We know nothing of their perceptions. They give us no account of their experience in the fire; they tell us nothing about the one 'like a son of the gods'. Their character is one that does not change through the course of the story. Even though the narrator has set up an ordeal structured like a rite of passage, a mythical hero's journey from old life to (symbolic) death to new life,[43] the ordeal so designed to bring about change brings about none for those who participate in it. Their faith is no stronger. They acquire no new powers. Their unchanged appearance so deliberately stressed by the narrator is symbolic of their unchanged character.

Besides being static, the character of Shadrach, Meshach, and Abednego is, like all the other characters in the story with the exception of Nebuchadnezzar, collective. The 'satraps, the prefects and the governors, the counselors, the treasurers, the judges, the officials and all the authorities of the province', the 'certain Chaldeans', the 'certain strong men' from the royal army, and the king's counselors all are completely uniform. They speak and act as one. No individual personalities emerge. Shadrach, Meshach, and Abednego, though they appear as heroic figures, are never portrayed as individuals.

Consequently, the story is never their story. It is not a story of their heroism. The story is about the effect of their heroism on the world around them, and in particular, on the king who has tried to transform them and, failing that, has tried to kill them.[44]

The consistent collective and static characterization of Shadrach, Meshach, and Abednego, as well as of the others, highlights the single individual in the story, King Nebuchadnezzar. The narrator has focused our attention on Nebuchadnezzar more than on any other character, and for the remainder of the story he again fills our range of vision. As the only one to have seen inside the furnace (not even the narrator admits to having witnessed what has transpired there), Nebuchadnezzar is now the one who offers testimony. Ironically, it is he, rather than Shadrach, Meshach, and Abednego, who is changed by the ordeal by fire. He acquires a new knowledge and it is around this acquisition of knowledge that the story turns.[45]

As Nebuchadnezzar shares his new knowledge of God, we realize how dependent we are on the characters for *our* knowledge of this god. The deity who answers Nebuchadnezzar's challenge is not presented as a character in the story at all. We know the power of this god because we see Shadrach, Meshach, and Abednego unharmed by the fire. We know the presence of this god, because Nebuchadnezzar has reported seeing a divine representative. Just as in Daniel 2, God's power has an effect on the story world, but God's character cannot be seen. Our vision of God in the story, like our vision of God in real life, is severely limited.

Nebuchadnezzar responds to what he has witnessed with 'Blessed be the god of Shadrach, Meshach, and Abednego who...delivered his servants who. . . gave their bodies because they would not serve nor would they pay homage to any god except their god' (v. 28). One might expect a version closer to the repetition we have heard before, something along the lines of 'they would not serve my gods nor would they pay homage to the gold image I have erected'. 'My gods' and 'the gold image that I have erected/made' has been preempted by 'any god except their god'. He is fairly reticent about his own involvement in the preceding ordeal. By making the issue strictly a religious one, by omitting all political elements, by exempting himself from culpability, he saves face (or perhaps one should say 'image').

The limits of Nebuchadnezzar's new knowledge become apparent as he continues his speech. As he does in Daniel 2, the king defines and identifies the divine in terms of the human. Though he recognizes the power of the Hebrew god, he does not even ask the name or nature of this god. Instead, he refers to the deity as 'the god of Shadrach, Meshach, and Abednego'. While he expresses amazement concerning the power of the Hebrew god, he never admits that his own power should be subject to this divine power. In fact, he immediately attempts to exert control over this deity by issuing a royal decree: 'I make a decree that any people, nation or language that says anything against the god of Shadrach, Meshach, and Abednego will be dismembered and his house will be laid in ruins because there is no other god who is able to deliver like this' (v. 29).

The structural balance of the story lends an ironic force to the climactic confession of Nebuchadnezzar. This decree concerning the god of Shadrach, Meshach, and Abednego mirrors the earlier decree concerning the gold image. Both order some type of religious subservience. Both threaten death for disobedience. Nebuchadnezzar is again in the business of controlling the religious attitudes of others by wielding his political power.

While his first decree is commission, the king's second decree is prohibition. The people are not required to worship the god of Shadrach, Meshach, and Abednego; they are merely prohibited from saying anything against this god. Although he has witnessed a miracle, it seems that the king's allegiance to this god, like his knowledge of this god, has its limitations. He, nevertheless, makes this god politically useful. Like the gold image, this god becomes a measurement of political fidelity: Whoever speaks against this god shall be 'punished as culprits against the realm'.[46]

The god of Shadrach, Meshach, and Abednego is now to be recognized because of the *deliverance* that has just taken place (vv. 28 and 29). The theme of deliverance harks back to the king's question of deliverance in v. 15 and produces a fitting irony: the same character who mockingly asks 'Who is the god who will deliver you from my hands?' is the one who answers his own question: 'There is no other god who is able to deliver like this'.

In v. 15 the king uses the verb *sezib* (deliver) which is repeated twice by Shadrach, Meshach, and Abednego (v. 17). The verb occurs again in v. 28 when Nebuchadnezzar blesses the god of Shadrach, Meshach, and Abednego for delivering his servants. In his final statement in the story, Nebuchadnezzar confesses, '. . . there is no other god who is able to deliver like this'. Here, however, he does not use the verb *šēzib*, but instead uses the verb *nṣl*. This is not a deliberate substitution on the part of Nebuchadnezzar; the substitution is part of the narrator's rhetoric. The verb *nṣl* is the same verb used in 2 Kings 18 and 19, the same verb used in Deut. 32.39: 'See now that I, even I, am he, and there is no god beside me; I kill and I make alive; I wound and I heal; and there is none that can deliver out of my hand'. Consequently, while Nebuchadnezzar comes to the realization that the god of Shadrach, Meshach, and Abednego is the 'highest god', the narrator, behind the backs of the characters, is communicating to the reader the message that this god who delivers is indeed the only god.

The royal decree shows also that Nebuchadnezzar still considers himself to be in control of life and death. In godlike fashion, he still decides the destinies of his subjects. The coda of the story also plays upon this point. Verse 30 tells us that 'the king made Shadrach, Meshach, and Abednego prosperous'. The sound of the verb *haṣlaḥ*, 'he made prosper', echoes the infinitive in the preceding verse, *lehaṣālāh*, 'to deliver'. The auditory similarity between the two words connects the two ideas. The king now acts as the god acts. Those whom this god delivers, the king makes prosper.

For Shadrach, Meshach, and Abednego, the word play suggests another ironic turn. The three men are indebted to their god for deliverance. Are they now indebted to their king for prosperity? Has the king not obligated them after all?

Excursus II: The Story as Metaphor

Of this story, James Wharton writes

> ... the story of the three men in the fire strikes us as a piece of
> surrealistic art. There is a kind of photographic realism about the
> way we are asked to imagine all the details of this story. Yet the net
> effect of the story is to call in question all our common sense
> perspectives about what is actually going on in the world. No
> tyrant is ever so explicitly anti-godly. No choice we make is ever
> quite so clear. No saint is ever so unambiguously saintly. No
> ending is ever quite as spectacularly happy as this one.[47]

The reality of the story world in Daniel 3 stands in tension with
what we perceive to be reality in the world around us. While we may
'willingly suspend disbelief' in order to enter into the story world, we
are not required to sustain disbelief when assessing what that world
means for our world. For most readers, Daniel 3 does not imbue
them with the confidence that, if they themselves were to walk into a
fire for similar reasons, they would be miraculously protected from
harm. Nor does Daniel 3 make most readers oblivious to the fact
that, in the real world, people burn everyday in the resistance against
tyranny. Most readers know that this is not the only story that can be
told of religious persecution (cf. 2 Maccabees 7).

I suggest that this story that is too good to be true, this story that
speaks of unequaled tyranny, unsullied faith, unflinching heroism,
and unquestionable divine presence is but a small paradigm of a
larger story of ambiguous politics, compromised faith, confused
response, and an elusive god. This story is a metaphor for exilic
experience. Lacocque writes: '. . . the three companions are Israel in
Exile saved through divine intervention'.[48] If this is a story of Israel
in Exile, then it must be recognized that this is an exceptionally clean
story of clear choices made by model characters. As Wharton points
out, our reality is not like that and, I suspect, neither was (is) the
reality of exile. The story, however, selects and organizes, only telling
part, never telling all, in an attempt to make sense of uncertainty, to
see with clarity what is blurred in real life. In short, the story as
metaphor offers an answer, offers a meaning, offers a lens with and
through which we can read a difficult text—the text of exilic
experience.

The key image of this metaphorical reading is that of the fiery
furnace. Both 'fire' and 'furnace' are metaphors known from Israel's

larger story, metaphors of captivity. In Deut. 4.20, the exodus from Egypt is described in terms of Yahweh's bringing Israel out of an 'iron furnace'.[49] In a speech of comfort to those in exile, Deutero-Isaiah uses the metaphor of fire to describe the exilic experience: 'When you pass through the waters I will be with you; and through the rivers, they shall not overwhelm you; when you walk through fire you shall not be burned, and the flame shall not consume you' (Isa. 43.2). By analogy, the fiery furnace in Daniel 3 is symbolic of exilic experience and, as Lacocque has observed, the three friends are Israel[50] faced with decision: They can conform and survive or retain their identity only to be persecuted and to die. As a metaphor, the story communicates that, despite all attempts to make them conform, the Jews endure exile unchanged, identity secure, integrity intact, loyal to their god.[51]

If Shadrach, Meshach, and Abednego had succumbed to Babylonian uniformity along with all the other 'peoples, nations, and languages', they would have lost their identities as Jews and there would have been no story to tell.[52] Likewise, if the Jews of the Babylonian exile (or any kind of exile for that matter) had conformed completely to the culture in which they found themselves, there would be no Jewish nation; there would be no story to tell. Consequently, Daniel 3 is, on the one hand, a celebration of a nation's endurance.

On another level, Daniel 3 is also an attempt to make sense of exilic experience, to reassess what it means to be Israel and to be in relationship with God. Daniel 3 portrays the exile as a test of both the people and God. For both Israel and God, exile tests fidelity. Can the people be faithful even when they cannot be assured of God's fidelity? Has God not abandoned them, 'given them into the hand' of Nebuchadnezzar of Babylon? Will God, in the end, keep faith with Israel? From the people's perspective, exile is also a test of God's sovereignty. If Israel claims their God to be sovereign, will their God indeed prove to be so? Will God be able to deliver? And will God be able to deliver in such a way that Israel's fidelity will be justified in the eyes of other 'peoples, nations, and languages'?

It is this third party that complicates the relationship between God and Israel. According to the metaphor of the story, exile is an opportunity for other 'peoples, nations, and languages' to acquire a knowledge of God. The captivity and testing of Israel is not for Israel alone. Like the narrator of Daniel 3, God is concerned, perhaps primarily, with the perspectives of those outside Israel, particularly those outside Israel with political power. Israel's God has become ambitious. It is no longer enough to be recognized by Israel alone. In order to be sovereign of the world, God must catch bigger fish than Israel. Israel becomes the sacrifice, the burnt offering without blemish, that is to secure the victory, the recognition of God's sovereignty by 'all peoples, nations and languages'.[53]

Finally, the metaphor of Daniel 3 suggests that, in exile, Israel discovers yet another side of their God. Their God's fidelity does not lie in preventing exile, just as in the story, God does not extinguish the fire or allow them to escape. Instead, their God joins them in the flames. As Lacocque comments, 'In Babylon as in Egypt, "he is with them *in* distress" (Ps. 91.15). . . '[54] God is 'with them in distress' not simply for their own sake, but for the sake of those who cause and witness their distress and, ultimately, for the sake of God's name. God is with Israel in distress, 'because he [Israel] knows my name (Psalm 91.14)'. Israel and God's name are inextricably bound together. (After all, how can the god of Shadrach, Meshach, and Abednego be recognized if there is no Shadrach, Meshach and Abednego? How can the god of Israel be known if there is no Israel?) Israel's endurance depends upon divine presence, but might it not also be the case that divine presence is also dependent upon Israel's endurance?

Chapter 4

DANIEL 3.31–4.34[1]

The Story

(31) Nebuchadnezzar the king to all peoples, nations and languages who dwell in all the earth: 'May your peace be multiplied! (32) It seems appropriate for me to disclose the signs and wonders that the most high God has worked with me.

(33) 'How great are his signs,
   How mighty are his wonders!
His kingdom is an everlasting kingdom
   And his rule is with generation after generation!

(1) 'I, Nebuchadnezzar, was content in my house and was flourishing in my palace. (2) I had a dream and it made me afraid. While I was upon my couch, the imaginings[2] and the visions of my head troubled me. (3) I issued a decree that all the sages of Babylon should be brought before me that they might make known to me the dream's interpretation. (4) The magicians, the enchanters, the Chaldeans, and the soothsayers[3] they came in and I told the dream to them, but they could not make known to me its interpretation.

(5) 'At last, Daniel came in before me—he whose name is Belteshazzar after the name of my god and in whom is the spirit of the holy gods—and I told him the dream: (6) "O Belteshazzar, chief of the magicians, because I know that the spirit of the holy gods is in you and that no mystery baffles you,[4] tell the interpretation of the visions of the dream that I have seen. (7) Here are the visions of my head as I lay upon my couch:

'"I was looking, and lo, a tree was in the midst of the land and its height was immense. (8) The tree grew great and mighty, its height reached to the heavens, and it was visible to the end of the entire earth. (9) Its foliage was fair, its fruit abundant, and in it was food for all. It shaded the beasts of the field beneath, in its branches dwelled the birds of the heaven, and from it all flesh was fed.

(10) '"While upon my couch, I was seeing in the visions of my head, and lo, a watcher[5] and a holy one descended from heaven. (11) He called loudly and thus he said: 'Hew down the tree and cut off its branches. Strip off its foliage and scatter its fruit. Let the beasts flee from beneath it and the birds from its branches. (12) Leave only the stump of its roots in the ground in a band of iron and bronze midst the grass of the field. Let him be wet with the dew of

heaven and let his lot be with the beasts mid the grass of the earth. (13) Let his heart change from that of a human and let the heart of a beast be given to him. Let seven times pass over him. (14) The sentence is by the decree of the watchers and the order is by the word of the holy ones in order that the living will know that the Most High rules in the human kingdom. To whomever he pleases he gives it and the lowest of persons he sets over it.'

(15) '"This dream, I, King Nebuchadnezzar, saw. As for you, Belteshazzar, tell the interpretation because all the sages of my kingdom are unable to make known to me the interpretation, but you are capable because the spirit of the holy gods is in you."'

(16) Then Daniel, whose name was Belteshazzar, was, for a moment, taken aback and his thoughts troubled him. The king responded, saying, 'Belteshazzar, do not let the dream or the interpretation trouble you'. Belteshazzar answered, 'My lord, may the dream be for those who hate you and its interpretation for your enemies!

(17) 'The tree you saw that grew great and mighty, its height reached the heavens, and it was visible to all the earth; (18) its foliage was fair and fruit abundant and in it was food for all; under it the beasts of the field found shade, and in its branches dwelled the birds of the heavens—(19) it is you, O King, who have grown great and mighty. Your greatness has grown and reaches to the heavens and your rule to the end of the earth. (20) Whereas the king saw a watcher and a holy one descend from the heaven and say, "Hew down the tree and destroy it. Leave only the stump of its roots in the ground in a band of iron and bronze amid the grass of the field. Let it be wet with the dew of heaven and let its lot be with the beasts of the field until seven times pass over him"—(21) This is the interpretation, O King: It is the decree of the Most High that has come upon my lord, the king. (22) You will be driven from the human community and your dwelling place will be with the beasts of the field. You will be fed grass as oxen are and you will be wet with the dew of heaven. Seven times will pass over you until you know that the Most High rules in the human kingdom and he gives it to whomever he pleases. (23) As they commanded to leave the stump of the roots of the tree, your kingdom is to remain for you from the time you know that heaven rules.

(24) 'Therefore, O King, may my counsel be acceptable to you: Break off your sins by doing righteousness and your evil by showing favor to the impressed. Perhaps there will a lengthening of your contentment.'

(25) All this came upon Nebuchadnezzar the king.

(26) Toward the end of twelve months, while he was walking atop the royal palace of Babylon, (27) the king said, 'Is this not great Babylon, which I have built as a royal residence by my mighty power and for the honor of my majesty?' (28) The words were still in the king's mouth when a voice fell from heaven, 'To you, King Nebuchadnezzar, it is spoken: The kingdom has

passed from you. (29) You will be driven from the human community and
your dwelling will be with the beasts of the field. You will be fed grass as
oxen are. Seven times will pass over you until you know that the Most High
rules in the human kingdom and gives it to whomever he pleases.'

(30) In that moment, the word was fulfilled upon Nebuchadnezzar. He was
driven from the human community and he ate grass as oxen do and his body
was wet with the dew of heaven until his hair grew long like eagles' feathers
and his nails like birds' claws.[6]

(31) 'At the end of the days, I, Nebuchadnezzar, lifted my eyes to heaven
and my reason returned to me and I blessed the Most High and I praised and
I glorified the one living forever:[7]

> 'His rule is an everlasting rule
> > and his kingdom is with generation after generation.
> (32) All the inhabitants of the earth are accounted as nothing
> > and he does as he pleases in the host of heaven
> > and among the inhabitants of the earth.
> There is no one who hinders his hand
> > or says to him, "What are you doing?"

(33) 'In that moment, my reason returned to me and, for the glory of my
kingdom, my majesty and splendor returned to me. My counselors and my
lords sought me and I was established over my kingdom and exceeding
greatness was added to me.

(34) 'Now, I, Nebuchadnezzar, praise and extol and glorify the king of
heaven for all his works are right and his ways are just and those walking in
pride, he is able to make low.'

The Reading

The fourth story of the book of Daniel orients us by first disorienting
us. It begins in the fashion of an epistle.[8] Cast as an official
proclamation, the piece has an air of reality, an atmosphere of
authority. Some readers may even suspend their expectation that
what is to follow will be fiction. On the surface, the epistolary
salutation indicates direct discourse: 'Nebuchadnezzar the king to all
peoples, nations, and languages who dwell in all the earth "May your
peace be multiplied!"' In this first sentence the author of the
discourse identifies himsef to be Nebuchadnezzar the king. Because
he does not refer to himself as 'king of Babylon', he implies that his
kingship extends over all to whom he speaks: 'all peoples, nations,
and languages who dwell in all the earth'. The author of this
proclamation views himself to be the ruler of the world. A ruler of the

world commands attention. His communication is authoritative.

The proclamation is intended for all the people of the world. The identification of the addressee throws us immediately into the ironic undertones of the piece. The addressee, 'all peoples, nations, and languages', is of course the narratee,[9] the audience that is part of the story world: the people under the rule of Nebuchadnezzar. In the story world, the king addresses his subjects, charging them to hear what he has to say.

However, 'all peoples, nations, and languages who dwell in all the earth' has another referent. The identification is broad enough to include the implied reader, the audience outside the story world to whom the story itself is directed as a communication.[10] Although never a vassal of Nebuchadnezzar, the implied reader can also hear a direct address, a communication from a speaker who seems to 'break the frame'.[11] Hence, the reader is called upon to adopt a more subjective relationship to the text than was necessary in the reading of chs. 1–3. For the reader, the speaker's voice is not the voice of our sovereign, but a voice from the grave, the voice of a king who once ruled but who rules no longer. Consequently, we hear two communications, one that is internal to the story world, another that crosses the boundaries of the story world. The first is what the ruler of the world commands his subjects to hear; the second is the speech of a king long deceased to readers familiar with his fate.

When, in 3.31 (Eng. 4.1), Nebuchadnezzar issues his proclamation to all the world extolling the signs and wonders of the most high God, we first think this praise of the most high God is the result of the signs and wonders that Nebuchadnezzar has witnessed in Daniel 3. His address, 'all peoples, nations, and languages' echoes his invocations regarding the gold image (3.4) and the god of Shadrach, Meshach, and Abednego (3.29). It occurs to us that, after reflecting upon the miraculous deliverance of the three Jews, Nebuchadnezzar has been persuaded of the sovereignty of this delivering god.[12]

Nebuchadnezzar ends his doxology only to assume the role of narrator. As he begins his narrative (4.1; Eng. 4.4), we realize that something other than the incident involving Shadrach, Meshach, and Abednego has brought about his conversion. The story we are about to hear will explain the king's song of praise to the Most High. Hence, we enter the story at the end. The pagan king is now a convert to the worship of the Most High. The distortion of the natural chronological order of the story's events effectively catches and retains the reader's curiosity. We see the outcome of the story, but we do not know what has happened in the meantime to bring it about.[13] We read on to piece together the puzzle of the past.

Nebuchadnezzar presents himself as a mediator, a spokesperson for the Most High. His purpose in speaking is to 'disclose the signs and wonders of the Most High'. We recall the frequent use of 'disclose' (*hawāh*) in Daniel 2, a story in which the subject to be disclosed is the dream and its interpretation, i.e. the message and intention of the Most High. In that story, only Daniel can disclose this knowledge of God. In Daniel 4 Nebuchadnezzar subtly claims the same power by using the same word in essentially the same context. Furthermore, the word invites the reader to see Nebuchadnezzar and Daniel, two characters who started out as opponents, now being focused closer together.

When occurring together, the words 'signs and wonders' in the Hebrew Bible refer specifically to acts or events that embody a communication from God.[14] Of the seventeen times that these words occur together in the Hebrew text, thirteen refer to the signs and wonders that Yahweh performed when bringing Israel out of slavery in Egypt.[15] Three of the others occur in the context of prophetic mediation.[16] By using this phrase, Nebuchadnezzar elevates his role of mediator, one who imparts divine knowledge to his people, and implies that his authority is derived (apart from his kingship) from the experience he is about to relate, an experience equal in importance to Israel's exodus from Egypt. Nebuchadnezzar's portrayal of himself as an authority on the Most High, as a special spokesperson for this god whom he did not even recognize in ch. 1, is more than a little ironic. In fact, the reader is still not sure whether Nebuchadnezzar associates the 'Most High' with the god of the Jerusalem temple, the god of Daniel, or the god of Shadrach, Meshach, and Abednego. The reader knows, nevertheless, that this is indeed one and the same god. The king, who has destroyed this god's house and has exiled this god's people, speaks now as this god's chosen representative. The reader might respond with resentment toward Nebuchadnezzar's unmitigated gall or the reader might suspect that Nebuchadnezzar is at the mercy of a hidden, implied narrator (a narrator behind the narrator, so to speak),[17] and so see a touch of humor in the absurdity of the situation.

Curiosity lures us into Nebuchadnezzar's story. How has this persecutor of the god of the Jews come to offer such a pious testimonial? After the doxology, Nebuchadnezzar begins to answer our question by taking us back into his past. He recalls an earlier time of contentment and prosperity. A troubling dream brings fear and alarm. This beginning of discontent is important to the conversion aspect of the story. Contented people are not easy converts. Furthermore, trouble's intrusion into self-contentment foreshadows later developments in the story, particularly the turn of events described in 4.26-30 (Eng. 4.29-33). The troubling dream also looks back to ch. 2. Nebuchadnezzar, it seems, is developing a history of nightmares. The reader might very well ask, has this one anything to do with the dream in ch. 2?

The reader immediately surmises that the dream has, at least, had something to do with the narrator's conversion. It is perhaps the key to the change that has taken place. What is this dream?, we wonder. But we must continue to wonder, because, rather than recount the dream to us at the same point in the past in which he dreamed it, Nebuchadnezzar waits.[18]

He summons his sages and we again see phantoms of ch. 2. We are not surprised, then, at the sages' inability to explain the dream nor are we surprised when Daniel comes to the king's assistance. Unlike Daniel 2, however, the request for interpretation is not absurdly difficult nor charged with tension. No one is threatened for failure; no one is accused of treason. When Daniel arrives, the king's expression of confidence in Daniel's ability is so strong, that we do not even doubt that Daniel will interpret the dream. Consequently, even though Daniel's ability is contrasted to the inability of the sages, the competition is not magnified and there is no warrant to classify the entire story as a 'tale of contest'.[19] The contrast element is peripheral because the story is not a story about courtiers. The occasion of the story is a particular experience of the main character, Nebuchadnezzar the king.

Daniel comes before the king as Belteshazzar, which is the name given to him by the Babylonian administration. The name Belteshazzar, the king tells us, is reflective of the name of the king's god. The king first tells us, and then tells Daniel, that he knows that 'the spirit of the holy gods' is in him. Nebuchadnezzar's impression of Daniel, established at the end of ch. 2, appears not to have changed. To him, Daniel is still a curious mixture of human and divine, a sage with an awe-inspiring ability to solve any mystery.

Daniel's presence is the occasion for the telling of the dream. The dream itself is something of a flashback within a flashback. The telling of the dream is a return to the beginning of the story, a second backtracking to the dreaming of the dream. In the story world the telling of the dream functions to bring Daniel up to date so that he can give the king an interpretation of what the dream means. As a communication to the reader, the telling of the dream is a piece of the past's puzzle. We learn the dream when Daniel learns it.

In his dream, Nebuchadnezzar sees a great tree extending over all the earth, giving nourishment and protection to all the animals. Then, a watcher, or a wakeful one, descends from heaven and commands that the tree be felled, leaving only the stump. The watcher gives further instructions that the heart of the tree be changed from that of a human to that of a beast and that this transformation remain until 'seven times' have passed.

The dream does not divulge to whom these instructions are given. We never know who is to carry out the felling, the binding, and the transforming of the tree. We are told, however, that these events are meant as a communication to the 'living'. 'By the decree of the watching ones is the sentence and by the word of the holy ones is the command in order that the living will know that the Most High rules in the human kingdom and to whomever he pleases he gives it and the lowest of persons he sets over it' (v. 14). To whom does 'the living' refer? The term, like 'all peoples, nations, and languages who dwell in all the earth', is broad enough to sustain our awareness of the multidimensional nature of this communication. The living most obviously refers to the dreamer (as he exists in the story world), but the term also includes the other characters in the story, the internal audience or the fictional narratee (i.e. those presumed in the story world) and the external audience or the implied reader (those living outside the story world to whom the story is addressed as a communication).

The great tree under the condemnation of a holy one is strongly reminiscent of the great image being shattered by the divine stone in the king's earlier dream. Might we safely guess, in this instance, that the great tree, like the head of gold, is none other than Nebuchadnezzar? The king himself anticipates this association in the beginning of the story when he says, 'I was content in my house, flourishing in my palace'.[20] The word *ra'anan*, 'flourishing', in the Hebrew Bible is always used (with the exception of Ps. 92.11) descriptively of plants, either literally or metaphorically.[21]

Hebrew prophetic tradition also invites us to associate the tree with the king. The great tree is a popular image in Hebrew prophetic tradition. Although the image of the tree has mythological backgrounds,[22] it is not used in Hebrew prophecy to speak of cosmology, but to describe and usually indict and pass judgment upon political entities.[23] On the one hand, the image of the tree has positive connotations. It is symbolic of messianic rule:

> There shall come forth a shoot from the stump of Jesse,
>> and a branch shall grow out of his roots.
> And the Spirit of the Lord shall rest upon him,
>> the spirit of wisdom and understanding, the spirit of counsel
>>> and might,
>> the spirit of knowledge and the fear of the Lord.
> And his delight shall be in the fear of the Lord...
> ... In that day the root of Jesse shall stand as an ensign to the peoples; him shall the nations seek, and his dwellings shall be glorious (Isa. 11.1-3, 10).

According to Ezekiel (17.22-24), the messianic tree is one that is planted and sustained by Yahweh:

> Thus says the Lord God: 'I myself will take a sprig from the lofty top of the cedar, and will set it out; I will break off from the topmost of its young twigs a tender one, and I myself will plant it upon a high and lofty mountain; on the mountain height of Israel will I plant it, that it may bring forth boughs and bear fruit, and become a noble cedar. Under it will dwell all kinds of beasts and, in the shade of its branches, birds of every sort will nest. All the trees of the field shall know that I the Lord bring low the high tree, and make high the low tree, dry up the green tree, and make the dry tree flourish. I the Lord have spoken, and I will do it.'

In Hosea 14 (vv. 5-7), the great tree is an image of God's salvation and continuing protection:

> I will be as the dew to Israel;
>> he shall blossom as the lily,
>> he shall strike root as the poplar,
> his shoots shall spread out;
>> his beauty shall be like the olive,
>> and his fragrance like Lebanon.
> They shall return and dwell beneath his shadow,
>> they shall flourish as a garden,
> they shall blossom as the vine,

their fragrance shall be like the wine of Lebanon.

On the other hand, the Hebrew prophets also use the image of the tree to pass judgment on the pride of political power. An Isaianic oracle against the sins of both Jerusalem and Assyria describes the punishment of the politically proud:

Behold, the Lord, the Lord of hosts will lop the boughs with
terrifying power;
the great in height will be hewn down and the lofty will be brought
low.
He will cut down the thickets of the forest with an axe,
and Lebanon with its majestic trees will fall (Isa. 10.33-34).

Ezekiel uses the tree image to describe the reign and fall of the Pharaoh of Egypt:

Behold, I will liken you to a cedar in Lebanon,
with fair branches and forest shade,
and of great height, its top among the clouds. . .
. . . All the birds of the air made their nests in its boughs;
under its branches all the beasts of the field brought forth their
young;
and under its shadow dwelt all the great nations. . .
. . . No tree in the garden of God was like it in beauty.
I made it beautiful in the mass of its branches,
and all the trees of Eden envied it that were in the garden of
God.

Therefore thus says the Lord God: Because it towered high and set
its top among the clouds, and its heart was proud of its height, I
will give it into the hand of a mighty one of the nations; he shall
surely deal with it as its wickedness deserves. I have cast it out.
Foreigners, the most terrible of the nations, will cut it down and
leave it. On the mountains and in all the valleys its branches will
fall, and its boughs will be broken in all the watercourses of the
land; and all the peoples of the earth will go from its shadow and
leave it. . . (31.3, 6, 8b-9, 10-12).

Just as the preceding oracles represent God's point of view, so, too, we might assume, does this dream. The dream in Daniel 2 was, after all, a message from God. If the tree is the vehicle through which God sees Nebuchadnezzar, then, the image of the tree itself suggests that the relationship between God and the king is indeed an ambiguous one. On the one hand, God must view Nebuchadnezzar as an agent, a protector and nourisher of all living things. Like the trees in Eden (a correlation suggested by Ezekiel 31), particularly the tree of life, the tree in the dream provides food. On the other hand, God must also view Nebuchadnezzar as an enemy, a mortal who, like the tree, reaches to heaven. Heaven represents God (v. 23; Eng. v. 26). The dream, then, portrays Nebuchadnezzar as one who grasps divinity for himself. Just as, in the Eden story, the tree of knowledge of good and evil represents the human desire to know all, i.e. to be like God, so, too, the tree in the dream is representative of a human being wanting to be like a god.[24] The dream implies that he considers himself above humanity, a tree of life nourishing the whole world. The existence of the entire world depends upon him. He acknowledges no other source of power besides himself. This is the sin for which he is to be punished.

As a message of divine judgment, the dream is remarkably like our synchronic reading of the dream in Daniel 2. In that dream, the image symbolizing human pride, accomplishment, and power is brought down by divine fiat. In this dream, the tree reaching heaven is to be hewn down by the order of the holy ones. The resemblance of this dream to the former one raises a question: If the dream embodies a message from God, why is Nebuchadnezzar being sent another dream so like the first?

I propose that Nebuchadnezzar must be shown the impending divine judgment again, because he did not perceive it the first time. We know that he does not perceive the dream in ch. 2 to be a judgment against him personally, because he neither says nor does anything to indicate repentance. In fact, he is so enraptured with the idea of his being the gold head of a gigantic image that he immediately constructs in ch. 3 a gigantic gold image that symbolizes his power. Why does he interpret the dream in ch. 2 to be a personal confirmation rather than a personal indictment? Because Daniel only explains the temporal dimensions of the dream and portrays the dream only as vision of posthumous events. Because Daniel does not tell the whole truth of the dream in ch. 2, God must repeat the message. If one indulges this reading of the overarching story, then one's interest at this point also revolves around what Daniel will say this time.

Nebuchadnezzar's lack of perception is symbolized in the ironic contrast between the king and God's representative in the dream. The one who descends from heaven is a 'wakeful one' who sees the shortcomings of Nebuchadnezzar, knows what is to become of him, and has the power to bring it about. The wakeful one stands in opposition to a 'sleeping' Nebuchadnezzar who does not recognize his sin, does not know what the dream means, and has no power to keep it from coming about. One might say that the 'watcher' has been keeping track of what has transpired with the king, has seen Daniel's lapse in announcing the judgment of the dream in ch. 2, and now utters the judgment himself.

We are told that, upon hearing the dream, Daniel is taken aback and his thoughts trouble him. With this omniscient insight, we begin to recognize a narrative voice other than that of Nebuchadnezzar. The presence of this external narrator[25] is confirmed in the next sentence when the king is referred to in third person. The shift in narrator is not disturbing to the reader, however. I daresay that many people upon a first reading do not realize that the shift has taken place.[26] The subtlety of the shift lies in the fact that, though the person shifts from first to third, the perceptual point of view remains the same—at least for the time being. We know that we are still seeing the events from Nebuchadnezzar's perspective because of the use of the name Belteshazzar in reference to Daniel. As far as Nebuchadnezzar is concerned, he is addressing the sage named Belteshazzar (not Daniel). Likewise when the sage responds (v. 16), he speaks as Belteshazzar, just as Nebuchadnezzar would have perceived him.[27]

Thus it happens that in v. 16 the external narrator (whose presence we have suspected since Nebuchadnezzar's absurdly pious doxology) joins the internal narrator in the telling of the story. The external and internal narrators balance the external (i.e. the implied reader) and internal narratees, and thus the process of communication is further complicated. Just as we realized earlier that the message of Nebuchadnezzar to the internal narratee is not exactly the same as his message to us, now we become aware that the message of the external narrator to us may not be the same as that of Nebuchadnezzar to us. In other words, the two narrators are not necessarily expressing the same point of view.

The interchange here between Daniel and Nebuchadnezzar is somewhat different from the one that takes place in ch. 2. When the king expresses his overwhelming confidence in Daniel, twice affirming his belief that Daniel is of divine spirit (vv. 6 and 15), Daniel says nothing to clarify the king's understanding. He issues no disclaimers, as he does in ch. 2, that it is not his wisdom but God in heaven who reveals mysteries. Nor does Daniel have to consult the God of heaven for his answers as he does in ch. 2. In this story Daniel knows the 'mind' of God. He knows instantly what God means by the dream. In short, Daniel's behavior in this scene simply ingrains the king's misunderstanding about Daniel's human status in the end of ch. 2: Daniel conveniently allows the boundary between divine and human ability to remain blurred.[28]

His role as mediator between God and Nebuchadnezzar places him in a delicate position. It is clear that, as soon as he hears the king's account of the dream, he knows (as well as we do) that it is a decree of judgment from God. The (implied) narrator tells us that Daniel 'was taken aback for a moment and his thoughts troubled him'. He is hesitant to tell the king what the dream means, possibly because he fears for his own safety as the bearer of ill tidings or possibly because he truly likes the king and is sorry to know what is about to befall him. After some encouragement from the king, he responds with 'My lord, may the dream be for those who hate you and its interpretation for your enemies!' Whether this is a heartfelt exclamation or simply safe protocol preparing the king for bad news, the statement communicates that what he is about to tell the king is not something that he himself would wish upon him. In other words, Daniel disengages himself from God's message by his gentle protest that the king's enemies, not the king himself, deserve the coming reprimand.[29]

Daniel tells the king what we have surmised all along, that the dream is a decree of the Most High (v. 21; Eng. v. 24). As he proceeds with the interpretation, he repeats the dream with subtle but significant variations. He refers to the hewing of the tree, but he omits the watcher's elaboration of the command: 'Cut off its branches. Strip off its foliage and scatter its fruit. Let the beasts flee from beneath it and the birds from its branches'. By omitting this portion, Daniel avoids telling the king of the complete loss of integrity, power, and influence that he is to experience. When Daniel recounts the next portion of the dream, he tells the king that he will, for seven 'times', live in the wild as the beasts do. He does not repeat to the king that his 'heart' will change from that of a human to that of an animal. Thus, he fails to communicate the extent of the humiliation that is in store for the king.

When he reiterates the reason for the divine decree upon the king which is, in the words of the watcher, 'in order that the living will know that the Most High rules in the human kingdom and to whomever he pleases he gives it and the lowest of persons he sets over it', Daniel changes 'the living' to 'you'. This change makes the decree appear to be strictly a personal issue between the Most High and the king. It ignores the fact that the king will not experience this humiliation in a vacuum; there will be spectators who will also learn from his experience. Consequently, the first change Daniel makes in his version of the reason for the decree is to ignore the public nature of the king's humiliation. The second change that Daniel makes is that he leaves out the phrase 'and the lowest of persons he sets over it (i.e. the human kingdom)'. Daniel, perhaps aware that the king could easily mistake the opinion of the Most High for that of Daniel himself, avoids calling Nebuchadnezzar 'the lowest of persons' to his face.

As he concludes his interpretation of the dream, he does not end his explanation as the dream itself ends, with the reason for divine judgment. Instead, he returns to the image of the stump left in the ground, the sole element of hope in the dream. He assures the king that the stump signifies that his power will be returned to him when he learns his lesson. In other words, the dream is not a message of utter destruction. The kingdom will be restored.

Daniel's variations in his interpretation of the dream add up to a substantial softening of the divine decree. In this sense, his interpretation here is like his interpretation in ch. 2: He tells the truth but not the whole truth. The reason for this softening might lie simply in his precarious position as the messenger of doom. However, the reason might also involve a conflict of interests. If Daniel's words in v. 16b. (Eng. v. 19b) hold any sincerity whatsoever, it is clear that he does not wish to see the dream come to pass. After all, what becomes of Daniel if the king who favors him so strongly falls from power? Consequently, he concludes his communication to the king with advice on how to keep the divine judgment from coming about: '... Break off your sins by doing righteousness, and your evil by showing favor to the oppressed. Perhaps there will be a lengthening of your contentment' (v. 24).

We are neither told nor shown Nebuchadnezzar's immediate response to Daniel's interpretation of the dream or to his counsel to repent. Perhaps Nebuchadnezzar, like the reader, is still a little unclear as to what 'doing righteousness' and 'showing favor to the oppressed' has to do with 'knowing that heaven rules'. While Daniel may be making some implicit connection between recognizing God's sovereignty and 'doing what the Lord requires', the connection would seem to be quite lost on this pagan king who knows nothing of what this god requires. After all, neither the dream nor Daniel's interpretation of it has said anything specific about being sinful, unrighteous, evil, or oppressive—the dream seems to be centered around the king's recognizing the sovereignty of the Most High.

Thus, the interchange between Daniel and Nebuchadnezzar abruptly closes with Daniel's counsel. The next notice we hear is the (implied) narrator's foreshadowing summary: 'All of this came upon Nebuchadnezzar the king'. With an explicit temporal ellipsis, the narrator takes us a year beyond the interview concerning the dream. We have no idea what Nebuchadnezzar has done in the course of this year.

Nevertheless, at the end of a year, Nebuchadnezzar walks atop his palace and utters the words that bring about his doom: 'Is this not great Babylon, which I have built as a royal house by my mighty power and for the honor of my majesty?' The words with which he intends to praise himself are heard in heaven as the words which condemn him.[30] In the moment that he claims the kingdom to be symbolic of his own glory, the voice from heaven declares the kingdom to be lost, the glory to be taken away. In this third repetition of the divine sentence, no mention is made of the great tree shading the earth or the stump that is to be left. The word is an unqualified word of judgment.

It is rather ironic that Daniel suggests to the king that the Most High will respond to a change in *behavior* (v. 24, Eng. v. 27), but this episode implies that *words* trigger divine response. The correlation between speech and action is never quite spelled out in this story. The seeming priority of affective speech makes the testimony of Nebuchadnezzar, in this reader's mind, suspect. In the end, has Nebuchadnezzar simply found that the right words will appease the divine?

Nebuchadnezzar's speech atop his palace exposes to us the attitude imaged by the dream. Like the city builders in Genesis 11 (who, incidentally, built in the same geographical location), Nebuchadnezzar has built his city Babylon (= Babel) for his own glory, in other words, to make a name for himself. The allusion to the tower of Babel underscores the condemnatory message of the dream. The height of the tree is reminiscent of the great tower. The tree, like the tower, reaches the heavens. The scattering of the peoples and the multiple languages that result from the building of the tower are reproduced in the dream when the fruit, the beasts, and the birds are scattered after the fall of the tree. The scattered ones in Nebuchadnezzar's world are the subjugated peoples, the peoples of many nations and languages to whom he addresses his correspondence.[31]

The voice from heaven announces that Nebuchadnezzar, too, will be 'scattered'. He is to be driven from society and become like a beast for 'seven times' until he 'knows that the Most High rules in the human kingdom'. The judgment is immediately fulfilled upon Nebuchadnezzar. Taken from the life of 'flourishing' luxury, he is left, exposed to the natural elements, living and eating with and like the beasts.

When, in this fourth repetition of the divine judgment against the king, the (implied) narrator directly communicates to the reader that the judgment does actually befall the king, the narrator elaborates on the king's bestial existence by adding: 'His hair grew long like eagles' feathers and his nails like birds' claws'. Here we are told that the loss of societal contact and of his mental faculties takes its toll physically. Rather than being like the great tree in the dream, Nebuchadnezzar takes on the characteristics of the dream's representations of his subjects—the birds and the beasts. He now acts like an ox and looks like a bird. This final repetition of the decree caps the theme of poetic justice: A man who thinks he is like a god must become a beast to learn that he is only a human being.[32]

At last we know what has brought about Nebuchadnezzar's new-found piety. The power of the Most High has made its mark on him personally. He has not witnessed the divine power in relation to someone else—i.e. in Daniel's ability or in the deliverance of Shadrach, Meshach, and Abednego he has experienced this power himself.[33]

With another temporal ellipsis, one that implicitly spans 'seven times', the narrative resumes, but under the direction of Nebuchadnezzar himself: 'At the end of the days, I, Nebuchadnezzar, lifted my eyes to heaven and my reason returned to me and I blessed the Most High and I praised and I glorified the one living forever...' (v. 31; Eng. v. 34).

Now that we have returned to the first-person narrator, perhaps it would be helpful to backtrack at this point and consider carefully how this story is being told. Because of its first-person narration and its use of such extensive flashback (the second device being obviously related to the first), Daniel 4 is unique to the Hebrew Scriptures.[34] Although first-person narration is utilized in some of the prophetic narrations, in Nehemiah's memoirs, in Qoheleth, and even in the latter part of the book of Daniel, Daniel 4 is the only instance of this occurring in a biblical short story, i.e. a literary unit containing a conflict and its resolution that is suitable to be read as fiction.[35]

Daniel 4 is, as we have noted, a complex mixture of narrative voices. The first-person narration of Nebuchadnezzar frames a substantial portion of third-person narration. It would appear that whatever is told in this middle portion of the story is controlled by Nebuchadnezzar, that is, he allows this material to be part of his proclamation to the world. When one steps back and considers ch. 4 in the context of Daniel 1-6, however, yet another level of narration is evident. The third-person (implied) narrator of 1-6 controls the voice of Nebuchadnezzar. This implied narrator allows Nebuchadnezzar to tell part of his story, but does not allow him to tell all. The question becomes, *Why* is Nebuchadnezzar not allowed to tell all? Before we can answer this question, however, an examination of the story's structure is in order.

William Shea has recently shown that the pattern in which Daniel 4 is told displays careful construction.[36] Shea has uncovered a chiastic structure of form and content[37] in Daniel 4 which can be summarized in the following diagram:[38]

> *Prologue*
> vv. 1-3
> Post-fulfillment proclamation
> Poem I
> > **A** vv. 4-7 Dream reception
> > > **X** vv. 8-9 Dialogue I—King to Daniel
> > > **B** vv. 10-17 Dream recital
> > > > **Y** Dialogue II
> > > > > vv. 18-19a King to Daniel
> > > > > v. 19b Daniel to King
> > > **B'** vv. 20-26 Dream interpretation
> > > **Z** v. 27 Dialogue III—Daniel to King
> > **A'** vv. 28-33 Dream fulfillment
>
> *Epilogue*
> vv. 34-38
> Post-fulfillment restoration
> Poem II

Although Shea points out quite clearly the narrative structure, he says nothing about how this structure helps to guide the reader into uncovering the story's meaning(s). His diagram invites us to consider certain parts of the story in association with one another. He points out the associations but he does not explore the significance of these associations or how these associations relate to other dimensions of the narrative, e.g. characterization, time, and point of view. In short, we are left wondering, what effect, if any, does this structure have upon the reader?

Usually, the focus of a chiasm—in this case represented by Y—, indicates some sort of turning point in the story. A major oversight of Shea's study is its failure to entertain the possible connections between Y as a structural point and what is being communicated at point Y. Obviously, Y does not contain a plot climax (the plot reaches a climax in vv. 26-30, Eng. vv. 29-33), but something else important is happening at this point. It is in the apex of the chiasm that a major shift in narrative voice, or narrative point of view, occurs. It is at this place in the story that the first person narration of Nebuchadnezzar is taken over by a third person narrator. The second half of the flashback (B', Z, A'), then, represents a different point of view than that expressed by the original narrator, i.e. Nebuchadnezzar.

What is the effect of having the implied narrator unveiled at point Y? To begin with, having the implied narrator report Daniel's interpretation of the dream reinforces the exclusivity of Daniel's knowledge and wisdom. The revealed presence of the implied narrator emphasizes that there is no way Nebuchadnezzar would have access to Daniel's knowledge and wisdom except that he be told. Furthermore, by allowing Daniel's speech to stand on its own (rather than being quoted by Nebuchadnezzar), the implied narrator allows Daniel's variation of the dream (B') to stand in relief against Nebuchadnezzar's recitation of the dream (B). If Daniel's version of judgment is, as I have argued, softer than the dream's (see the above discussion of Daniel's variations), then we can be assured that this diluted version is Daniel's doing and not Nebuchadnezzar's.

The control of the implied narrator allows Nebuchadnezzar's point of view to remain limited. Just as Daniel's interpretation (B') presents a slightly different point of view from the dream (B), so Daniel's encouragement to repent (Z) represents a different view of Nebuchadnezzar's situation than Nebuchadnezzar himself has (X).

The Nebuchadnezzar of the pre-humiliation past has, to hear him tell it, no concept of himself as unrighteous, sinful, evil, or oppressive. For Nebuchadnezzar, the troubling dream comes at an arbitrary moment, while he is 'flourishing', content in his home. The untimely dream is a mystery to be solved by someone in whom is the 'spirit of the holy gods'. Daniel, however, views the king's lifestyle to be in need of correction.

The issue of reliability requires that the events that follow Daniel's interpretation also be told by the implied narrator. Nebuchadnezzar's proud speech, his desire to see himself in the most glorious light possible, suggests that he cannot be relied upon to relate the words of condemnation. Nor can he be relied upon to relate his subsequent downfall because a madman is an unreliable narrator.[39] The voice of the implied narrator, then, reinforces the mental incompetence of the beast-like king. The king is an unreliable witness of these events. Moreover, the account is 'protected' from the self-interests of Nebuchadnezzar who, even after regaining his sanity, might not want to portray himself in such a humiliating light.

Finally, I would like to suggest that there is an inherent irony in the control of the implied narrator. Nebuchadnezzar may think himself sovereign of the world, but he is not even sovereign of his own story. This powerful king who has conquered the world needs a little help recounting his experience. Just as the dream (as well as Daniel's explanation) is intended to help him see himself more clearly, so the third person narration functions to help him to get his story straight, to help him to remember what he may not want to remember, and to force him to tell the narratees the events, the details of which he may not want them to know.

When Nebuchadnezzar regains his reason, he is allowed to resume his story. Now that he is mentally competent, he can continue. He tells of the moment in which he lifts his eyes to heaven and blesses the Most High and praises and glorifies the one living forever. At this point his speech breaks into another doxology:

> His rule is an everlasting rule
> > and his kingdom is with generation after generation.
> All the inhabitants of the earth are accounted as nothing
> > and he does as he pleases in the host of heaven
> > and among the inhabitants of the earth.
> There is no one who hinders his hand
> > or says to him 'What are you doing?'

Perhaps he utters this doxology when he regains his sanity (i.e. it is the blessing, praise, and glorification that he vocalizes when he lifts his eyes to heaven). But it is also possible that, prompted by the memory of restoration, he utters this doxology in the present narration. The reader cannot be certain.[40] In either case, his blessing, praise, and glorification of the Most High is preceded by the phrase, 'my reason returned to me', and succeeded by the echo, 'In that moment my reason returned to me'. The double placement of this phrase makes the chronology unclear. Does his reason return *before* he articulates his praise of the Most High or does his reason return *after*, i.e. *as a result of*, his words of praise.

The voice from heaven has implied that it will be his acknowledgment of God's sovereignty that will bring an end to his punishment. Is God simply responding favorably to the king's declaration of divine praise just as God responded unfavorably to the king's declaration of self-praise? If we are to see in this event that, again, *words* evoke divine response, God's preoccupation with human speech is cast in a rather ironic light. Is God satisfied with words acknowledging divine sovereignty even when they come from a madman? If the madman is Nebuchadnezzar, king of 'all peoples, nations and languages', God is satisfied with verbal acknowledgment. Because, in order for the 'the living' (both internal and external narratees) to know that the Most High rules in the human kingdom', 'the living' must hear the human king say so.

Nebuchadnezzar's language from this point on resounds with allusion and irony. We hear the words of Job in this pious speech of Nebuchadnezzar. Job says of God: 'Behold he snatches away; who can hinder him? Who can say to him, "What are you doing?"' (Job 9.12). The language associates Nebuchadnezzar with Job.[41] Job and Nebuchadnezzar, fellow sufferers at the hands of the Most High, one a blameless, upright man, the other an infamous destroyer, one a man of righteous behavior, the other a man of only words, one a man who remains faithful to God in spite of his suffering, the other a man who declares faithfulness to escape his suffering. By comparison, Nebuchadnezzar appears transparent; his piety is without depth.

In the words of Nebuchadnezzar we also hear echoes of Qoheleth.[42] Eccl. 8.1-11 reads:[43]

> Who is like the *sage*?
> And who *knows* the *interpretation* of a thing?

Wisdom makes one's face shine,
and the hardness of one's countenance is *changed*.

Keep the *king's* command and because of your oath of *the gods do not be troubled*. Go from his presence. Do not wait when the word is adverse, for *he does whatever he pleases*. For the word of the king *rules* and *who can say to him, 'What are you doing?'* The one who keeps the command will not know an adverse thing and the heart of the sage will know time and judgment. For every matter has a time and judgment although (or because) human adversity is great. For no one *knows* what is to be because who can tell how it will be? No one *rules* over the *spirit* and there is no *rule* in the day of death; there is no discharge from war, nor will wickedness deliver those who are given to it. All this I saw while applying my heart to all that is done under the sun while one human being *rules* over another bringing adversity.

Then I saw the wicked buried; they used to go in and out of the holy place, and were praised in the city where they had done such things. This also is vanity. Because *sentence* against an evil deed is not executed speedily, the human heart is fully set to do evil. . .

This text shares with Daniel 4 the scenario of counselor before king. It deals with the same motif: the sage's dilemma when the word he is asked to interpret is a message of ill-fortune. The text offers a word of encouragement to the sage, to say what must be said without fearing the consequences. Admittedly, the text is ambiguous at several points, but it appears that the main reason why the sage should do this has to do with a duty to obey the king. One should not fail to obey the king because the king is like god, 'he does whatever he pleases. For the word of the king rules and who can say to him, "What are you doing?"' These are the words Nebuchadnezzar speaks concerning the Most High: 'He does as he pleases in the host of heaven and among the inhabitants of the earth. There is no one who hinders his hand or says to him, "What are you doing?"' The attitude that the king has toward God is the attitude that the subjects have toward their king.

In one sense, Nebuchadnezzar turns the words of Qoheleth around. Qoheleth emphasizes the king's authority: 'The word of the king rules'. In the *content* of his speech, Nebuchadnezzar defers his own authority. The Most High, rather than the king's word, rules. God, rather than the king, is the one who cannot be questioned. The speech's *effect*, however, shows the skeptical Qoheleth to be correct: it is *the word of the king* that renders authority to God. In other words, the word of the king still rules as far as the audience of the story world is concerned. If the king says that the rule of the Most High is 'an everlasting rule and his kingdom is with generation after generation', then that must be so. The word of the king legitimates the rule of the Most High through worldwide proclamation.

Although Ecclesiastes 8 brings up minor issues similar to ones in Daniel 4 (for example, the ideas that 'every matter has a time and judgment' and 'no one knows what is to be'), Qoheleth's major concern in this passage has to do with the situation where 'one human being rules over another bringing adversity' or literally, 'for evil'. Eventually, adverse situations are corrected, i.e. there is a time and a judgment, but 'because sentence against an evil deed is not executed speedily, the human heart is fully set to do evil'. This is certainly true in Daniel 4. The one who rules does not, according to Daniel, do righteousness nor does he favor the oppressed. Moreover, his major offense is his arrogant pride. Because the *sentence* of the holy ones is not executed speedily—a year passes—his heart is fully set to be arrogant.

Nebuchadnezzar's doxology, like the one that prefaces the epistle, is also the language of the Psalms:

> All your works shall give thanks to you, O Lord,
> and all your saints shall bless you.
> They shall speak of the glory of your kingdom,
> and tell of your power,
> to make known to humanity your mighty deeds,
> and the glorious splendor of your kingdom.
> Your kingdom is an everlasting kingdom,
> and your dominion endures throughout all generations.[44]

Nebuchadnezzar has discovered not only the right thing to say to this most high God; he has learned the right way to say it. From the hymnic tradition of Israel, he speaks the form and content most appropriate for communicating with God. Should we construe the ease in which the words trip off his tongue to be evidence of genuine piety? Or should his smooth, culturally correct, language be cause to suspect his sincerity?[45]

Nebuchadnezzar concludes his flashback with an account of his reestablishment upon the throne: 'In that moment my reason returned to me and, for the glory of my kingdom, my majesty and my splendor returned to me. My counselors and my lords sought me and I was established over my kingdom and exceeding greatness was added to me' (v. 33; Eng. v. 36). In speaking of his reestablishment, his pious language disappears, at least temporarily. Here even the *content* of his speech betrays him. No longer does he speak of God's rule, God's kingdom, or the greatness of God's signs and wonders. Instead he speaks of 'the *glory* of *my* kingdom', '*my majesty* and *my* splendor', '*my* exceeding *greatness*'. There is no word about God's part in his restoration. In fact, the words are reminiscent of the very speech that brought about his downfall: 'Is this not *great* Babylon, which *I* have built as a royal house by *my* mighty power and for the *glory* of *my majesty*?' As far as Nebuchadnezzar is concerned— 'exceeding greatness was added to me'—he is greater than ever before.

As we listen to Nebuchadnezzar's words, we realize that we have heard many of them before. In his first doxology (3.33; Eng. 4.3) Nebuchadnezzar speaks of how 'great' and 'mighty' are the signs and wonders of the Most High God. The next few times these words appear (4.8, 17, 19; Eng. 4.11, 20, 22) they describe the great tree that represents Nebuchadnezzar. They then appear in subsequent speeches of the king. First, 'Is this not *great* Babylon which I have built as a royal house by my *mighty* power...?' Finally, when his ordeal is over, he reports his restoration: '...for the glory of my kingdom, my honor and my splendor returned to me...and exceeding *greatness* was added to me'. 'Exceeding greatness' is 'added' to what Daniel describes as a greatness that already 'reaches the heavens' (4.19; Eng. 4.22). The words that are used to describe God are the same words used to describe Nebuchadnezzar in the dream, in Daniel's speech and in the speeches of the king himself.[46] Not only does the king praise himself with the same terms that he uses to praise God, but his self-praise grows even more strident at the end. He cannot completely break away from his sin of hubris.

Other often repeated words that apply to both human and divine sovereign are words of political control, 'rule', 'king', and 'kingdom'. The question, Who rules in the human kingdom?, is indeed the heart of the story. In his opening doxology Nebuchadnezzar says of the most high God, 'His kingdom is an everlasting kingdom and his rule is with generation after generation'. But, as we have seen in the recounting of the story, the king has not always been of this persuasion. Daniel's interpretation of the dream implies that both the king and his subjects have perceived the king to be in command: 'It is you, O King, who have grown great and mighty. Your greatness has grown and reaches to the heavens and your rule to the end of the earth' (4.19; Eng. 4.22). The decree from heaven has been issued in order that everyone may learn otherwise, that 'the Most High rules in the human kingdom and to whomever he pleases he gives it' (4.14, 22, 23, 29; Eng. vv. 17, 25, 26, 31). When Nebuchadnezzar acknowledges this, his kingdom is given back as promised. He declares at the end in a slight rearrangement of his opening doxology: 'His rule is an everlasting rule and his kingdom is with generation after generation'. When Nebuchadnezzar recognizes the kingdom of the Most High, his own kingdom is restored to him with more glory and splendor than before. When he acknowledges the Most High as the 'King of heaven' (4.34; Eng. 4.37), he himself is restored to kingship and 'exceeding greatness is added' to him.

Does Nebuchadnezzar perceive that there is a kinship among kings? Yes, says the language that overlaps human and divine sovereignty. Mary Daly has pointed out the danger of using singular models for God in an elliptical but critical statement: 'If God is male, then the male is God'.[47] The same principle applies in this character's perception. If 'greatness', 'might', 'kingdom', and 'rule' are the kingly attributes of God, then these attributes, when applied to a human being, become godly. If God is king, then the king is God. Whether the association is conscious or unconscious on the part of Nebuchadnezzar, he somehow connects God's glory and power with his own. Thus the acknowledgment of sovereignty has come full circle.

When he jumps back to the present (v. 34, Eng. v. 37) he resumes his pious language, but he chooses his words carefully: 'Now, I, Nebuchadnezzar, praise and extol and glorify the king of heaven for all his works are right and his ways are just. . . ' He does not repeat the words of the watcher: 'the Most High rules in the human kingdom. . . and the lowest of persons he sets over it'. Instead Nebuchadnezzar talks of God's ability to bring down 'those walking in pride' or perhaps 'those walking in majesty'—the meaning of the term is somewhat ambiguous.[48] The point is that Nebuchadnezzar is impressed with God's ability to bring 'down' those who are 'high'. He certainly does not want to be brought down again. Consequently, his pious language might be seen as insurance against this happening. I am not suggesting that he is taking the divine display of power lightly. Quite the contrary, nothing impresses those with power like those with more power. But if pious language is what it takes to keep this powerful god at bay (and to keep the human king himself in a position of sovereignty), then pious language is what this god will get. And the reader asks, Who's ruling whom?

So, what is the reader to make of this pious testimony of the king who destroyed Jerusalem and its temple and exiled its people? He has said the right words in the right way. Does he convince us that he recognizes divine sovereignty? Does he convince the God of heaven, for that matter? Or, in the words of Qoheleth, does the word of the king rule after all? Does Nebuchadnezzar control the 'signs and wonders' of God by commanding the attention of the world? Does he not leave us with a vision that blurs 'the glory of my kingdom' with the 'everlasting kingdom' of the Most High?

But Qoheleth also reminds us: 'there is no rule in the day of death'. Eventually, 'the wicked are buried'. This is an ironic comment indeed on the voice of the dead king in Daniel 4. As we listen to Nebuchadnezzar's voice from the grave, we are reminded that, eventually, all oppressors are brought down, not just temporarily, but ultimately. And so it is in Daniel 4: In the storyteller's world, the fate of Nebuchadnezzar is left unspoken and yet is abruptly disclosed. When Nebuchadnezzar closes his testimonial, there is no coda. The next sentence is the first sentence of the story that follows: 'King Belshazzar made a great feast...' Somewhere between the ending of Daniel 4 and the beginning of Daniel 5, Nebuchadnezzar is no more.[49]

Perhaps the most ironic aspect of this communication lies in the reader's realization that Nebuchadnezzar says, or is made to say, in death what the historical Nebuchadnezzar never would have said in life.[50] He is made to utter praise (however ambiguous) for a god for whom the historical king had no respect. In its confrontation with the historical Nebuchadnezzar, the Israelite community was impotent. But years later a member of this once impotent community played a joke on the infamous king of the exile by creating a new memory of Nebuchadnezzar, a memory of which the historical king would have never approved. I daresay, in the minds of most readers, the new memory overshadows the old. And thus we see what the author of this story must have known, that the human imagination is able to overpower human history.[51]

Chapter 5

DANIEL 5

The Story

(1) King Belshazzar made a great feast for a thousand of his lords and in the presence of the thousand he drank wine. (2) Upon tasting the wine,[1] Belshazzar commanded that the gold and silver vessels that Nebuchadnezzar his father had taken from the temple in Jerusalem be brought and the king and his lords, his wives and his concubines would drink from them. (3) Then the gold vessels which were taken from the temple which is the house of God that is in Jerusalem were brought and the king and his lords, his wives and his concubines drank from them. (4) They drank the wine and they worshipped the gods of gold and silver, bronze, iron, wood and stone.

(5) In that moment, the fingers of a human hand came forth and wrote before the candlestick upon the plaster of the wall of the king's palace and the king saw the hand that wrote. (6) Then the king's color changed, his thoughts troubled him, his loins gave way,[2] and his knees knocked together. (7) The king cried loudly to bring the enchanters, the Chaldeans, and the astrologers. The king said to the sages of Babylon, 'Anyone who can read this writing and can disclose its interpretation will be clothed in purple, the chain of gold will be put upon his neck, and he will rule as third[3] in the kingdom'. (8) Then all the king's sages came in, but they were not able to read the writing or to make the interpretation known to the king. (9) Then King Belshazzar became very troubled, his color changed, and his lords were perplexed.

(10) The queen, on account of the words of the king and his lords, came into the drinking hall. The queen said, 'O King, live forever! Do not let your thoughts trouble you or your color change. (11) There is a man in your kingdom who has in him the spirit of the holy gods, and in the days of your father, illumination, insight, and wisdom like the wisdom of the gods was found in him. And King Nebuchadnezzar your father elevated him to chief of the magicians, enchanters, Chaldeans, and astrologers,[4] (12) because an excellent spirit, knowledge, and an insight to interpret dreams and to disclose riddles and to solve problems[5] were found in him, in Daniel whom the king named Belteshazzar. Let Daniel be called and he will disclose the interpretation'.

(13) Then Daniel was brought before the king. The king said to Daniel 'You are that Daniel, one of the exiles from Judah, whom the king my father

brought from Judah. (14) I have heard of you, that the spirit of the gods is in you, and light, insight, and excellent wisdom have been found in you. (15) The sages and the enchanters were brought before me who were to read this writing and to make known to me its interpretation, but they were not able to disclose the interpretation of the matter. (16) I have heard about you, that you are able to give interpretations and to solve problems. If you are able to read the writing and to make known to me its interpretation, you will be clothed in purple, the chain of gold will be upon your neck, and you will rule as third in the kingdom'.

(17) Then Daniel answered before the king, 'Your gift can remain yours; give your reward to another. Nevertheless, I will read the writing to the king and I will make the interpretation known to him. (18) You, O King: the most high God gave the kingdom and the greatness and the glory and the majesty to Nebuchadnezzar your father. (19) And on account of the greatness that he gave to him, all peoples, nations and languages came to tremble and fear before him. He killed whomever he pleased and he kept alive whomever he pleased; he raised up whomever he pleased and he put down whomever he pleased. (20) When his heart was lifted up and his spirit grew strong to make him presumptuous, he was brought down from the throne of his kingdom and his glory was taken from him. (21) He was driven from the human community and his heart became like that of the beast and his dwelling was with the wild asses and he was fed grass as oxen are and his body was wet from the dew of heaven, until he knew that the most high God rules in the human kingdom and he sets over it whomever he pleases.

(22) You, his son, Belshazzar, have not lowered your heart even though you knew all of this. (23) You have lifted yourself to the lord of heaven, and the vessels from his house have been brought before you, and you and your lords, your consorts and your concubines have drunk wine from them, and you have praised the gods of silver and gold, bronze, iron, wood, and stone who do not see and who do not hear and who do not know. And the God who has your breath in his hand and whose are all your ways, you have not glorified.

(24) Then from his presence the hand has been sent and this writing has been inscribed. (25) This is the writing which is inscribed: Mene, Mene, Tekel, and Parsin. (26) This is the interpretation of the word: Mene—God has numbered the days of[6] your kingdom and he has finished it. (27) Tekel—you have been weighed in the balances and you have been found wanting. (28) Peres—your kingdom has been broken in two and given to Media and Persia'.

(29) Then Belshazzar gave a command, and Daniel was clothed in purple, the gold chain was put upon his neck, and a proclamation was made concerning him that he was to be the third ruler in the kingdom.

(30) That night Belshazzar the Chaldean king was killed.

(31) And Darius the Mede took[7] the kingdom. He was sixty-two years old.

The Reading

In many ways the story world of Daniel 5 is similar to those of Daniel 2 and 4. The casts of characters are almost identical: There is a king, a group of incapable sages, and a successful sage. To a large degree, the plot of Daniel 5 follows the folktale pattern outlined by Niditch and Doran.[8] The king has a problem that must be solved. He offers a reward to the one who can provide the solution.[9] There is a 'contest'[10] among the sages. Only one sage succeeds in solving the problem and that sage is duly rewarded.[11] The sage capable of accomplishing the assigned task is, of course, Daniel.

Besides these structural features, there are also other familiar elements in Daniel 5. In Daniel 5, as in Daniel 2 and 4, the narrator tells us that the king is distressed about his problem. In fact, the same words are used in every case to describe the king's reaction: 'his thoughts troubled him'. In Daniel 5 as well as in Daniel 2, a mediator brings Daniel to the king's attention. In both of these cases, Daniel is introduced seemingly as if he were being presented to the king for the first time. Furthermore, in Daniel 5, as in Daniel 4, the prophetic element of the king's 'problem' is fulfilled, at least for the most part.

Most of these elements are evident even on a surface perusal of the story. Readers who are familiar with the preceding stories in Daniel easily recognize these features and naturally develop certain expectations concerning the story, namely, that Daniel will eventually be called upon to solve the mystery and that he will, indeed, be successful.

In spite of these similarities to preceding stories, Daniel 5 is unique. Not only does Daniel 5 contain distinctive material,[12] but even its familiar material takes on different significance when read in light of the rest of the story's content. Furthermore, Daniel 5 has affinities to stories other than Daniel 2 and 4, stories, as we shall see, that have nothing to do with sages and royal mysteries *per se*. The distinctive features of Daniel 5 resist any attempts to categorize or paraphrase the story conveniently in terms of a 'court tale of contest' or a folk story about a successful sage.

The story begins abruptly: 'King Belshazzar made a great

feast...' The reader must immediately come to attention. We realize
that the narrator is not giving us much time or information with
which to get our bearings in the story.[13] The action begins before we
know who Belshazzar is, when this is happening, why he is giving a
feast, or what has happened to Nebuchadnezzar, the king with whom
we have been dealing up to this point. The abruptness of the
beginning is so pronounced that the alert reader may be reminded of
a story recently read that begins just as impulsively. Daniel 3 opens
with: 'King Nebuchadnezzar made an image of gold...' In neither of
these stories do we have a temporal clause to ease us into the story, as
we do in Daniel 1 and 2, nor do we have an epistolary formula to
orient us to the narrator and narrative, as we do in Daniel 4.

Once we make the association between the opening phrase of
Daniel 5 and that of Daniel 3, we notice that more connects these
two than just the fact that they are both disjointed beginnings. There
is a duplication of grammatical structure as well as of vocabulary:
Daniel 5.1 reads 'Belshazzar *the king made*...' Daniel 3.1 reads
'Nebuchadnezzar *the king made*...' One makes a great feast; the
other makes a great image.

The similarity of structure and content raises the question: Are the
sentences similar in function? Obviously both sentences establish the
context of the events that follow, but do they do more than that? In
our discussion of Daniel 3 we noted that the first sentence reports the
first event, the strategic event that initiates the plot. The first
sentence of Daniel 3 introduces the first element of the conflict that
must be resolved. Can the same functions be seen in the opening
sentence of Daniel 5? Perhaps Belshazzar's feast is not simply the
setting of the story, but is something more significant. Let us, for the
moment, keep this question open.

The similarity between the two opening sentences is further
sustained in that both sentences continue beyond the point quoted
above with a description of excess. Nebuchadnezzar builds an image
'of gold whose height was sixty cubits and its width six cubits'.
Belshazzar makes the feast 'for a thousand of his lords and he drank
wine in front of the thousand'. The parallels do not end here. Once
the image is erected, Nebuchadnezzar demands the assembly of a
whole cast of political officials for the dedication of the image. With
verbatim repetition, even of the list of officials, the narrator reports
that the king's demand is fulfilled. In similar fashion, once Belshazzar
inaugurates the feast, he commands that the vessels from the

Jerusalem temple be brought in order that he and his guests can drink from them. The narrator reports that this is carried out exactly as commanded and, as the narrator does in Daniel 3, even repeats the list of the guests who are present. Furthermore, it is at this point in both stories that the people assembled pay homage to idols.

These parallels between Daniel 5 and 3 are more intricate than the broad plot parallels sketched above between Daniel 5 and Daniel 2 and 4. The parallels between 5 and 3 exist on both the levels of content and narrator's style and technique. Granted, the parallels between Daniel 5 and 3 do exist in terms of the plot, that is to say, the same *kinds* of events are taking place. In addition to the similar events, there is the common atmosphere of festivity and celebration and the common scenario involving a king, his political underlings, and the worship of images. However, what seals the association between the two stories is the way in which the similar content is presented. The opening parallels between Daniel 5 and 3 are underscored by the narrator's word choice, sentence structure, repetition, and organization of the presented material.

All of these parallels occur at the same point in the narrative structure. They are contained within the expositions or beginning movements of the stories. Inasmuch as these parallels invite us to consider Daniel 3 as we read Daniel 5, they do so at the very beginning of our reading of Daniel 5. It is at the beginning of Daniel 5 that we are most plagued by the gaps in our knowledge: Who is Belshazzar and what has he to do with Nebuchadnezzar? What is the nature and purpose of this feast? Why does he send specifically for the Jerusalem temple vessels? Daniel 3 can aid us in filling these gaps if we recognize the presence of its shadow from the beginning of our reading of Daniel 5.

Hence, as we begin our reading, two characters and their actions are paired: Belshazzar and Nebuchadnezzar. Both are kings. Both 'make' grand things. Both invite a multitude of subjects to admire and/or participate in these things. The second sentence of the story gives us information that formally links the two kings: 'When he tasted the wine, Belshazzar commanded that the vessels of gold and silver that Nebuchadnezzar his father had taken from the temple in Jerusalem be brought. . . ' Consequently, we learn that the two kings are not simply being paired; they fall into a chronological pattern: One comes after the other. One knows of the other and imitates. A son models his father.

So, what was his father doing in ch. 3? We deduced from our reading of Daniel 3 that Nebuchadnezzar's golden image represented his attempt to insure political and religious unity in his kingdom. His command to all his officials to pay homage to the image is symbolic of a requirement that they swear complete political allegiance to him.

What then of Belshazzar's feast? Does it not serve the same function? Is it not like the feast given by Adonijah in 1 Kings 1, a feast designed to allure the political allegiance of subjects and to consolidate political power?

However, lest we think too quickly 'like father, like son', we should consider how the two differ. The focus of Nebuchadnezzar's assembly is the image that he made. Whatever the image stands for,[14] the accent falls on the fact that it is Nebuchadnezzar's accomplishment—and appropriately so, for Nebuchadnezzar has achieved political power through accomplishment.[15] Belshazzar, on the other hand, has accomplished nothing significant as far as we know. The focus of his assembly is himself. He centers the attention upon himself by 'drinking wine in front of the thousand'. The narrator's language supports the centrality of the king. Everyone present is described in terms of the king: *his* lords, *his* wives, *his* concubines.

Furthermore, the two kings handle their power in significantly different ways. Nebuchadnezzar commands the allegiance of his officials with the threat of death; Belshazzar cajoles his lords with wine and merriment. Nebuchadnezzar assumes power; Belshazzar still needs affirmation of power. Consequently, Belshazzar is much like Adonijah son of David in 1 Kings 1.[16] Although Belshazzar already has the title of king while Adonijah is attempting to claim such a title, the two characters are alike in that they both are having to deal with the reputations of their fathers. Neither son has done anything to compare with the accomplishments of his father, yet each wants his father's power and position. They have done nothing to command respect and political support so they buy respect and support with food, wine, and entertainment by giving feasts to celebrate themselves.

If Belshazzar has accomplished nothing worthy of note thus far, then perhaps the feast will provide the context by which he can confirm himself before his lords. And indeed, the feast does provide the opportunity for him to do something quite extraordinary: 'When he tasted the wine, Belshazzar commanded that the vessels of gold and silver that Nebuchadnezzar his father had taken from the temple in Jerusalem be brought and they, the king and his lords, his wives and his concubines, would drink wine from them'.

Why does he specify these particular vessels from the temple in Jerusalem? Has he simply always fancied them? Are they somehow grander, more ornate than other vessels, even other temple vessels? Is he at odds with the god to whom these belong and is he overtly defying this god? Is he equating vessels of gold and silver with gods of gold and silver[17] or does he consider himself simply to be using sacred things to serve sacred subjects, i.e. the gods of gold and silver, bronze, iron, wood and stone?

A clue to this question concerning the vessels might be found when one compares Belshazzar's command with the narrator's report of its fulfillment. Belshazzar's command concerns 'the vessels which Nebuchadnezzar his father had taken from the temple in Jerusalem'. The narrator's report describes the vessels as the 'vessels that were taken from the temple which is the house of God that is in Jerusalem'. The variances between these two statements are subtle but significant. The two statements represent two different points of view: the first of Belshazzar, the second of the narrator. In Belshazzar's point of view, the importance of the vessels for his purpose lies in the fact that *Nebuchadnezzar his father* had taken them. But, for the narrator, and likewise for the reader, the vessels are significant because they are from *the house of God* in Jerusalem.[18]

Our interest in the vessels (which, in turn, arouses our sense of foreboding) stems from our investment in 'the god in Jerusalem'. Belshazzar, however, has no such investment. He has no quarrel with the god of Jerusalem. He has no reason to try to prove that the god of Jerusalem is a 'phony'.[19] Nor does the text give us any indication that Belshazzar is trying 'to reassure himself by degrading what frightens him'.[20] Belshazzar is a religious man. He worships all sorts of gods. If he is anxious to gain the favor of the gods of gold, silver, bronze, iron, wood and stone, why should he seek to offend any one god, particularly the god of Jerusalem?[21]

Belshazzar's motive lies in something else. He sends for the vessels which Nebuchadnezzar his father had captured. This allusion takes us back to the introduction of Daniel 1, of Daniel 1-6, of the book of Daniel as a whole. Daniel 1.1-2 reads:

> In the third year of the reign of Jehoiakim king of Judah, Nebuchadnezzar king of Babylon came to Jerusalem and besieged

> it. And Adonai gave Jehoiakim king of Judah into his hand, with
> some of the vessels of the house of God; and he brought them to the
> land of Shinar, to the house of his god, and he placed the vessels in
> the treasury of his god.

In our discussion of this text in Chapter 1, we noted the disparity
between the narrator's point of view and Nebuchadnezzar's point of
view concerning the conquest of Jerusalem. For Nebuchadnezzar,
the capture of the city, its king, and its temple's vessels is the result of
his military expertise and the support of his personal god. The
narrator and the reader know, however, that Adonai has *given* to him
the Judean king and the temple vessels. To Nebuchadnezzar, the
vessels symbolize his success and, implicitly, the success of his god.
He does not realize, as does the reader, that the vessels are a *gift* from
the god to whom they belong.[22] Nevertheless, it is to his credit that
he does realize the sacred nature of the vessels and he respects that
sacredness by placing them in the treasury of his god.

What the above excursus has to do with Belshazzar is this: In the
story world of Daniel 1–6 (which is the nationally self-centered world
of the Hebrew narrator), the capture of Jerusalem and its temple is
portrayed as Nebuchadnezzar's major military conquest, despite the
fact that Nebuchadnezzar does not realize how this success came
about. Granted, this conquest assumes this importance by default—
it is the only one mentioned. Nonetheless, it is, for the narrator,
Nebuchadnezzar's most noteworthy achievement. The temple vessels
are the symbol of this success. Belshazzar, the son who has
accomplished nothing, has to vie with the reputation of his father. He
tries to show himself superior to his father as a means of gaining
credibility in the eyes of his subjects. He tries to outdo his father by
taking his father's accomplishments and values lightly.[23] Hence, he
sends for the vessels, not because they belong to the god of Jerusalem,
but because they represent his father's greatest accomplishment. He
belittles his father's achievement by using the vessels as if they were
ordinary vessels.[24] He discredits his father's values by showing that,
what his father considered to be sacred is not sacred to him. And
finally, he shows himself to be more courageous than his father in
that he is doing something his father would never do—drinking from
a vessel that has been dedicated to a god. And let us not forget,
though the vessels have come from the house of God in Jerusalem,
they have since been dedicated to Nebuchadnezzar's god. By
drinking from these vessels, Belshazzar is saying, like Rehoboam in

1 Kings 12, 'My little finger is thicker than my father's loins'.

The narrator makes a point of telling us that Belshazzar sends for the vessels *biṭēm ḥamrā'*, 'when he tasted the wine' or 'under the influence of the wine'.[25] The phrase is ambiguous. Has he simply tasted the wine or is he, at least to some extent, inebriated? His sending for these particular vessels is too deliberate to be the act of a drunkard or even the impulse of one who has taken just a sip of wine. Belshazzar's act is premeditated.[26] He knows exactly which vessels he wants and he knows exactly what he wants to do with them. The command is given before a thousand of his lords; it is not a request whispered to a butler. His act claims authority over Nebuchadnezzar his father; his act must be witnessed to have its desired effect. This scenario has its parallel. In 2 Samuel 16 Absalom has mounted a rebellion against his father and has taken over Jerusalem. When Absalom seeks counsel concerning what he should do next, he is told: 'Go in to your father's concubines, whom he has left to keep the house; and all Israel will hear that you have made yourself odious to your father, and the hands of all who are with you will be strengthened'. The text says that Absalom complied: 'So they pitched a tent for Absalom upon the roof; and Absalom went in to his father's concubines in the sight of all Israel'. The word of his counselor is all the encouragement Absalom needs to do what he does. For Belshazzar, the wine is his encouragement. The wine steels him to do what he has decided to do; it is his 'shot of courage'. As Absalom profanes his father's concubines, Belshazzar profanes the vessels of his father's conquest, the vessels that have been dedicated to his father's god.

Furthermore, as Absalom and Adonijah claim the authority of kingship with the offering of sacrifices (cf. 2 Sam. 15.7-12 and 1 Kgs 1.9, 19), so, too, Belshazzar invites divine blessing with the offering of praise (and perhaps wine also) to the gods of gold and silver, bronze, iron, wood, and stone. Such a list of deities suggests that Belshazzar is seeking favor from seemingly every quarter.[27] Could this excessive solicitation of divine favor signify political insecurity?

The narrator connects the next event to the preceding one, not causally but chronologically. 'In that moment' the fingers of a human hand appear and write upon the palace wall. The king sees the hand as it writes. The narrator describes, in detail and not without touches of irony and humor, the visual effect this sight has upon the king: 'Then the king's color changed, his thoughts troubled him, the knots of his loins were loosened, and his knees knocked against each other'.

In Daniel 2 and Daniel 4, after dreaming significant dreams King Nebuchadnezzar, too, is afraid. In these stories the narrator describes the king as having a troubled spirit, being unable to sleep, or being troubled by the visions of his head. Never once does Nebuchadnezzar allow his fear to be manifested physically in public view. Belshazzar, on the other hand, loses his composure. He shows all the signs of being overcome by what he has just witnessed.[28] His face pales, his knees knock and, depending upon how one understands the image 'the knots of his loins were loosened', either his legs give way or he loses control of certain bodily functions. The man who would surpass Nebuchadnezzar is 'turned to water'.[29] The king who would be powerful shows himself to be weak.

As is to be expected, the king calls for the Babylonian sages at this point. Even in this stereotypical reaction, however, the narrator's choice of words sustains a contrast between Belshazzar and Nebuchadnezzar. In Daniel 2, Nebuchadnezzar *commands* that the sages *be called* (*wayōmer hamelek liqrō'*). In Daniel 4 Nebuchadnezzar *issues a decree* that the sages *be brought* (*śîm ṭeʿēm lehanʿālāh*). In Daniel 5, however, Belshazzar *cries loudly* for the sages *to be brought* (*qārę' malkā' beḥayîl leheʿālāh*). Although in a state of anxiety in both Daniel 2 and Daniel 4. Nebuchadnezzar acts authoritatively. He commands; he issues decrees. Belshazzar, on the other hand, responds in panic. He cries out loud.[30]

The contrasts continue: When Nebuchadnezzar summons his sages in Daniel 2, he promises them reward for success, but only after he has threatened them with death for failure. He is an uncompromising king who uses his power as he wills. In Daniel 4, the performance of the sages as well as their appearance falls under the command of the king's decree (Dan. 4.3, Eng. 4.6). In Daniel 5, Belshazzar only promises reward, and rather excessive reward at that, to any sage who can explain the writing to him. Considering the task—at least there is visible writing on the wall; no one is required to recount someone else's dream—he acts with decidedly less assurance than does the character of King Nebuchadnezzar.

When the royal sages fail to comply (which comes as no surprise to the reader), the king becomes even more troubled and his color changes further. Upon hearing of the excitement at the banquet, the queen comes into the drinking hall to speak to the king. Beginning with Josephus, most commentators on this text have agreed that the queen here is the queen mother.[31] The story world supports this identification. The narrator has told us that the wives and concubines of Belshazzar are already present. The queen speaks to him with familiarity and a certain degree of authority. Furthermore, the queen's knowledge of Nebuchadnezzar and his reign indicates that she is more likely the wife or mother of Nebuchadnezzar than the wife of Belshazzar.

As Lacocque has observed,[32] the queen plays a role like that of Arioch in Daniel 2. She brings Daniel to the attention of the king. Though her role is primarily that of an agent[33] the narrator uses her to bring several important dimensions to the story. Notice her first words to the king: 'O King, live forever! Do not let your thoughts trouble you or your color change'. Because her language echoes that of the narrator, the reader knows that, at least to some extent, her perception of the king's condition is correct. Her language, however, is double-edged. While on the one hand, her words *speak* a message of comfort, on the other hand, her words *function* to bring attention to the king's discomfort. If any of those present have missed the king's display of fear, she makes sure that they now take note of it.

She sees for herself, upon entering the room, what we have been told to see in the preceding movement of the story. However, her perception of the situation is not entirely complete. As she continues her speech, she tells the king of Daniel and expresses her confidence that he can show the interpretation. She never mentions the strange appearance of the hand or the actual event of the writing. She connects the king's anxiety strictly with the fact that the writing has not been interpreted. Her attitude is such that, once the writing is interpreted, the problem will be solved, the crisis will be over, the matter settled. One might say that, on the surface, the queen's speech reflects the 'folktale type 922' mentality. Her words lead the audience to look to the solving of the mystery as the focal point of the story.[34] She does not speculate on what the mystery has to do with the situation at hand or how the interpretation might affect the lives of the people involved.

Another contribution that the queen's speech makes to the story is her detailed description of Daniel. Her speech allows us to see the character of Daniel from her point of view. Her impression of Daniel borders on hero worship: He has 'the spirit of the holy gods', 'illumination and insight and wisdom like the wisdom of the gods', 'an excellent spirit and knowledge and an insight to interpret dreams and to disclose riddles and to solve problems'. Not only do her direct statements concerning his having 'the spirit of the holy gods' and 'wisdom like the wisdom of the gods' identify Daniel with the divine, but some of her other words as well play off of descriptions of the divine. In the queen's point of view, Daniel has 'light' or 'illumination' which, as we learned in Daniel's prayer of thanksgiving in ch. 2 (2.22) is an attribute of God. Furthermore, the phrase 'to solve problems' literally reads 'to loosen knots'. The repeated phrase connects Daniel's ability to solve problems with the 'loosened knots' of the king. We cannot be sure whether or not the queen is aware of her word play, but we cannot help but wonder, at the suggestion of her words, if she has not only noted the color of the king's face, but also a puddle at his feet! The funny little word play foreshadows Daniel's ironic role in the story. If the hand writing on the wall has 'loosened the knots of the king's loins', what does the queen think Daniel's interpretation will do? Does she suspect that Daniel will only increase the king's fear? She seems somewhat removed from the king's problem, but we have yet to figure out why.

An important aspect of the queen's characterization of Daniel has to do with her connection of him to the reign of Nebuchadnezzar. Daniel's abilities, she tells Belshazzar, were discovered 'in the days of your father'. And 'King Nebuchadnezzar, your father', she continues, recognized his superior ability and elevated him to 'chief of the magicians, enchanters, Chaldeans, and astrologers'. According to the MT, she even repeats at this point the phrase 'your father the king'. Again her language *does* more than it *says*. On the surface, she is communicating Daniel's credibility: She recommends him on the basis of his service to Nebuchadnezzar. However, by using the phrase 'your father the king', the queen also communicates two kinds of hierarchy. Fathers command the respect of sons and kings command the respect of subjects. By referring to Nebuchadnezzar as 'the king', she undermines Belshazzar's own title. Might we hear her words implying that Nebuchadnezzar was a real king while Belshazzar has yet to prove himself? Furthermore, she tells Belshazzar that the king (that is, Nebuchadnezzar) gave Daniel the name Belteshazzar.[34] Not only is she informing Belshazzar that Daniel was highly regarded during the reign of Nebuchadnezzar, but by quoting Nebuchadnezzar's own words concerning 'the spirit of the holy gods' being in Daniel (cf. 4.5, 6, 15; Eng. 4.8, 9, 18), she communicates specifically Nebuchadnezzar's attitude toward Daniel. Indeed, she is the voice, and perhaps not such a welcome voice, of the dead king Nebuchadnezzar.

It appears from her speech, that the queen is introducing a person unknown to Belshazzar. As we noted above, she seems to be functioning, as Arioch does in Daniel 2, to inform the king of a resource of which he is unaware. Some commentators have noticed the incongruity of this situation. How can Belshazzar not know of the sage who ranked so highly in his father's administration? Anderson argues that the incongruity is 'no more than a literary device', albeit 'an effective one'. 'The calling in of the unknown hero, though of course anything but unknown to the reader, and his success, where the readily available professionals have failed, add lustre to the cause being championed by the author'.[35] Lacocque, on the other hand, explains the problem in terms of Belshazzar's character: 'As for the "ignorance" of Daniel's existence professed by Belshazzar, it is part of his psychological "block" and is in parallel with Exod. 1.8: "Now there arose over Egypt a new king who did not (want to) know Joseph". . .'[36]

Both of these comments are helpful but not entirely satisfactory. Anderson is correct in that the introducing of an unknown hero is a common plot motif as can be seen in Daniel 2 as well as in the Joseph story, and in the stories introducing Saul and David. The motif comes to the story as a commonly known literary device. However, this appeal to the story's mechanics does not resolve the incongruity: It still does not make sense that Belshazzar is unfamiliar with his father's chief sage. Lacocque suggests that Belshazzar does not want to be familiar with Daniel. This reading shows promise, but before we can resolve this issue, we must read further.

The queen's last words are: 'Now let Daniel be called and he will disclose the interpretation'. Knowing our narrator's love for repetition, we might expect the narrator to report at this point something like 'And so the king called for Daniel in order that he might disclose the interpretation'. But, oddly enough, Belshazzar does not call for Daniel nor does he say anything in answer to the queen. Daniel is simply 'brought' upon the queen's suggestion. The queen's enthusiasm sweeps the plot along at this point. Belshazzar has, for the moment, lost control. Daniel is brought without the king's bidding.

When Belshazzar speaks to Daniel, he repeats much of what has happened thus far as well as part of what the queen has said. In our

preceding discussions of stories in Daniel, we have noted that
repetitions and their variations often reveal surprising dimensions to
situations and characters. This case is no exception. Belshazzar's
first sentence to Daniel shows us that we have been deceived by the
motif of the unknown hero. The king says: 'You are that Daniel, one
of the exiles from Judah, whom the king my father brought from
Judah'. The queen has not mentioned that Daniel is an exile from
Judah. Belshazzar knows this already. He not only knows of Daniel
and Daniel's background, but he describes Daniel with the stigma of
his own obsession: 'one of the exiles from Judah, whom *the king my
father* brought from Judah'. Moreover, he refuses to use the name
given to Daniel by his father.[37]

Hence, Lacocque is correct in that Belshazzar does know of Daniel
and does indeed resist acknowledging him. At the same time,
however, Lacocque is not attentive to the text. Belshazzar never
professes 'ignorance of Daniel's existence'. Nor does Belshazzar fail
to remember Daniel because of some sort of 'mental block' or
'psychological barrier'.[38] Belshazzar remembers Daniel quite well;
he remembers well enough to know that he is an exile from Judah.

So, what is going on between the sovereign and the sage? I propose
the following reading: Belshazzar has overtly shunned Daniel
because Daniel is a symbol of his father's regime. First of all, Daniel,
being an exile, falls into the same category as do the temple vessels.
They were brought from Judah by Nebuchadnezzar, the king, the
father. Daniel, like the vessels, symbolizes the success of Nebuchadnezzar, a success that Belshazzar would like to belittle. Secondly,
Daniel was respected and admired by Nebuchadnezzar's administration. What Belshazzar has attempted to show with the vessels, he has
also attempted to show with Daniel: What was important to his
father is not important to him.

One might also see an association between Daniel and the queen.
Neither were invited to Belshazzar's banquet. The queen comes
unbidden. Perhaps she has not been invited because she, too, is too
closely identified with the rule of Nebuchadnezzar. The reader
recalls the situation that Bathsheba describes to David in 1 Kings 1.
The ones who threaten Adonijah's power have not been invited to his
banquet.

When Belshazzar speaks to Daniel, he ignores Daniel's former
position even though the queen has just gone to great lengths to
remind him of it.[39] Rather than saying, 'You are that Belteshazzar,

one of the sages, whom my father the king promoted to be chief of the magicians, enchanters, Chaldeans, and astrologers...', he says instead, 'You are that Daniel, one of the exiles of Judah, whom my father the king brought from Judah'. His word choices minimize Daniel's status.

It is very difficult to determine the tone of the remainder of Belshazzar's speech. Since he disregards Daniel's former status in his opening address, one should not imagine that his tone is one of a 'friendly welcome and proposal'.[40] If, as I have argued, Belshazzar has shunned Daniel up to this point because he is too closely associated with his father's regime, then it seems logical that Belshazzar would not be very happy about Daniel's presence. The two are face to face, however, 'before the thousand'. The king keeps his composure. He is torn between wanting to understand the writing and yet not wanting his father's chief sage to be the successful interpreter.

This ambivalence is borne out by the fact that, while Belshazzar uses many of the queen's glowing descriptions of Daniel and even words that Nebuchadnezzar his father used in ch. 4, he never expresses such confidence himself. He speaks of Daniel's having 'the spirit of the gods', and of 'light, insight and wisdom' having been found in him and of Daniel's ability 'to interpret' and 'to solve problems', but he never uses these words as direct statements of confidence in Daniel. In ch. 4 Nebuchadnezzar says to Daniel, '... *I know* that the spirit of the holy gods is in you...' Belshazzar says, '*I have heard of you*, that the spirit of the gods is in you and light and insight and excellent wisdom have been found in you'. In ch. 4, when Nebuchadnezzar has finished relating the dream to Daniel he says, 'And you, Belteshazzar, disclose the interpretation, because all the sages of my kingdom are not able to make known to me the interpretation, but *you are able* for the spirit of the holy gods is in you'. Belshazzar also speaks of the failure of the sages, but notice that he does not contrast so starkly their failure with Daniel's ability:

> Now, the sages and the enchanters were brought before me who were to read this writing... but they were not able to disclose the interpretation.... *I have heard about you, that you are able* to give interpretations and to solve problems. Now, *if you are able* to read the writing and to make known to me its interpretation, you will be clothed in purple and the chain of gold will be upon your neck and you will rule as third in the kingdom'.

There is a pattern to Belshazzar's speech:

A   You are that Daniel, one of the exiles from Judah whom the king my father brought from Judah

> B   *I have heard of you*, that the spirit of the gods is in you and light and insight and excellent wisdom have been found in you.

>> C   The sages... were not able to disclose the interpretation of the matter

> B'   *I have heard of you*, that you are able to give interpretations and to solve problems.

A'   Now, if you are able... you will rule as third in the kingdom

Belshazzar's speech moves from pointing out Daniel's humble status to dangling before him the possibility of a position at the other end of the spectrum. Encased in this frame are two statements concerning Daniel's ability. They are not declarations of confidence, however,[41] but statements of hearsay, statements that challenge Daniel to prove whether or not the descriptions of his ability are indeed correct. In the center of the speech, Belshazzar describes the failure of the other sages. At this pivotal point, the accent falls on *inability*. It is up to Daniel to prove himself different from the other sages. If he fails in this, he loses not only his so-called reputation, but a chance at power and prestige.

One might read Belshazzar's speech as one tinged with skepticism, perhaps even sarcasm, but at the very least, it is a speech of challenge. It has its counterpart in the speech of Nebuchadnezzar to Shadrach, Meshach and Abednego in ch. 3. In ch. 3, accusation brings the three men before the king. In ch. 5, recommendation brings Daniel before the king. In ch. 3 the king questions the truth of the accusation. I propose that in ch. 5 the king is questioning the truth of the recommendation. In ch. 3 the king is forced, on account of his earlier ultimatum, to threaten Shadrach, Meshach, and Abednego with death for their failure to obey. In ch. 5 the king is forced on account of his earlier promise, to offer Daniel a reward for his success. Just as Nebuchadnezzar is surely not anxious to learn that his top officials, whom he himself appointed, have been disobedient to his command, so Belshazzar is not anxious to see his father's chief sage succeed (particularly if the writing is an ill-omen) where his own sages have failed.

On the other hand, Belshazzar is a man divided. He has just seen an apparition that has terrified him, and the fact that the apparition has not yet been explained has increased his anxiety even more. Perhaps, as Lacocque suggests, Belshazzar does suspect that the writing is a negative pronouncement.[42] If this is the case, then we must suppose that Belshazzar reacts as do most people concerning ill tidings: He does not want to know the bad news, but not knowing is worse. He needs to find out what the writing says, but he does not want Daniel to be the one to tell him. He is desperate, he is vulnerable, and he resents having to depend upon Daniel, the man who most represents his father's power and success.

If one reads Belshazzar's speech as a complex mixture of skepticism, challenge, desperation, and resentment rather than a 'friendly welcome'[43] a 'kindly invitation'[44] and an 'expression of confidence',[45] then the brusqueness of Daniel's reply makes more sense.[46] Daniel is not returning indictment for courteous greeting; he is not railing against Belshazzar as an answer to compliments and expressions of confidence. Daniel is meeting the challenge. He hears the skepticism. He hears the disregard for his former status. He sees Belshazzar dangling the bait of reward.

Daniel waves aside the reward with an air of disdain: 'You can keep your gifts; give your rewards to another'. Porteous notices that this refusal is out of character for Daniel. Obviously, he has no aversion to accepting rewards in ch. 2. The reward itself is not the problem. The problem for Daniel is the person offering the reward. Daniel's refusal is designed to offend. His refusal is motivated not by his humility,[47] but by his pride.

When Heaton marvels that Daniel's 'attitude is in striking contrast... with his generous concern for Nebuchadnezzar previously',[48] he hits upon the key to understanding Daniel's response. A closer examination of this contrast is in order. In our discussion of Daniel 4 we noted that Daniel is indeed 'generously concerned' for Nebuchadnezzar. When called upon to interpret the dream that he knows to be negative in content, he responds with tactful hesitancy. He does not want to explain to the king the dream's message and, when pressed by the king to do so, he wishes aloud that the dream and its meaning would not befall the king. His opening sentence is a parallel structure: 'My lord, may the dream be for those who hate you and its interpretation be for your enemies!' When Daniel responds to Belshazzar in ch. 5, he again uses a parallel structure, but this time without tact or protocol: 'Your gifts can remain yours; give your rewards to another'. He offensively refuses the king's reward but hurriedly volunteers to read and interpret the writing, writing that he knows to predict Belshazzar's downfall. He never hesitates, but enters into his task of indictment with unsurpassed zeal.

After he agrees to read and interpret the writing, he begins as he has begun many times before: 'You, O King. . . ' (cf. Dan. 2.29, 31, 37, 38; 4.19). From our experience with this phrase, we expect him to start talking about the king's vision (Dan. 2.29, 31) or about how the king's vision relates to his power (Dan. 2.37, 38; 4.19). Since all of the dreams and visions thus far have been concerned with royal power, we might expect something like we find in Dan. 2.37: 'You, O King, to whom the God of heaven gave the kingdom, the power, the might and the glory. . . ' And indeed, Daniel's address starts this way: 'You, O King, the most high God gave the kingdom and the greatness and the glory and the majesty to—Nebuchadnezzar your father'. With these words, Daniel stings Belshazzar in the most sensitive spot. What the young king has desired most—power, prestige, authority— has not been attributed to him, but to the one whose memory he has tried to defeat—his father.

In all of Daniel's dealings with Nebuchadnezzar, the issue has been the recognition of the divine source of royal power. As he recapitulates the god-given power of Nebuchadnezzar and Nebuchadnezzar's experience of humiliation when he grew presumptuous, Daniel is communicating several things. First, he is reminding Belshazzar and the audience that Nebuchadnezzar's problem was, indeed, acknowledging the most high God as the source of his power. Second, he is taunting Belshazzar with the extent of his father's power: '. . . all the peoples, nations, and languages came to tremble and fear before him. He killed whomever he pleased and he kept alive whomever he pleased; he raised up whomever he pleased and he put down whomever he pleased. . . ' Daniel's language is surprising.[49] He is describing the power of Nebuchadnezzar with language that is normally used only to describe the power of God.[50] With these words, Daniel flaunts the power of the former king to the son who desires to surpass it. Of course, Daniel makes a point of mentioning that the most high God gave this divine-like power to Nebuchadnezzar. But Daniel's mention of this implies a contrast, which is the final point of his recounting the information about Nebuchadnezzar: The most high God has given such power to Nebuchadnezzar; but God has given no such power to Belshazzar. Belshazzar has tried to grasp what will never be his.

Daniel implies that, because the power given to Nebuchadnezzar was so great, the overextension of his pride was inevitable. After describing his power in divine terms, Daniel says '*When* his heart was lifted up. . . ' Instead of saying 'then (*bē'dayin*) his heart was lifted up' or 'on account of his greatness (cf. 5.19) his heart was lifted up', Daniel uses the word 'when' (*kedî*), as if royal presumption were only a matter of time given the kind of power that Nebuchadnezzar had. Thus, in a sense, Daniel excuses Nebuchadnezzar for the fact that, eventually, his spirit was hardened. Just as in ch. 4, Daniel refrains from passing personal judgment on Nebuchadnezzar.

Daniel has continued on about Nebuchadnezzar for four long verses and has yet to come to the problem of the writing on the wall. His role thus far has not been that of a sage but of an indicting prophet.[51] This portrayal of Daniel has been compared to the portrayals of Amos, Jeremiah before Zedekiah, and Nathan before David.[52] There is, however, an important difference between this speech of Daniel and the speeches of the aforementioned prophets. Daniel makes no effort to clarify his speech as the 'word of the Lord'. Daniel speaks on his own cognizance. His praise and memory of Nebuchadnezzar is reflective of the 'generous concern' and admiration that Daniel has expressed to Nebuchadnezzar in both chs. 2 and 4.

As he moves from citing the occurrences of the past to accusing Belshazzar directly, his tone changes. He has no problems of conscience as he has in ch. 4 when he is required to relay the message of judgment to Nebuchadnezzar. He makes no effort to soften the tidings or to disengage himself from the indictment; he is in complete agreement with his message. How curious that Daniel's attitude toward the king corresponds directly to his position and esteem (or, in this case, lack of position and esteem). When he is the king's chief sage, his message is one of discretion, even when it means underreading the judgment of God. When his position is ignored, when he is ostracized from the administration, Daniel's word is a harsh word, delivered without tact, without respect. Daniel's objectivity is questionable.

His indictment reveals that he, too, knows many things that he has not been told. Belshazzar has not told him any of the events that have led up to the writing. He has not mentioned the vessels, the drinking, or the worship of idols. He has not even told Daniel about the hand. Daniel, upon entering the banquet hall, has obviously assessed the situation for himself. Since Belshazzar does not put the writing in context, Daniel does. The writing has to do with Belshazzar's behavior.

Notice that, in his indictment of Belshazzar, Daniel does not single out the desecration of the vessels as the reason for judgment. All of the statements of accusation stand on equal ground:[53]

> You... have not lowered your heart... and you have lifted yourself
> to the lord of heaven... and the vessels from his house have been
> brought... and you and your lords, your wives and your concubines
> have drunk wine from them and you have praised the gods of silver
> and gold, bronze, iron, wood, and stone... and you have not
> glorified the God who holds your breath in his hand and whose are
> all your ways.

Daniel has an investment in the very content of his message as well. Belshazzar has not respected the king to whom Daniel had had such a strong allegiance. Belshazzar has desecrated the vessels that are sacred to Daniel and his people. And finally, Belshazzar has ignored Daniel's God. As does the lord of heaven, Daniel takes offense at Belshazzar's behavior.

Daniel's speech not only tells us something about Daniel's character, but in the indictment of Belshazzar we glimpse also how Daniel views Belshazzar's character. According to Daniel, Belshazzar's character, and consequently his punishable behavior, must be understood in light of the character of his father. The emphatic 'You' loosely parallels and contrasts the indictment portion of the speech with the recounting of Nebuchadnezzar's glory and subsequent pride and humiliation.

You, O King, the most high God gave the kingdom, the greatness, the glory, and majesty to Nebuchadnezzar your father.	You, his son, Belshazzar, have not lowered your heart though you knew all of this.
On account of the greatness that he gave him, all peoples, nations and languages trembled and feared before him.	You have lifted yourself to the lord of heaven and the vessels of his house have been brought before you and you and your lords, your wives and concubines have drunk wine from them

He killed whomever he pleased and he kept alive whomever he pleased. He lifted up whomever he pleased and he put down whomever he pleased.

And when his heart was lifted up and his spirit grew strong to make him presumptuous, he was brought down from the throne of his kingdom and his glory was taken from him. He was driven from the human community and his heart became like that of a beast and his dwelling was with the wild asses. He was fed grass as oxen are and his body was wet from the dew of heaven, until he knew that the most high God rules in the human kingdom and he sets over it whomever he pleases.

and you have praised the gods of silver and gold, bronze, iron, wood and stone who do not see and who do not hear and who do not know. And the God who has your breath in his hand and whose are all your ways, you have not glorified.

Then from before him the hand has been sent and this writing has been inscribed. This is the writing which is inscribed: Mene, mene, tekel, and parsin. This is the interpretation of the word: Mene—God has numbered the days of your kingdom and has finished it. Tekel—you have been weighed on the balances and have been found wanting. Peres—your kingdom has been broken in two and given to Media and Persia.

Several opposing images recur in this roughly paralleled speech: lifting and lowering, life and death, power and impotence, taking and giving. The opposing images reinforce Daniel's message that Belshazzar the son stands in direct contrast to Nebuchadnezzar the father. According to Daniel, Nebuchadnezzar had lifted his heart with understandable reason: God had given him divine-like power, power over life and death itself. In contrast, Belshazzar has lifted himself without reason; he does not truly comprehend life and death, much less have power over them. His lack of knowledge and his subsequent impotence are evidenced. In Daniel's point of view, by his trust in idols. The gods that he considers to be alive 'do not see, do not hear, and do not know'. Conversely, the God who is the source and controller of life, he does not even recognize.

Nebuchadnezzar had to be brought down in order to learn that the power was a gift from a sovereign higher than he.[54] But rather than learning a lesson from this and lowering his heart, Belshazzar has tried to lift himself higher than his father by attempting to take what was *given* to his father as a *gift*. This action is symbolized by the taking and using of the captured vessels. The power was a gift to his father. The vessels were a gift to his father. In his attempt to surpass his father, he has collided with the only sovereign more powerful than his father—the lord of heaven. In his attempt to seize the gifts, he has offended the giver.

The power of Nebuchadnezzar set him apart from his subjects: 'All peoples, nations, and languages trembled before him'. Daniel points out that Belshazzar, on the other hand, is not set apart from his subjects. Not only do he and his subjects all engage in the same behavior, 'You and your lords, your wives and your concubines have drunk wine from them (i.e. the vessels)', but Belshazzar himself has led his subjects into behavior that is offensive to the divine. In his concern to glorify himself, he has had no regard for his people. He leads his people to treat as common what is holy and to treat as holy what is in fact common (gold, silver, bronze, iron, wood, stone). His acts (as pointed out above) reinforce the fact that his leadership is based upon lack of knowledge and impotence.

Daniel sees Belshazzar as an audacious, but weak king. In fact, to Daniel, Belshazzar *is* audacious *because* he is weak. (In other words, some presumption is excusable if one is truly strong, as in the case of Nebuchadnezzar.) Daniel's characterization of Belshazzar is, to some extent, supported by the narrative itself. Belshazzar's problem with his father is itself a sign of the young king's insecurity. His inability to conceal his fear, his failure to be authoritarian when addressing his sages (he does not command, he 'cries aloud'; he promises excessive reward; he does not threaten punishment as Nebuchadnezzar might have done, cf. ch. 2), his allowing the queen mother to take control of the situation all can be construed as evidences of weakness on the part of the king.

Consequently, the meaning of the writing on the wall lies not in any mysterious historical referents,[55] but the meaning of the writing must be understood in the context of the story world. The actual words of the writing, Mene, mene, tekel, and parsin,[56] are ambiguous in that they not only represent weights of coinage,[57] but they also play upon the verbs 'to count or number', 'to weigh', and 'to divide' as can be seen in Daniel's interpretation. Furthermore, the word *perēs* plays upon 'Persian'.[58] The image of coinage and the verbs themselves (in other words, the words on the wall and Daniel's interpretation of them) both suggest that the issue is one of *value*. And, indeed, the problem of value has been the crux of the story. Belshazzar has not valued his father's example. He has not valued the captured vessels. He has not valued his father's chief sage. He has not valued his father's God. Instead, he has valued the services of incapable sages. He has valued gods who do not see, who do not hear, and who do not know.

Furthermore, the portrayal of Belshazzar as a weak king communicates the irony that the one who has inappropriate values is himself of little value. He is of little value to Daniel; he is of little value to God. Thus the images of weights and balances fit comfortably with the images of lifting and lowering: the weak king of little value has tried to lift himself, i.e. make himself valuable, but to no avail. 'You have been weighed in the balances and have been found wanting', says Daniel. Weighed against whom? According to this reading—Nebuchadnezzar. If Nebuchadnezzar is a minah, Belshazzar is only a shekel (a ratio of 60 to 1) and while the Medes and Persians (half-minahs) may not be as valuable as was Nebuchadnezzar, they are a good deal better than Belshazzar.

Value answers the question that centuries of readers have posed to this story: Why, when the notorious Nebuchadnezzer is given a chance to repent, is Belshazzar not also allowed repentance? Surely, after seeing the dislocated hand writing on the wall, he would be an easy convert! The answer that the violation of holy things is unforgivable is not entirely satisfactory.[59] If it were simply the act of desecration itself, like the desecration of Israel's ancient ark of the covenant (cf. 1 Sam. 6.19; 2 Sam. 6.6-7), then all the people participating would be liable. All would be condemned. Instead, Belshazzar alone is condemned.

Belshazzar's sin is not so much a ritual sin as it is a sin of presumption. Lacocque's reading of the text, that Belshazzar intends to challenge God directly when he calls for and uses the vessels, is, nonetheless, unconvincing. Lacocque writes, 'Through his profanatory act, the king has "desired" the writing on the wall. He has challenged God and his challenge has been accepted. It is solely an affair between God and Belshazzar...'[60] The problem with seeing Belshazzar's act as a direct challenge to God is that, in order to challenge someone, one must at least implicitly acknowledge the existence of the person one is challenging. Part of Belshazzar's transgression is that he has not acknowledged, he has not glorified the God who gives and controls life.

Furthermore, though his act is obviously offensive to the lord of heaven, the transgression is not an issue strictly between Belshazzar

and God. Nebuchadnezzar haunts this exchange: He is the standard
that Belshazzar has tried to surpass; he is the standard by whom
Belshazzar is to be judged. Their sins are the same. However,
Nebuchadnezzar was valuable enough to God to have been spared in
spite of his presumption. His redeeming quality was his strength.
Strong kings can be successful agents. Furthermore, the issue is one
of sovereignty. The conversion of Nebuchadnezzar, a great king, a
king who lifts up and puts down whomever he pleases—just as God
does—is a notable stroke for the sovereignty of God. Belshazzar, on
the other hand, is a weak king and, because he is weak, his
presumption is magnified. He is of no use to God. He is 'found
wanting' and though, after seeing the vision, he might be an easy
convert, he is not worthy of divine investment. His kingdom is to be
finished, his account to be settled. The gift of the kingdom is to be
taken away and given to someone else, because after all, 'the most
high God rules in the human kingdom and sets over it whomever he
pleases'.

In discussing this attitude, one must recognize that the narrator is
also, to some extent, appeasing the audience. The ancient Jewish
audience obviously had to wrestle with the success of the historical
Nebuchadnezzar. Why did God allow such a destroyer continued
success? The Jewish people have had no such problem with the
relatively unknown historical Belshazzar.

Not only does Nebuchadnezzar cast his shadow over this 'affair
between God and Belshazzar', but so does Daniel. From the minute
he opens his mouth to speak, Daniel demands our attention and, in
so doing, he controls the story. The question arises, what is the
extent of Daniel's control, both over the story world and over our
reading of the story world? In determining the answer to this
question, we might explore another: What might we expect in the
interests of a unified plot? In Daniel 2, 3, and 4, the divine message or
the theophany is designed to evoke the response of the king. In these
stories, God speaks a word of judgment, God communicates in order
to bring about a change in understanding, in order to redeem, if you
will. In Daniel 5, however, Belshazzar is given no final word; we are
not allowed to see his reaction. Instead, Daniel fills the stage. Daniel
cuts off the possibility of response in two ways: First, if there *is* a way
that Belshazzar can avoid or escape punishment (as there is in Dan.
4.24; Eng. 4.27), Daniel does not tell him of it. Second, Daniel opens
no ears to confession.

Consequently, the role of Daniel and the role of God become blurred just as do the words of Daniel and the words of God. Daniel himself certainly never bothers to distinguish between his words and those of God. What motivates Daniel's indictment of Belshazzar? All of this speech cannot be derived from the four words written on the wall. Like the reader, Daniel is in the business of filling gaps. However, since no one else can read the text, i.e. the words on the wall, who can determine to what extent Daniel's reading represents the divine text and to what extent his own? Daniel's complaint is the same as that of the lord of heaven. Belshazzar has ignored both of them. He has failed to glorify Daniel and he has failed to glorify Daniel's God.[61] Instead, he has trusted in gods incapable of doing what Daniel's God can do, just as he has trusted in sages who are incapable of doing what Daniel can do. Does Daniel's arrogance mirror God's impatience with the weak and stupid king? Or is Daniel's resentment being projected upon God? Daniel and God are so closely aligned, how can one clearly separate between them?

We must rely on Daniel not only to interpret the words on the wall, but also to tell us what the words are. He does not pray for revelation as he does in ch. 2; he already knows what the writing says. He does not feel the need to attribute his ability to God. Everyone knows that he has the spirit of the holy gods in him. He does not even bother to clarify that the spirit is of but one holy god. Daniel may as well be the hand that writes upon the wall; they function the same way, as the curious word play, 'to loosen knots' suggests: The anxiety incurred by the vision of the hand is anxiety verified in Daniel's solving of the problem of the writing. Daniel's word confirms that the word on the wall is a word of death. If Belshazzar's 'knots are loosened' at the appearance of the hand, surely Daniel's words have loosened them further.

How ironic that Daniel grows ever more like his friend Nebuchadnezzar. He wields the words of life and death as easily as Nebuchadnezzar (5.19) wields power over life and death. Moreover, it appears at least from chs. 4 and 5, that Daniel, like Nebuchadnezzar, 'lifts up whom he pleases' and 'puts down whom he pleases'. In both cases, authority is God-given, but both have trouble making the source of their authority clear.

Daniel does not simply read and interpret for us the writing on the wall. He interprets for us the story itself. Just as he puts the writing on the wall in the context of the drinking feast, he puts the character

Belshazzar in the context of his past. He confirms our suspicion that the character of Belshazzar is to be read in light of the character of Nebuchadnezzar. He suggests to us that we should find, as he does, Nebuchadnezzar's sin excusable but not Belshazzar's.[62]

When Daniel's speech is finished, Belshazzar confers upon him the promised reward. As many commentators have noticed, it is rather odd that Daniel accepts the reward now, when previously he had refused it. Perhaps it is indeed that the folktale plot requires that the successful sage must receive his reward.[63] However, one must recognize that this part of the plot is quite expendable, as we have seen in Daniel 4. Furthermore, even what may be included in the narrative in the interests of a unified plot has an effect upon how one reads character. If one wants to read Daniel's initial refusal as an act of humility or an example of 'what the attitude of Jewish sage to a heathen potentate ought to be',[64] then one is forced to suppress this later acceptance. In fact, any discussion of Daniel that interprets his character to be completely flawless,[65] must ignore or qualify this part of the text. Daniel accepts the reward now, when Belshazzar, after hearing the stinging, condemning message of doom, cannot possibly be happy to give it.[66] Perhaps this is the reason why he accepts it; allowing Belshazzar to do what he obviously does not want to do is Daniel's final blow of retaliation. Perhaps he takes the honor and position now as a symbol of victory over Belshazzar. Belshazzar has previously ignored his position as chief sage; Daniel now overcomes the king's attempt to ostracize him. Perhaps he accepts the honor and position now because he, too, values power and prestige.

The story ends almost as abruptly as it beings: 'That night Belshazzar, the Chaldean king, was killed. And Darius the Mede took the kingdom. He was sixty-two years old'. The narrator connects these two events only chronologically; the reader must make the causal connections. We are not told who kills Belshazzar or how he dies, but simply that he is killed. We are not told how Darius takes the kingdom, simply that he does. The information continues the ironic thread of the story. First, the young king, so anxious to prove himself, is defeated by an old king. Second, the word *qabēl*, 'to take' also means 'to receive'; hence we are given two alternative ways to read the coda, a choice which sustains the ambiguity of the king's perception and leaves the reader uncertain as to the exact nature of the turn of events. In Darius's point of view, is the kingdom a conquest or is it a gift? Does Darius take the kingdom or does he receive it from another hand? If from another hand, whose? The hand of the lord of heaven or the hand of the third ruler in the kingdom?

The end of the story is a reflection upon Daniel's prophetic credibility. The Chaldean kingdom is finished. The kingdom is given to the Medes. Where the Persians are we are left to wonder. Daniel's interpretation of the writing is, in essence, something of an overreading. This time he has told more than the truth.

No matter how negatively Daniel interprets the character of Belshazzar to be, the ending of the story is somewhat unsettling. Perhaps this is because the oppositions in the story are not so clear. Divine sovereignty and human sovereignty do not stand opposed to one another as one might expect. Instead, they are in a hierarchical relationship: Divine sovereignty takes priority over human sovereignty. At the same time, however, the hierarchy is twisted in that the two cannot always be distinguished, as we have seen in the description of Nebuchadnezzar's power, in the description of Daniel's ability and as we have heard in the ambiguously motivated words of Daniel himself.

Furthermore, the two entities, the divine and the human, are inconsistent within themselves. One is led to think that, in the realm of humanity, there also exists an opposition between humility and pride, as is imaged so well in the lifting and lowering language of Daniel's speech. God desires both humility and pride. On the one hand, the human sovereign is to be humble in relation to God. On the other hand, God respects, desires the human sovereign to be proud and powerful in relation to other humans. But here, too, the two elements are not strictly opposed to one another; they relate hierarchically. According to Daniel 4 and 5, (religious) humility is a more desirable quality to God than is pride. Divine sovereignty and its counterpart, human humility, may be the priorities of the narrative, but the hierarchy keeps breaking down. What cracks the hierarchy is the fact that (humble) humans (the characters, the narrator, the reader) must confer sovereignty on the divine in order for divine sovereignty to emerge as the point of the text. In other words, the fact that divine sovereignty is dependent upon human acknowledgment undercuts the idea that God authorizes and controls human sovereignty.[67]

Another twisted relationship between the human and the divine in the stories of Daniel 4 and 5 has to do with revelation and interpretation. Divine knowledge and wisdom takes priority over human knowledge and wisdom. However, while Daniel's ability is dependent upon God's revelation, God is dependent upon Daniel's ability to interpret in order that divine revelation can be made known. Moreover, the problem of perspective (or point of view) further muddles the hierarchy. If the other characters do not clearly distinguish between Daniel's wisdom and divine wisdom, then how can they perceive that God's wisdom is indeed sovereign?

Divine revelation and human interpretation present yet another unsettling irony. Daniel (as God's representative) dramatizes the tenuous connections among sovereignty, revelation, and the issue of life and death. The God who speaks judgment in Daniel 4 speaks to redeem. The divine word of judgment brings a new understanding, a new knowledge of God. In the case of Nebuchadnezzar, the new knowledge feeds back into God's sovereignty. The greatness of the spokesperson contributes to the greatness of God. However, the God who speaks judgment in Daniel 5 speaks to kill. A testimony from Belshazzar would add nothing to the sovereignty of God. Consequently, pride and humility fall into a double bind: One must be proud in order for one's humility to be valued by God! And Daniel, in his wisdom, in his godlike knowledge, issues reprieve in one instance and a sentence of death in the other (and, I might add, in the latter case, without a word of humility). It is at the end of Daniel 5 that we realize that there is contradiction in the nature of God and likewise, in the nature of human beings.

We began our discussion of Daniel 5 by noticing the relationship of this story to the story in Daniel 3. The analogies we have found between this story and Daniel 3 have helped us to answer some questions that we have asked of the text. There are other analogies between Daniel 5 and 3 that have not been discussed, broader analogies that perhaps raise more questions than they answer. We pointed out earlier that, in each story, the worship of images plays a strategic role. Shadrach, Meshach and Abednego are condemned because they do not worship the image of gold. The three Judean exiles do not worship the king's god. In Daniel 5 there is an ironic reversal. Belshazzar is condemned because he does worship images and because he does not worship the exiles' god. In Daniel 3 the king asks the three men before him, 'Who is the god who will deliver you from my hands?' In Daniel 5, there are also hands at work, not the hands of the king, but the hands of God: One hand holds breath and life; the other silently writes words of death. In Daniel 3 the king passes a death sentence upon the exiles; in ch. 5, an exile passes a death sentence upon the king. In Daniel 3, the exiles are allowed to defend themselves; in Daniel 5, the king is not. In Daniel 3 the exiles are saved from religious persecution; in Daniel 5, the king is not.

As these broader comparisons and contrasts indicate, there are little needles in this theme of sovereignty. The issue of power touches not only the kings, but the exiles as well. The powerless exiles grow progressively more powerful with each story. The God of the conquered proves with each episode, as in the repeated hardenings of Pharaoh's heart, to be the victor. And the victorious God's representatives grow more and more self-secure, self-secure in their judgment, self-secure in their indictment, self-secure in their interpretation. These are the representatives entrusted with making divine revelation known.[68] Must it take sovereigns to make sovereignty known?

Chapter 6

DANIEL 6 and EPILOGUE

The Story

(1) Darius the Mede took the kingdom. He was sixty-two years old.

(2) It seemed good to Darius that he establish over the kingdom a hundred and twenty provincial officials who would be throughout all the kingdom. (3) He placed over them three prime ministers, of whom Daniel was one, to whom the provincial officials would give report that the king would not suffer injury. (4) Then this Daniel distinguished himself over the prime ministers and the provincial officials because of the excellent spirit in him and the king planned to establish him over all the kingdom. (5) Then the prime ministers and the provincial officials sought an occasion to find Daniel opposed to the kingdom. They were not able to find any occasion or corruption because he was faithful, nor could any neglect or corruption be found concerning him. (6) Then these men said, 'We will not find any occasion against this Daniel unless we find it concerning the law of his god'.

(7) Then these prime ministers and provincial officials made a commotion before the king and thus they said to him, 'O King Darius, live forever! (8) All the prime ministers of the kingdom, the prefects, the provincial officials, the counselors, and the governors have agreed the king is to establish an ordinance and to authorize a prohibition that anyone who petitions any god or human being for thirty days, other than you, O King, will be cast into a den of lions. (9) Now, O King, you must establish the prohibition and sign the document so that it does not change according to the law of the Medes and Persians which does not pass away'.[1] (10) Subsequently, King Darius signed the document and the prohibition.

(11) Daniel, upon learning that the document had been signed, went to his house where he had windows in his upper room facing Jerusalem and, three times a day, he knelt upon his knees, praying and giving thanks before his god just as he had done before this.

(12) Then these men came in a commotion and they found Daniel petitioning and seeking favor before his god. (13) Then they approached and said before the king, concerning the prohibition, 'O King, did you not sign a prohibition that any one who petitions any god or human being for thirty days, except you, O King, will be cast into the den of lions?' The king

answered, 'The word is true according to the law of the Medes and Persians which does not pass away'. (14) Then they answered before the king, 'That Daniel who is one of the exiles from Judah shows no deference to you, O King, or to the prohibition that you have signed. Three times a day he makes his petition'. (15) Then when the king heard the word, it was very displeasing to him and, concerning Daniel, he set his heart to deliver him. Until the setting of the sun he struggled to rescue him.

(16) Then these men made a commotion before the king and they said to the king, 'Know, O King, that it is a law of the Medes and Persians that any prohibition or ordinance that the king has established is not to change'.

(17) The king commanded and Daniel was brought and he was cast into the den of lions. The king said to Daniel, 'May the god whom you serve continually deliver you!' (18) A stone was brought and placed upon the mouth of the den. The king sealed it with his signet and with the signet of his lords that nothing would change concerning Daniel.

(19) Then the king went to his palace and he passed the night fasting. No diversions[2] were brought before him and sleep fled from him.

(20) Then, at the break of dawn, the king arose and went, troubled, to the den of the lions. (21) As he approached the den of Daniel, he cried out in an anguished voice. The king said to Daniel, 'Daniel, servant of the living God, has your god whom you serve continually been able to deliver you from the lions?' (22) Then Daniel spoke with the king, 'O King, live forever! (23) My God sent his angel and he shut the mouths of the lions and they could not harm me because I was found to be innocent before him and also before you, O King. I have done no harmful act'.

(24) Then the king was very glad and he commanded that Daniel be brought up from the den. No harm was found upon him because he was faithful to his god.

(25) The king gave a command and those men who had accused[3] Daniel, their children, and their wives were cast into the den of lions. They had not reached the bottom of the den when the lions overpowered them and broke all their bones to pieces.

(26) Then Darius the king wrote to all peoples, nations and languages who dwell in all the earth: 'May your peace be multiplied! (27) I issue a decree that in all the rule of my kingdom there is to be trembling and fearing before the god of Daniel,

> for he is the living God
> > and established forever.
> His kingdom is one which cannot be harmed
> > and his rule is until the end.
> (28) He delivers and he rescues;
> > he works signs and wonders
> > in heaven and in earth.
> For he delivered Daniel from the hand of the lions'.

Thus Daniel prospered in the kingdom of Darius and in the kingdom of Cyrus the Persian.

The Reading

As the book's final narrative account about a Hebrew sage and his foreign sovereign, ch. 6 attempts to bring the 'story of stories' about Daniel and his friends to a close. Daniel 6 shows its allegiance to the preceding stories by utilizing many of the motifs, themes, narrative structures and devices that we have seen thus far in Daniel 1-5. Its closest affinities are, of course, to Daniel 3 which is also a story of deliverance[4] or a tale of conflict.[5] In both stories there is a conspiracy against Hebrew officials who are subsequently sentenced to execution for disobeying the king's law. The officials are miraculously delivered and the king passes some sort of decree concerning the power of their god.[6]

In some ways, however, ch. 6 does not completely end the story of stories about sages and sovereigns. The very same motifs, themes, narrative structures and devices that bind ch. 6 to what has gone before also open a door to the remainder of the book. While chs. 7–12 are obviously not a primary focus of this study, it does no harm, I think, to peek through the door should it be found ajar.

The exposition of Daniel 6 (vv. 1-6) tells us several things. First, Darius, busy setting up his new regime, decides to decentralize the government. He appoints 120 provincial officials and three prime ministers to whom the officials answer. Daniel is one of those three. Daniel distinguishes himself (which is no surprise to the reader) above the other two ministers and Darius intends to set him over the kingdom. The jealousy of the other officials provides the story's conflict. When they cannot find any fault in Daniel about which they can tattle to the king, the officials scheme to entrap Daniel in his piety.

This exposition echoes with reminiscences of other stories in the book. The transitional information 'Darius the Mede took (or received) the kingdom' ends the story of Belshazzar while beginning the story of Darius. This union insures that neither story easily ignores the other's presence. Young king and old king, rejected sage and distinguished sage, a kingdom's end and a kingdom's beginning all stand linked through the transition. If one sustains the reading of animosity between Belshazzar and Daniel in ch. 5, one might see

Daniel's political progress in ch. 6 as a sign of his final ascendancy over the young king. Daniel, like Nebuchadnezzar before him, has been ostracized from the administration and returns with even greater power and prestige, while the one who had tried to exclude him from power has passed into oblivion.

Darius's appointment of three prime ministers plays upon Belshazzar's begrudging promotion of Daniel to 'third ruler in the kingdom', giving the impression that Darius is simply adopting part of the existent political structure of the newly acquired kingdom. Daniel does not have to be introduced to Darius; he is already part of the power structure. In fact, Darius is so well disposed toward Daniel that one might suspect that Daniel, as third ruler in the kingdom, at the very least, has welcomed with open arms Darius's takeover. The narrator, after all, tells us that Daniel 'distinguished himself. . . because of the excellent spirit in him'. Daniel's 'excellent spirit' heretofore has referred to his ability to interpret mysteries. He has not been called upon, as far as we know, to interpret anything for Darius. In the context of Daniel 6, the excellent spirit appears to refer to political ability. However, the last time we saw Daniel's excellent spirit at work (5.12, 14ff.), he was not only interpreting mysteries but also undermining Belshazzar's rule. Might this particular occasion of the manifestation of Daniel's excellent spirit be what now brings him distinction?

In a sense, the rule of Darius represents a return to the latter days of Nebuchadnezzar as portrayed in Daniel 4. We cannot help noticing that the phrase 'it seemed good' begins both the stories in Daniel 6 and in Daniel 4. In Daniel 4, 'it seems good' to Nebuchadnezzar to render authority to the Most High. In Daniel 6, 'it seems good' to Darius to render authority to other people, in particular, to Daniel. The hint of parallel prompts us to observe a more substantial similarity. Both stories depict the relationship between sage and sovereign to be one of amiability and cooperation, unlike the stories found in Daniel 3 and 5 in which the relationship between sage and sovereign is not without friction and opposition. Both Nebuchadnezzar of ch. 4 and Darius of ch. 6 have the utmost respect for Daniel's ability. Of course, by ch. 6, Daniel's ability has advanced from personal interpretive and counseling skills (ch. 4) to political expertise.

Daniel's ability and the king's admiration of it give rise to obvious jealousy on the part of the other ministers and officials. Although they try to catch Daniel in a subversive act, they are unsuccessful because, as the narrator tells us, Daniel is 'faithful and neither neglect nor fault could be found regarding him'. They know, however, that Daniel has a certain religious allegiance and while this does not normally conflict with his political allegiance, the officials scheme to set these allegiances on a collision course.

The next episode finds the ministers and officials coming before the king to put their plan into action. The odd word (*rgš*) describing the assembly of these men has an indeterminable meaning[7] that ranges from the rather innocent connotation of 'in company',[8] to the idea of 'conspiracy',[9] to the notion of 'rage'.[10] All of these nuances are at play in the context of Daniel 6. The ministers and officials obviously assemble themselves before the king. They are, as we know from vv. 5-6, conspiring against Daniel. Considering that there are 122 of them, it seems unlikely that they could gather together without causing a certain amount of disturbance!

Their reason for coming before the king is clear to the reader; the narrator has already given us indication of what is about to transpire. Their reason, however, is not clear to the king. The pairing of *rgš* (which I am translating 'to make a commotion') with the multipurpose preposition *'al* reflects what is, from the king's point of view, an ambiguous reason for the assembly. The ministers and officials are making a commotion *to* (or before) the king which, obviously, he perceives since they have come to him with their suggestion. The king might also interpret the men to be making a commotion *over* him since their request has to do with his own exaltation. What the king most likely does not consider, however, is the possibility that the men are making a commotion *against* him.

The officials come, addressing the king with the appropriate etiquette ('O King, live forever!'), and inform him that

> 'All the prime ministers of the kingdom, the prefects, the provincial officials, the counselors and the governors have agreed that the king should establish an ordinance and enforce an edict that anyone who makes a petition to any god or human being for thirty days—except to you, O King—will be cast into a den of lions. Now, O King, you must establish the edict and sign the document so that it does not change according to the law of the Medes and Persians which will never pass away.'

Several observations can be made concerning this speech, the first of which is that the men are lying to the king about the persons involved in this agreement. Obviously Daniel has not consented to this idea. We also know from the story's exposition that only the two other prime ministers and the provincial officials have discussed the matter: The prefects, the counselors and the governors have not been consulted. The lie is a tactic of persuasion. The men lead the king to believe that this opinion poll is exhaustive and unanimous.

Second, the content of the speech belies its intent. We know that this suggestion to the king has as its goal the entrapment and destruction of Daniel. Nothing on the surface of the proposal betrays this, however. The speech appears to be a political proposal aimed at getting the king to confirm publicly his personal authority. This interpretation of the proposal, which is obviously one that the men want the king to adopt, is brilliant in the context of the newly established kingdom and in light of Darius's plans for the way in which the kingdom is to be ruled. Darius has decentralized the government, an action which may be more efficient in the long run, but which also diminishes his own power. The officials' proposition suggests that there may be a hidden danger in the king's plan: A powerful appointee might easily sway the people's allegiance away from the king. The proposal looks as though it is designed to rectify any threats to royal power that might be inherent in the king's political strategy. Thus, the vehicle of conspiracy is presented, ironically, as a protection *against* conspiracy!

This overture to the king has a delicately balanced appeal. The officials are taking into consideration Darius's propensity toward the redistribution of power. They are aware that he is not a rigid authoritarian at heart. Consequently, when they propose that he alone be the focus of his subjects' petitions, they suggest it as a temporary condition. After all, the kingdom is new and, to some extent, unstable. The king should firmly establish his hold at the very beginning, the men are implying; then, when the new government is stable, the king can relax his grip. Darius, desiring, as any king would, to make his kingdom sound, is willing to accept this temporary measure despite the fact that it runs counter to his political policy.

Darius appears to be oblivious to the implicit absurdity of the proposal. How can an ordinance in effect only thirty days be an edict that 'cannot change'? How can a human being replace the divine—and for only thirty days at that, as if one could put on and take off divinity as one would a suit of clothes? One could argue[11] that the proposal of ultimate sovereignty appeals to Darius's ego, but I think the issue is not simply one of a man wanting to be a god. The thirty-day limitation offsets the desire for divinity as a possible motivation for consenting to the edict. Besides, the wording of the edict, 'to make a petition' or 'to make a request' (from *be‘ā'*, 'to ask' or 'to seek'), is ambiguous: It may, but does not necessarily, specify the worship of Darius. If the edict appeals to his ego (which it certainly has to, to some extent), the appeal lies more likely in the idea that Darius interprets both the proposal and the crowd before him to be indicative of his subjects' overwhelming support.

The situation abounds with irony. The dramatic irony—the disparity between what the characters know and what we, the readers, know—allows us to recognize the verbal irony—the use of words to express something other than what they seem, on the surface, to mean.[12] Because we know more than Darius does, we are able to recognize what he does not, namely, that the proposal is a ruse. While the edict seems to be protecting the interests of the kingdom, it is in fact subverting those interests. While the officials seem to be placing all power into the hands of the king, by signing the edict, the king is actually falling into the power of the officials. Darius perceives that the men are making a commotion *over* him, but in fact they are making a commotion *against* him. He thinks that he is the focus of their proposal, but in fact the focus of their proposal is Daniel. When he signs the edict without discussion, he understands himself to be doing a sensible thing; we know, however, that he is doing a foolish thing that will surely come back to haunt him.

In the next episode, when Daniel learns of the new edict, he goes with deliberateness to his house to say his daily prayers. The narrator tells us that Daniel customarily prays three times a day in an upper chamber before an open window facing Jerusalem.[13] Because his practice is observable and on a consistent schedule, the other ministers and officials have no difficulty catching him in the act.

The men find Daniel making petition to his god and they waste no time bringing the matter to the king's attention. Like the 'certain Chaldeans' in ch. 3, the men come with an accusation. However, unlike the Chaldeans who state the situation forthright ('You, O king, made a decree. . . '), the officials in ch. 6 begin by addressing a question to the king: 'O king, did you not sign an edict that anyone who makes a petition to any god or human being for thirty days—

except to you, O King—would be cast into a den of lions?' The king replies, 'The word is true according to the law of the Medes and the Persians which will never pass away'.

The form of this interchange is reflective of the way in which these men have carried out their conspiracy. By persuading the king to sign the edict in the first place, the officials have tricked the king into unknowingly participating in the conspiracy against his favorite administrator. It is the king's edict that ensnares Daniel. Likewise, the question that the men direct to the king lures the king into confirming the accusation against Daniel. The king's answer seals Daniel's fate.

Once the king has committed himself with his response, the officials spring the trap: 'That Daniel, who is one of the exiles from Judah, shows no deference to you, O king, or to the edict that you signed. Three times a day he makes his petition'. The men bring the formal accusation[14] against Daniel with words that disparage and malign. He is not Daniel the prime minister, but Daniel the exile. He does not simply disregard the edict; he shows no deference to the king whatsoever. The men have equated the edict with some sort of oath of loyalty. Disobedience makes Daniel a complete traitor to the king. Besides, the fact that he is an exile makes him all the more suspect: Prisoners of war would be more inclined to subversion.

Although the reader recognizes the accusation to be a gross overstatement, the reader also knows that there is some truth to it: Daniel does petition his god three times a day. Perhaps Darius, too, is aware of Daniel's piety and this is why he does not ask the men for clarification when they fail to mention the nature of Daniel's daily petition. This episode raises questions about the preceding episode. If Darius is conscious of Daniel's religiosity (as are the other officials), one wonders how can he believe the men when they tell him (in v. 8) that *all* the prime ministers agree on the edict. If he knows about Daniel, has he temporarily forgotten? Is he so swept along by the crowd that he does not consider the ramifications of this decree? Does he think that Daniel is willing to make an exception for thirty days? Why does he not notice that Daniel is not among the men before him?

If Darius knows, or at least remembers, Daniel's piety when the men make their accusation, then perhaps this explains why Darius, unlike Nebuchadnezzar in ch. 3, does not call the accused before him for a hearing. If Daniel's worship habits are known, there is no reason to allow him to defend himself. This reading does not explain, however, why Darius does not even question the unqualified charge 'he shows no deference to you'. Does this part of the indictment not sink in? Possibly—but perhaps this indictment, too, is credible from Darius's perspective. Consider Daniel's relationship to the last king. Daniel certainly 'showed no deference' to Belshazzar. Could there be, in Darius's mind, the slightest suspicion of Daniel's political allegiance, a little gnawing suspicion that contributes to his 'displeasure' upon hearing the accusation? Darius wrestles with himself concerning Daniel, but he grants Daniel no hearing.[15]

The narrator says that Darius 'set his heart upon Daniel to deliver him and until the setting of the sun, he was struggling to rescue him'. What the king's options are, we are not told at this point. We are not sure of the nature of the king's struggle. There must have been some alternative, however, because in the next scene the officials feel the need to coerce the king to see the sentence through. The men again make a commotion, and the king is surely aware by this time that they are making a commotion, not innocently *to* him and certainly not *over* him, but indeed *against* him. The men drop all protocol; they make no effort to be polite. They speak with an imperative: 'Know, O King, that it is a law of the Medes and Persians that any edict or ordinance that the king establishes is not to change'. Is it indeed the case that the law *cannot* be changed? Why must the men remind him and in such an unpleasant tone? Is it not the case that their imperative carries with it a veiled threat, an implicit ultimatum? What is the law? It is the opposite of anarchy. The law that does not change represents stability. If the king changes the law (and doubtless there are loopholes or the king would have nothing about which to wrestle), the kingdom is weakened. His power is questionable. Are the men not telling Darius that, if he changes the law, they will bring his power into question in a very tangible way? They are many; they are organized (the fact that they are portrayed as a collective character reinforces their unity); and, despite the fact that they are *supposed* to be 'throughout the kingdom', they are all present in the capital city ready to make a political move, if need be.

Darius cannot afford to endanger his kingdom even for the sake of a favorite, particularly if the loyalty of that favorite is in doubt. The king commands that Daniel be brought and be thrown into the lions' den. Though Daniel probably cannot hear him from within the pit, the king, nevertheless, offers a kind of wistful petition of his own:

'May your god, whom you serve continually, deliver you'. The king's statement is a mixture of respect, displeasure, and pathos. His admiration for Daniel's courage to serve his god in spite of the edict is clear. He seems to think that Daniel's courage certainly deserves just reward from his god. But whether or not Darius is truly convinced that Daniel's god will save him is another matter. He fears, I think, that Daniel's god will be of no avail; he laments that Daniel's allegiance has brought him to such an end. Might he not realize, sadly and perhaps a little bitterly, that if Daniel had served his king (rather than his god) continually, his king could have and would have gladly delivered him.

A stone is put over the mouth of the den and, with a gesture of finality, Darius seals the stone with his signet and with the signet of his lords. The use of the royal signets symbolizes that Daniel's fate is sealed for the sake of the kingdom's stability.

If Daniel's night with the lions is, implicitly, wakeful, Darius's night in his palace is, explicitly, sleepless and stressful. Just as in ch. 3 we were not allowed to see inside the furnace, so, too, here we are not allowed inside the pit. We must spend the night with Darius and, for the first time in the story, we know no more than Darius does. Darius spends the night fasting and without diversions. Whether or not his fasting has religious significance is debatable. I think it more likely that he has trouble stomaching food knowing that his friend Daniel *is* himself, this very night, food for the lions.

When the day breaks, the king returns to the den, perhaps on the chance that Daniel has survived the night, perhaps so that he can claim any of Daniel's remains for burial. The king is troubled and he cries out in an anguished voice, 'Daniel, servant of the living God, has your god, whom you serve continually, been able to deliver you?' Darius's utterance is not an expression of confidence in Daniel's survival; it is a cry of distress.[16] As David, in 2 Samuel 19, cries out (*z'q*) to the dead Absalom, the Absalom who was guilty of treason, so Darius cries out (*z'q*) to Daniel, the Daniel who was supposedly executed for the suspicion of treason.

In this context of lament, Darius's use of the term 'living God' is rather unexpected. It seems unlikely that, during the night, the king has experienced a religious conversion. Rather, Darius's words are further commendation of Daniel's religious fidelity. Darius would never have known of this god save for the fact of Daniel's servanthood. If Daniel is willing to die for this god, this god must indeed be worthy, indeed, a 'living God'.

When Daniel speaks from the pit of death—which comes, no doubt, as a surprise to the king[17]—he also uses language of life: 'O King, live forever! My god sent his angel and he shut the mouths of the lions. They could not harm me because I was found to be innocent before him and also before you, O King. I have done no harmful act'. At this point in the story, many analogies between what has been going on inside the pit and what has been going on outside the pit become apparent. As Darius has sealed the *mouth* of the pit, so God has shut the *mouths* of the lions. During the night, Darius has not been able to eat; likewise, neither have the lions. The lions are not allowed to *harm* Daniel because Daniel has done nothing to *harm* the king.[18]

Daniel's dual allegiance to both God and king is expressed in his language. While Darius refers to Daniel's god as the 'living God', Daniel immediately says that his king, too, 'lives forever'. Daniel is anxious to convince the king that he is innocent not only before his god but also before his king. He is innocent, he claims, not because he has not broken the edict—that transgression is undeniable—but because he has done nothing that would harm the king. The fact that he has not harmed the king is, he explains to Darius, the reason why the lions have not harmed him.

When, in the next verse, the narrator reports to the reader Daniel's removal from the pit, the narrator clarifies the situation: No harm is found upon Daniel, not because he was faithful to his king, but 'because he was faithful to his god'.[19]

After Daniel is brought up from the lion pit, the king issues a command and Daniel's accusers are thrown in—they, their children, and their wives. Those who had 'eaten the pieces' of Daniel are themselves torn to pieces and eaten by the lions. This folkloristic 'overkill'[20] is more than poetic justice and has been problematic for many interpreters.[21] Porteous comments: 'The author of our book had not learnt everything that God had to teach about the nature of justice'.[22] The execution of this multitude says not so much about the author, I think, as it says about the king who orders it and perhaps about Daniel who does nothing to stop it or even to qualify it. Darius's motives for this mass execution are ambiguous. Does he give this command to establish justice for Daniel? Or do personal reasons motivate this drastic action? After all, the men have subverted his power; but, more than that, they have made a fool of him. Darius never takes responsibility for his part in the entrapment of Daniel; he never acknowledges that his own gullibility, his own pride, and perhaps his own suspicion of Daniel should share the blame for the preceding course of events. By placing all the blame on the officials and by obliterating them and their families, Darius not only punishes the criminals, but he also rids himself of any reminder of his own stupidity.

As for Daniel—obviously, Daniel is no longer in the business of rescuing the innocent as he was in ch. 2. He allows the blameless to die with the guilty. His religious conscience may move him to make a stand for his god in the face of political power, but it does not move him in the face of political power to protect fellow human beings.[23]

The 'rite of passage' structure that has appeared in chs. 1, 3, and 4 is present in the story as well. Daniel is separated from society, sent down to the pit of death, and then is brought back among the living. Just as in ch. 3, this rite of passage brings about no change in the one who undergoes it. In ch. 3, the king is the one who is transformed by the experience; so, too, in this story the king is, to some extent, changed by the experience. Of course, one might see in the parallel experiences of Darius and Daniel that the king, too, endures a rite of passage. He separates himself from society, spends a sleepless night fasting, and regains his happiness when he finds Daniel safe.

The primary change that takes place, however, is a change in culture or in societal structure. After witnessing the survival of Daniel, Darius passes new legislation ordering that 'in all the rule of my kingdom, there is to be trembling and fearing before the god of Daniel'.[24] This decree ironically cancels out the king's original edict that there be no petitions made to anyone other than the king for thirty days. The law that is not to change changes with the stroke of a pen. Thus, we see that the king's struggle in v. 15 had not so much to do with whether or not the king *could* save Daniel, but whether or not he should.[25]

While Darius's second decree reconstitutes society, its relationship to the first decree undermines the reconstitution of society. To begin with, the second, like the first, legislates religious allegiance. Daniel's transgression shows the first to be ineffective. The second is just as likely to be ineffective. There will always be a Daniel, a Shadrach, a Meshach, an Abednego who will show fidelities other than the ones that are legislated.

In the second place, both decrees also legislate political allegiance:

the first explicitly, the second implicitly. The first edict makes the king the focus of allegiance; the second makes the god of Daniel the focus of allegiance. This god is not called Yahweh Elohim, the Most High, or the God, Lord, or King of heaven. This god is represented by and defined by Daniel. The power of this god is manifested in Daniel's very existence ('for he delivered Daniel from the power of the lions'). To worship Daniel's god is to align oneself politically with Daniel. The king's original intent to place Daniel over the kingdom is implicitly fulfilled in the edict that all worship Daniel's god. Consequently, the society at the end of the story is not so very different from the society at the beginning.

The ease with which Darius replaces one law with another produces further irony. The passing of law is the attempt to establish permanence, but the fact that one can make a law points to impermanence. What is to keep Darius from replacing this latter law with yet another law insisting upon the worship of yet another god? Even supposing Darius does not change the law, what is to keep some other king from changing it?[26]

One might interpret this striving for permanence, in spite of all its confessional trappings, as bordering on blasphemy.[27] When the worship of a god is established by the law, then the law out-powers the deity. The law inspires the fear that the deity itself cannot. God is reduced to an ordinance and thus the language of Darius's decree plays: The word he uses to declare that the god of Daniel is *established* (*qayyām*) forever is reminiscent of the language used earlier (v. 8 and cf. also v. 16) to speak of establishing an ordinance (*leqayyāmāh qeyām*). But for the lengthening of a vowel one might read that the god of Daniel is an ordinance forever. As the text stands, the language merely plays with us, but the question remains: What then is really god—deity, legality, or monarchy?

Finally, Darius's decree that all fear and tremble before the god of Daniel collapses the two 'laws' that, in the beginning of the story, the conspirators seek to put at odds. The conspirators realize that they will find no complaint against Daniel unless they find it 'concerning the law of his god'. Their trap is designed to pit the law of Daniel's god against the law of his king. In the end, the two laws are essentially one: The king's law embraces the law of Daniel's god. Daniel's allegiance to the law of his god is what brings about his downfall and, conversely, 'the law of his god' confirms his return to power. Not only is the law of Daniel's god portrayed as somewhat utilitarian, but as long as Daniel's survival and success image the power of his god, then, by the fact of sheer visibility, Daniel himself will always eclipse Daniel's god. After all, what is the result of Darius's legislation?—That everyone converts to the worship of the most high God and declares this god ultimate sovereign? No. The result of Darius's legislation is that *Daniel prospers*. The legislative enforcement of Daniel's religion sets him up for life.

Epilogue: Observations from the Threshold

Besides ironically mirroring the story's initial decree, Darius's decree at the end of ch. 6 participates in two major progressions that run throughout the first six chapters and also extend into the second half of the book. The first theme that runs throughout the Daniel stories is the political advancement of the Hebrew hero. We have seen the Hebrew sage climb the political ladder from captive prisoner to initiate to sage (ch. 1) to chief sage (ch. 2) to administrator over the province of Babylon (chs. 2–3) to the king's personal adviser (ch. 4) to third ruler in the kingdom (ch. 5) to the prime minister that the king himself intends, at the beginning of ch. 6, to set over the entire kingdom and does implicitly set over the kingdom at the end of ch. 6. Even the mention of Daniel's prosperity during the reign of Cyrus in 6.29 might suggest that Cyrus's decision to let the Jews return home was influenced by none other than Daniel. The theme of political advancement is carried into ch. 7 albeit in a more general strain. The interpreter of Daniel's vision promises that 'the people of the holy ones of the Most High' will receive 'the kingdom and the rule and the greatness of the kingdom's under the whole heaven' (v. 27, cf. also vv. 18, 22).

The sage wins political promotion through deception (Daniel 1), cooperation (Daniel 2, 4, 6) and conflict (Daniel 3, 5) with his liege. In every story in Daniel 1–6, the sage is called upon to hold to values that somehow oppose the existent political authority. The story of deception in ch. 1 lays the ground work for the remaining stories. In this first story, the young Judeans, by refusing to eat the food from the king's table, affirm that, though they are willing to serve the king, the source of their wisdom and the subject of their ultimate fidelity is their god, not their king. In this story and the ones that follow, the sages show that they are ready to oppose political power for higher values—whether this challenge entails speaking the truth about an unpleasant dream or vision (chs. 4, 5) or disobeying the command to pay ultimate allegiance to some king who thinks his sovereignty to be supreme (chs. 1, 3, 6).

The irony involved in all of this courageous resistance, however, is that every instance of resistance to political authority, every affirmation of priorities other than the priority of political power is rewarded—how?—with the bestowal of more political power. When one looks at the overall picture of Daniel 1-6, the so highly valued piety and wisdom of our Judean heroes become means to political ends. The world of Daniel is a world of political ambition. While our Judean sages busily assist the Most High in teaching lessons to the kings concerning the ways in which pride corrupts the powerful, the sages themselves are consistently being promoted to positions of greater power.

In the final analysis, political power is not just the concern of kings, but it is also the concern of the Judean sage. The fact that Daniel becomes even more like a king is seen not only from the pattern of his political advancement, but also from the narrative structure. In ch. 6 Daniel's experiences are very similar to those of his old friend Nebuchadnezzar in ch. 4. Nebuchadnezzar's troubles are brought on by a decree from the holy ones; Daniel's problems are brought about by a decree from the king. Both decrees involve the recognition of sovereignty. In both stories, after learning of the decree, the protagonists go to similar places and say and do things that bring their respective sentences to pass. Nebuchadnezzar goes up to the roof of his palace; Daniel goes up to an upper room in his house. Nebuchadnezzar looks out over Babylon; Daniel looks toward Jerusalem. Nebuchadnezzar praises himself and his accomplishments; Daniel makes petition before his god. (I think it no small coincidence that the only 'vision' in the latter half of the book that is set during the reign of Darius is Daniel's petition and vision in ch. 9 concerning the religious [9.24] *and political* [9.25] restoration of Jerusalem.) In ch. 4, a voice from heaven interrupts Nebuchadnezzar and the decree is fulfilled; in ch. 6, the officials interrupt Daniel and the edict is enforced.

The sentencing of both protagonists involves the temporary loss of political position and an association with beasts. Nebuchadnezzar is driven from society; Daniel is thrown into the pit. Nebuchadnezzar exists with the wild beasts; Daniel passes the night with the lions. Nebuchadnezzar is fed the food of beasts; Daniel is to be the food of beasts. Nebuchadnezzar is delivered because he acknowledges the Most High; Daniel is delivered because he is faithful. Both protagonists are restored: Nebuchadnezzar is reestablished upon his throne with even more greatness than before; Daniel is restored to royal favor and Daniel's god and Daniel as divine representative enjoy the respect that was to be bestowed, at the beginning of the story, only upon the king.

A common vocabulary shared by the two stories broadens the analogous narrative contexts. The language that Nebuchadnezzar uses in his first doxology in 3.31-33 is echoed by Darius at the end of ch. 6. Both kings address their messages to 'all peoples, nations and languages who dwell in all the earth'. Both use the common expression 'May your peace be multiplied' to greet their subjects. Both praise God's signs and wonders. Both speak of the endurance of God's kingdom and rule.[28]

Both of these doxologies with their common vocabulary occur at strategic places in the overarching literary structure. Nebuchadnezzar's first doxology in 3.31-33 (Eng. 4.1-3) is ambiguously placed.[29] On first reading, the doxology looks as though it concludes the story in ch. 3, just as Darius's doxology concludes ch. 6. In fact, because chs. 3 and 6 are so similar, a closing doxology on the part of Nebuchadezzar in ch. 3 would be just as appropriate as Darius's closing hymn in ch. 6. Both kings have just witnessed the miraculous deliverance of their Judean administrators. Both kings are impressed by the power of this god. If one reads 3.31-33 (Eng. 4.1-3) in the context of ch. 3, one finds in the expanded block of material 3.29-33 (Eng. 3.29-4.3) the same elements (though not in the same order) as is found in 6.26-29 (Eng. 6.25-28): There is a decree concerning worship, a notice that the heroes prosper, and a doxology.

Of course, we have seen that Nebuchadnezzar's doxology in 3.31-33 also functions as the introduction to ch. 4. It would seem that this doxology, like the transitional sentence in 6.1, is a piece of material that easily closes one story while opening another. In ch. 4, Nebuchadnezzar's opening doxology is followed by a first-person account of a flashback. The king tells of having a night vision and of one (Daniel/Belteshazzar) coming to interpret it. Because of its similarities to 3.31-33, 6.26-28 (Eng. 6.25-27) can be seen to function in much the same way. The passage obviously closes ch. 6, but it also looks ahead to ch. 7. Darius's doxology is followed (though not immediately) by a flashback to the days of Belshassar, by Daniel's first person account of a night vision and of one coming to interpret it. The analogies between the two accounts are remarkable: Both men are 'troubled' (4.2 [Eng. 4.5]; 7.15, 28). Both visions are about kings being overthrown. Both contain judgments or decrees from heaven (4.14 [Eng. 4.17]; 4.21 [Eng. 4.24]; 7.10, 26). Both contain doxologies uttered later in the experience by the respective personae (4.31b-2 [Eng. 4.34b-5]; 7.14; cf. also the doxology uttered by the interpreter, 7.27). Both of these doxologies utilize the same type of language that describes the enduring nature of God's kingdom, the everlasting nature of God's rule. In both accounts there is a reference to 'all peoples, nations and languages'. In both accounts kings are anomalous beasts: In ch. 7, four beasts rise from the sea having the characteristics of various kinds of animals. In ch. 4 Nebuchadnezzar becomes like a beast. He dwells with the beasts of the field and he eats grass as oxen do; yet, he also resembles a bird with long feathers and claws. In both accounts divine judgment is passed upon a king because of what he says (4.26-28 [Eng. 4.29-31]; 7.8, 11, 20, 25-26). Furthermore, in neither chapter can the visionary interpret his own vision; someone else must explain it to him.

Throughout the short stories of Daniel, signs and wonders (visions and deliverances) have taken place for the benefit of the king. The Hebrew sages have functioned as agents who assist in bringing new knowledge to the king. Starting with ch. 7, however, the visions are for Daniel's benefit. He is never told to report what he has seen to any of the kings. If anything, he is told to keep what he has seen to himself. It is as though Daniel becomes a full-fledged character as the stories end and the visions begin. Daniel takes over what the narratives (chs. 2, 4, 5) have set up as the king's role. Now it is Daniel rather than the king who sees images of the fantastic, the anomalous, the bizarre, images of greatness established and greatness fallen.

Just as the kings' visions and their witnesses to deliverances reveal to them the limitations of their power; so, too, Daniel is reminded in the vision of ch. 7 that foreign power is limited and temporary. The kingdom will not always belong to the beasts; some day it will be given to the people of the holy ones of the Most High. Does Daniel not also count himself among these people who are to receive the kingdom? As a person faithful to his god, why should he not also be allowed to participate in the coming kingdom of his god and people? In fact, might it not occur to him that the 'one like a son of man' to whom will be given control of the kingdom will be none other than

Daniel himself? After all, he is of royal, or at least of noble, seed. And who has more wisdom and political expertise than Daniel? Besides, why should God send such visions to Daniel specifically if not to ready him for the coming kingdom?

My reading suggests that, at least through ch. 7, Daniel fully expects to participate in the establishment of God's kingdom and—what is an equivalent in Daniel's mind (ch. 9)—in the physical, religious, and political restoration of Jerusalem. This reading of the text colors what we have read thus far as well as what lies ahead in the later chapters of the book. As we reflect on chs. 1-6, we see, on the surface, a story of stories that show how one can be a faithful Jew and, at the same time, be politically successful.[30] But what we might also see, if we put aside our positivistic lenses, is that complementary interests can also be compromised interests. While Nebuchadnezzar on his roof praises Babylon, Daniel in his upper chamber prays for (ch. 9) and toward Jerusalem. One cannot pay equal allegiance to Babylon and Jerusalem. One cannot be completely faithful to a king when one has political aspirations of one's own. And, on the other hand, we might also see that when one is trying, not just to survive, but to succeed in a foreign political system, one's religious allegiance may also be compromised. How easy it is to underread divine judgment (chs. 2 and 4) when one faces a violent and temperamental king! How easy it is to overread divine judgment (ch. 5) when one has been insulted by a weak, childish king who is about to be overthrown anyway!

A politically aspiring Daniel also informs the way we understand his behavior in the latter chapters of the book. Not only is he preoccupied with the question of 'How long, O Lord?',[31] but Daniel faints or grows ill seemingly whenever he is told that his visions of a restored kingdom will not come to pass in his lifetime, but in 'the time of the end', 'many days hence' (cf. 8.17-18, 26-27; 10.14-15). The vision of ch. 7 allows his political hopes to be sustained, but the visions that follow accent Daniel's inability to understand what is actually being shown to him. It is not until the very end of the book that Daniel receives any sort of assurance of his role in the kingdom: 'Go your way till the end, and you shall rest, and shall stand in your allotted place at the end of the days'. Whether this answer satisfies Daniel, we are not told.

Daniel's obvious and somewhat impotent struggle to understand his visions reveals a more poignant limitation as far as his character is concerned—the limitation of his wisdom. Throughout the stories of Daniel, Daniel has become increasingly more self-assured in matters of wisdom and interpretation. Since the ending of ch. 2, he has allowed his wisdom and abilities to be praised without disclaimer. He has interpreted and advised seemingly without assistance. But, lest we become too enamored with Daniel and his ability, the implied narrator shows us another side of Daniel. Beginning with ch. 7, Daniel is like Nebuchadnezzar who dreams dreams and is troubled. He is like Belshazzar who sees visions and is afraid. He is like the other sages who are powerless to discern divine communication. The sage who would interpret the dreams and visions of others cannot interpret his own.

The goal of political power is not limited to being a human concern in the world of Daniel. Political power is even the concern of God. Look at how God shows divine sovereignty with the signs and wonders of bringing down the mighty and delivering the troubled. In the world of Daniel, God deals only with politically important people. God only deposes and delivers people who have political authority (kings [ch. 4], administrators [ch. 3], prime ministers [ch. 6]). Why? Because in order for people to believe in divine sovereignty, the divine sovereign has to have high visibility. It does not count to simply whisk the heroes away, to deliver them to another world, so to speak. It does not count to depose kings without an explanation of why they are being deposed and who is bringing it about. In order to be effective, God's action must have witnesses—and the more politically prestigious the witness, the more wonderful the sign, the more significant the wonder. Perception is everything. An anonymous god who does anonymous work is no god at all. Religion cannot cope with secret sovereigns.[32]

Consequently, the second progression of the narratives that is capped by Darius's decree at the end of ch. 6 is the increasing recognition of the god of the Judean exiles as the sovereign of sovereigns. From ch. 1 in which the king is totally unaware of this god, there is growing affirmation of this god on the part of the kings. At the end of ch. 2, Nebuchadnezzar says, while paying homage and offering incense to Daniel, 'Truly your god is a god of gods and a lord of kings and a revealer of mysteries that you are able to reveal this mystery'. At the end of ch. 3 the king not only affirms but legislates against the blasphemy of this god: 'Therefore I make a decree: Any people, nation, or language that speaks anything against the god of

Shadrach, Meshach, and Abednego shall be dismembered, and their houses laid in ruins: for there is no other god who is able to deliver in this way'. In ch. 4 the king makes a personal confession of belief in the power of this god who has shown sovereignty over the sovereign and who, consequently, is appropriately entitled the 'Most High' and the 'king of heaven'. The confession of ch. 4, while not legislative, is couched in the form of a national proclamation. By the time we reach the end of ch. 6, Darius's legislation is even more stringent than the legislation of ch. 3: 'I make a decree that in all my royal rule, everyone will tremble and fear before the god of Daniel. . .'

In each of these proclamations, God is defined relationally. God is given no personal name.[33] God is the god of Daniel or the god of Shadrach, Meshach, and Abednego. Even Nebuchadnezzar's use of the appellatives 'Most High' and 'king of heaven' reflects the relationality of God: Nebuchadnezzar is 'high'—that we have learned from the image of the great tree. He reaches to heaven and he is, obviously, king. The god who has brought him down, however, is 'higher' than he. Anyone whose might is greater than Nebuchadnezzar's is indeed 'king of heaven'. This naming of the divine reveals how God is understood in the story world of Daniel. Except in ch. 1, God is not a character that we see and hear. God's presence is always mediated: Characters report it, holy ones and heavenly voices represent it, sages interpret it, kings confess it and legislate the recognition of it; but the presence of God is not visible in the form of a distinct, divine character. We know what we know of God by watching what happens to the human characters, and in the case of Daniel, it is difficult to keep from fusing divine and human, as we see from Nebuchadnezzar's treatment of Daniel at the end of ch. 2.

Like the decree before it, the decree of Darius that everyone is to worship the god of Daniel is (since it is an edict established by the king) one that 'cannot be changed according to the law of the Medes and Persians which will not pass away'. Just as the identity of God is confined by relational terms, so, too, the sovereignty of God is limited by the royal legislation. The legislation that *confers* the recognition of sovereignty *controls* the recognition of sovereignty. Having the god of Daniel recognized in the legislation of a powerful regime like that of the Medes and Persians is indeed impressive and suggests, of course, that the recognition of the sovereignty of the Most High, because it is now law, will never pass away. But the *law* of the Medes and Persians is one that will not pass away only as long as the *rule* of the Medes and the Persians does not pass away. When the rule of the Medes and Persians passes away, then so does the law—and so does the recognition of the sovereignty of the Most High. Thus, the world of Daniel contains an ironic circle of sovereignty. God may establish kings and kingdoms and 'allow them to pass away' (2.21; 4.28 [Eng. 4.31]; 5.20), but when they 'pass away', God must start again the struggle to gain recognition. In other words, human sovereignty depends upon divine sovereignty, but conversely, divine sovereignty is dependent upon the recognition of human sovereigns.[34]

At least Daniel 7 discerns the maddening circle; Daniel's first vision is a vision of a world in which the cycle will be broken. A kingdom will finally be established in which the sovereignty of God is not dependent upon the attitudes of human monarchs, but is immediately recognized by everyone. The one who is 'ancient of days' will become a visible presence. A kingdom will finally be established that really does have legislative authority. As can be seen in the court scene in Daniel 7, divine and human sovereigns will be put in their rightful places: The divine will be passing legislation concerning the human and not vice versa. The legislation of this kingdom is indeed what the legislation of human kingdoms cannot be: It is the law that cannot pass away, the divine decree that cannot be changed—it is written and sealed in the book (Dan. 12.1, 4, 9).[35]

But the circle is no sooner halted than it starts again. There must be 'one like a son of man', a Gabriel, a Michael, an anointed prince, holy ones to take care of the business of the kingdom or, theologically speaking, to mediate the presence of God. The 'fire' of God cannot immediately and constantly be borne. The kingdom is handed back to the people—the people of the holy ones of the Most High.

The ultimate irony, then, in the book of Daniel is that the kingdom as Daniel envisions it—whether mediated or otherwise—never manifests itself. The events that are decreed to take place in 'the time of the end' never come to pass. This ultimate irony is, I think, tied up in the political web of Jewish sage and foreign sovereign that is portrayed in Daniel 1–6. When one stands up to political authority because of religious values, the reward is more political power. Where there is political power, there is hierarchy; where there is hierarchy, there is always the threat of corruption—the hierarchy itself becomes god. Perhaps this is why, in visions of the kingdom, God must sit one throne removed. God's kingdom is perhaps a dangerous metaphor for those who value political power as the most prized form of reward. The envisioned kingdom is not for Daniel to experience. Daniel stands on the brink of the kingdom; he sees it as Moses sees the promised land. But kingdoms, like Canaans, can be corrupted and corrupting. The purity of the kingdom is preserved only in its elusiveness.

In the end of Daniel, there is no end. The 'end' does not come; the kingdom that will never pass away is not manifested—at least not in the pattern of kingdoms that we have been shown thus far in the book. The promise (decree?) that does stand, however, is that the people of the holy ones, those who turn many to righteousness, the wise ones will 'shine like the stars'. Their endurance is the sign of hope; more likely, their endurance is the sign of the kingdom itself. Just as Daniel's survival of the lions represents the indestructibility of God's kingdom (Dan. 6.26-27), so too, the people who survive other beastly powers are manifestations of the kingdom. The beasts who rise from the sea in Daniel 7 and the king who is a beast in Daniel 4 allow us to see Daniel's survival in the lion pit as a paradigm of his survival of exile. Daniel has survived not only the foreign rulers,[36] but all parties who are jealous of and hostile to him and his friends, to use the text's pun, those who 'eat the pieces of' Daniel and his friends. Daniel survives exile just as he survives the lions: He survives because he is faithful both to his god and to his king.

Likewise, his god and his king survive because he is faithful. Just as kings do not last very long without faithful subjects, neither do gods. As the psalmist says,

> What profit is there in my death,
>   if I go down to the pit?
> Will the dust praise you?
>   Will it tell of your faithfulness?[37]

God and humanity are interdependent. The faithfulness of human beings renders God visible, and that is why God cannot let the faithful ones completely perish. If God lets Daniel, or the community of Israel, perish in exile, or in any other historical crisis, what becomes of the sovereignty of the God of Israel? Who would proclaim it? Who would see it? Who would understand?

NOTES

Notes to Introduction

1. The study of poetics has been around at least since Aristotle. However, poetics has only recently become a popular subject of investigation in biblical studies. I point the reader to Adele Berlin's definition of poetics as 'the science of literature' which 'describes the basic components of literature and the rules governing their use' (p. 15) and her helpful discussion of the topic in *Poetics and Interpretation of Biblical Narrative* (Sheffield: Almond, 1983) 13-22.

2. For an introduction to the recent developments in literary criticism and how they are influencing biblical studies, see Edgar V. McKnight, *The Bible and the Reader: An Introduction to Literary Criticism* (Philadelphia: Fortress, 1985).

3. There are exceptional instances, however, when the sense of the MT cannot be determined, in which cases I have followed suggested textual emendation.

4. For an excellent discussion and extensive bibliography on this genre, see John J. Collins, 'Introduction to Apocalyptic Literature', *Daniel with an Introduction to Apocalyptic Literature* (FOTL 20; Grand Rapids: William B. Eerdmans, 1984) 2-24.

5. Consequently, I did not choose, on linguistic or structural grounds, to work on chs. 2-7 (cf. the work of A. Lenglet, 'La structure littéraire de Daniel 2-7', *Bib* 53 [1972] 169-90) or, on the basis of a reconstructed tradition and redactional history, to work on smaller blocks within Daniel 1-6 (cf. the recent work of Ernst Haag, *Die Errettung Daniels aus der Löwengrube: Untersuchungen zum Ursprung der biblischen Danieltradition* [SBS 110; Stuttgart: Katholisches Bibelwerk, 1983]).

6. For a survey of such issues, see Klaus Koch (with T. Niewisch and J. Tubach), *Das Buch Daniel* (Darmstadt: Wissenschaftliche Buchgesellschaft, 1980); Ferdinand Dexinger, *Das Buch Daniel und seine Probleme* (SBS 36; Stuttgart: Katholisches Bibelwerk, 1969); or P.R. Davies, *Daniel* (Sheffield: JSOT, 1985).

7. See George Coats, 'Tale', in *Saga, Legend, Tale, Novella, Fable: Narrative Forms in Old Testament Literature*, ed. George Coats (JSOTSup 35; Sheffield: JSOT, 1985) 63-70.

8. See W. Lee Humphreys, 'Novella', in *Saga, Legend, Tale, Novella, Fable*, 82-96, esp. 83-85. Although these two scholars use different labels, clearly they are describing the same narrative characteristics. The term

'short story' will henceforth be used as the generic label for the individual narratives in Daniel 1–6.

9. For a complete list, see Koch, 88-92.

10. 'Märchen, Legende und Enderwartung: Zum Verständnis des Buches Daniel', *VT* 26 (1976) 338-50.

11. Collins, 113.

12. Ibid., 41.

13. See particularly, M. Delcor, *Le Livre de Daniel* (Paris: J. Gabalda, 1971) 23-25, and his discussions on individual chapters; André Lacocque, *The Book of Daniel* (Atlanta: John Knox, 1979) 1, and his discussions on individual chapters; Louis Hartman and Alexander A. DiLella, *The Book of Daniel* (Garden City, New York: Doubleday, 1978) 53-54.

14. A.G. Wright, *The Literary Genre Midrash* (Staten Island: Alba House, 1967) 74.

15. John Gammie ('On the Intention and Sources of Daniel 1–6', *VT* 31 [1981] 282-92) has oberved some interesting connections between the materials in Daniel 1–6 and other parts of the Hebrew Bible, particularly, Proverbs, Job, and 2 Isaiah (see especially 286-92). His work on intertextuality, however, is, for the most part, devoted to reconstructing the redactional history of Daniel 1–6.

16. In this case, the intertextuality of the Hebrew Scriptures. Julia Kristeva describes intertextuality as 'a permutation of texts', 'in the space of a given text, several utterances, taken from other texts, intersect and neutralize one another'. See 'The Bounded Text', in *Contemporary Literary Criticism: Modernism through Post-Structuralism*, ed. Robert Con Davis (New York, London: Longman, 1986) 448-66, see 448.

17. Cf. Peter Miscall's strategy of reading parallel texts, *The Workings of Old Testament Narrative* (Philadelphia: Fortress, 1983; Chico, California: Scholars, 1983) 2-3.

18. First suggested by Ronald M. Hals, 'Legend: A Case-Study in OT Form-Critical Terminology', *CBQ* 34 (1972) 166-76, see 173, and recently adopted by Collins, 42, 44, 49, 55, 62, 67, 71.

19. Collins, 111.

20. Coats, 63-64.

21. Collins, 111.

22. *Saga, Legend, Tale, Novella, Fable*, 83. Many of these points are also covered by Coats (pp. 63-70), in the same volume. I am taking Humphreys as my point of departure, not only because of his convenient lists, but also because his discussion of novella might prove to be useful in talking about the entire narrative unit of Daniel 1–6.

23. Humphreys, 83.

24. Cf. Coats's discussion of exposition, 64-65.

25. Humphreys, 83.

26. For a provocative discussion of the alternative modes of literary borrowing and the various ways the audience can relate to such borrowing, see Peter J. Rabinowitz, '"What's Hecuba to Us?" The Audience's Experience of Literary Borrowing', in *The Reader in the Text: Essays on Audience and Interpretation*, ed. Susan R. Suleiman and Inge Crosman (Princeton: Princeton University, 1980) 241-63.

27. Humphreys, 83; Coats, 70.

28. This does not preclude, however, elements of the fantastic or supernatural. A story's quality of mimesis has to do with presenting something—anything—that is true about life and living.

29. Here Humphreys also refers to James Joyce's description of the short story having an 'epiphany quality' (p. 84).

30. The affinities of this material with the Joseph story and the book of Esther have been widely recognized. A. Meinhold ('Die Gattung der Josephgeschichte und des Estherbuches: Diasporanovelle, I, II', *ZAW* 87 [1975] 306-24; 88 [1976] 79-93) has proposed that these pieces are to be classified as *diaspora novella*. The designation *novella*, when applied to the Joseph story and the book of Esther, is accurate, but Collins (p. 42) is correct to note that the qualification 'diaspora' ignores non-Jewish parallels, for example, the story of Ahiqar.

31. 'A Life-Style for Diaspora: A Study of the Tales of Esther and Daniel', *JBL* 92 (1973) 211-23.

32. Apparently, Humphreys would also see the stories' origins as a qualifying element, but he simply assumes that the story world is an accurate reflection of the situation in which the stories were produced. Consequently, for him, these stories originate in the post-exilic diaspora (p. 223), which may indeed be the case, but how can that proved? And more important—how would establishing that case solve the question of genre?

33. Ibid., 219.

34. Ibid., 222.

35. Ibid., 223. This latter function (or intention) is, of course, dependent upon the *Sitz im Leben* of diaspora, see above note 32. The stories do entertain and they do present a particular lifestyle; however, they do much more than this as we shall see in following reading.

36. 'The Success Story of the Wise Courtier: A Formal Approach', *JBL* 96 (1977) 179-93.

37. Type 922 in A. Aarne and S. Thompson, *The Types of Folktale* (Folklore Fellows Communications 184; Helsinki: Suomalainen tiedeakatemia, 1964).

38. Type 922 falls under the heading 'Clever Acts and Words' in Aarne and Thompson.

39. For a more detailed summary of this study, see 'Excursus I: Formal Characteristics of Daniel 2', 60-62.

40. Humphreys, 'Life-Style', 220; Niditch and Doran, 190-91.

41. For the structures of these story types, see Davies, 51-52.

42. Ibid., 52.

43. Coats, *Saga, Legend, Tale, Novella, Fable*, 11.

44. On methodological pluralism in literary criticism, see Wayne C. Booth, *Critical Understanding: The Powers and Limits of Pluralism* (Chicago: University of Chicago, 1979).

45. For an overview of New Criticism, see David Robey, 'Anglo-American New Criticism', in *Modern Literary Theory: A Comparative Introduction*, ed. Ann Jefferson and David Robey (London: Batsford Academic and Educational Ltd, 1982) 65-83; for the political background and a helpful critique of New Criticism, see Terry Eagleton, 'The Rise of English', in *Literary Theory: An Introduction* (Minneapolis: University of Minnesota, 1983) 17-53. For a less than kind review of New Criticism, see Meir Sternberg's comments scattered throughout his chapter 'Literary Text, Literary Approach', in *The Poetics of Biblical Narrative: Ideological Literature and the Drama of Reading* (Bloomington: Indiana University, 1985) 1-57.

46. For an introduction to structuralism that includes discussion of how structuralism relates to other types of literary theory, see either Eagleton, 'Structuralism and Semiotics', in *Literary Theory*, 91-126 or Ann Jefferson, 'Structuralism and Post-Structuralism', *Modern Literary Theory*, 84-112.

47. Ferdinand de Saussure's work was collected and published posthumously in 1916 as *Cours de linguistique générale*; it has been translated into English as *Course in General Linguistics* (New York: McGraw-Hill, 1966).

48. Let me venture an example: The word *tree* is a linguistic sign that unites a form which signifies, that is, a particular pattern of the letters t, r, e, e, and an idea of a tall plant with (probably green) leaves and a (probably brown) wooden trunk and branches. The form (signifier) and the idea (signified) are distinguishable from any actual tree that is actually growing in the real world.

49. For an overview of the linguistic foundation of structuralism, see Jonathan Culler, *Structuralist Poetics: Structuralism, Linguistics, and the Study of Literature* (Ithaca, New York: Cornell University, 1975) 3-31.

50. For a more thorough discussion of the theory of how binary opposition creates story, see Robert Scholes, *Structuralism in Literature: An Introduction* (New Haven and London: Yale University, 1974) 102-108.

51. There seems to be no general consensus on what deconstruction is exactly. It has been 'variously presented as a philosophical position, a political of intellectual strategy, and a mode of reading' (Jonathan Culler, *On Deconstruction: Theory and Criticism after Structuralism* [London: Routledge & Kegan Paul, 1983] 85), not to mention a 'literary theory' as it is billed in recent introductions to literary criticism and theory.

52. Cf. David Jobling's observation that structuralism tends toward

deconstruction, 'Structuralism, Hermeneutics, and Exegesis: three Recent Contributions to the Debate', *USQR* 34 (1979) 135-47, see especially 142-43.

53. See Culler's discussion of recent critical works that explore this deconstructing principle of unstable hierarchy, *On Deconstruction*, 227-42.

54. Robert Con Davis, 'The Poststructuralist "Texte"', in *Contemporary Literary Criticism*, 409-14, 410.

55. Barbara Johnson, 'The Critical Difference: BartheS/BalZac' in *Contemporary Literary Criticism*, 439-46, 441.

56. Culler, *On Deconstruction*, 178.

57. On the general theory of indeterminacy or textual gaps, see Wolfgang Iser, 'The Reading Process: A Phenomenological Approach', in *The Implied Reader: Patterns of Communication in Prose Fiction from Bunyan to Beckett* (Baltimore: Johns Hopkins University, 1974) 274-95. For the theory in biblical literary studies, see Sternberg, *The Poetics of Biblical Narrative*, and the more popular work of Terence Keegan, *Interpreting the Bible* (New York: Paulist, 1985).

58. Eagleton, 194-217.

59. On the 'parasitical' nature of deconstruction, see J. Hillis Miller, 'The Critic as Host', in *Deconstruction and Criticism*, H. Bloom et al. (New York: Continuum, 1984) 217-53.

60. This is also the basic assumption underlying Sternberg's work. See *Poetics*, 7-23.

61. Ibid., 51. Although Sternberg would not, I place an emphasis on the qualifying portion of that sentence. More work needs to be done on the issue of the reliability of biblical narrators.

62. Sternberg describes this as moving between the truth and the whole truth, (pp. 184-85).

63. Peter Miscall writes, 'There is seldom much trouble in determining what OT narrative is narrating or describing even though the significance for the overall narrative of what is narrated or described may be difficult to determine, if it can be determined at all' (p. 7).

64. Sternberg, 186.

65. Ibid., 190-219.

66. Ibid., 206-207.

67. A helpful and quite readable discussion of plot can be found in Seymour Chatman, *Story and Discourse: Narrative Structure in Fiction and Film* (Ithaca: Cornell University, 1978) 43-95.

68. Even events that occur fortuitously are usually temporally connected with other events in the story. On sequence, see Chatman 45-48.

69. On narrative plot in general, see Robert Scholes and Robert Kellogg, *The Nature of Narrative* (Oxford/London/New York: Oxford University Press, 1966) 207-39; Rene Wellek and Austin Warren, *Theory of Literature*

(New York: Harcourt, Brace & World, 1956) 216-18. On plot structure in a
biblical 'tale', see Coats, 63-70, 64-67.

70. Sternberg, 264.

71. Ibid., 264-65.

72. On foreshadowing, see Sternberg, 268-70.

73. There are, of course, exceptions: For example, in the story of the
binding of Isaac, the narrator prefaces the conflict with 'After these things
God tested Abraham'. One could argue, in this case, that the theologically
problematic subject matter demands such clarification in advance.

74. Paradigms are not all narrative structures. A foreshadowing paradigm
might be a divine law, for instance, or a literary formula. See Sternberg's
discussion of paradigmatic formula in Judges as foreshadowing device
(p. 269).

75. Ibid., 268

76. Cf. the beginning of Judges 2.

77. Sternberg, 284.

78. On suspense and surprise, see Chatman, 59-62.

79. Sternberg, 259-60, 309-20.

80. The following categories are those designated by Berlin, 23-24.

81. Chatman, 117, 119.

82. Actually, to the narratee or implied reader. The multiple audiences
will be addressed in the section on point of view.

83. Berlin, 34-37.

84. See also Robert Alter's helpful discussion of this in 'Characterization
and the Art of Reticence', in *The Art of Biblical* Narrative (New York: Basic
Books, 1980).

85. Berlin, 40-41.

86. Sternberg, 130.

87. A most helpful study of point of view in literature and art is Boris
Uspensky, *A Poetics of Composition: The Structure of the Artistic Text and
Typology of a Compositional Form*, trans. V. Zavarin and S. Wittig (Berkeley:
University of California, 1973).

88. Berlin, 43; Sternberg, 84-99.

89. Sternberg claims that the narrator knows the 'whole truth' but only
tells 'part' of the truth; but this is an assertion (in fact, in Sternberg's case,
one might call it a confession of faith), not an argument. If the narrator only
communicates partial knowledge, only recounts the thoughts of some but not
all of the characters, why should we assume complete omniscience when we
observe only partial omniscience?

90. See Berlin's discussion and excellent examples of the various intensities
of the narrator's voice (pp. 57-59).

91. See Wayne Booth, *The Rhetoric of Fiction* (Chicago: University of
Chicago, 1961, 1983) 149-63, 169-205.

92. See Keegan's discussion of this construct in relation to biblical narrative, (pp. 95-96).

93. On naming as an indicator of point of view, see Berlin (pp. 59-61).

94. Ibid., 64-72.

95. Cf. Wolfgang Iser's chapter 'Grasping a Text', in *The Act of Reading: A Theory of Aesthetic Response* (Baltimore: Johns Hopkins, 1978) 107-34.

96. On the concept of implied reader, see Iser, *The Act of Reading*, 27-38.

97. Cf. Gerard Genette's discussion of intradiegetic and extradiegetic narrators and narratees, *Narrative Discourse: An Essay in Method*, trans. J.E. Lewin (Ithaca: Cornell University, 1980) 259-62.

98. For example, compare the use of the word *gdl*, 'great' or 'big', in the book of Jonah.

99. A repetition can be varied in several ways: the addition or subtraction of words, the change of word order, grammatical transformation, e.g. from active to passive voice, the substitution of one term with another, etc. See Sternberg, 390-93.

100. Berlin, 64-73.

101. In addition to the discussions of repetition and variation by Berlin and Sternberg, see Jacob Licht, *Storytelling in the Bible* (Jerusalem: Magnes, Hebrew University, 1978) 51-95.

102. The classic study of ambiguity is William Empson, *Seven Types of Ambiguity* (New York: New Directions, 1930; reprint, 1966).

103. Cf. above discussion on foretelling.

104. As biblical rhetorical critics painstakingly show us.

105. Iser, *The Act of Reading*, 142.

106. See Genette, 86-112, and Licht, 96-129.

107. Genette, 87, 109-12; Licht, 97.

108. Genette, 95-99.

109. Ibid., 99-106.

110. Ibid., 106-109.

Notes to Chapter 1: Daniel 1

1. The subject of the infinitive is omitted in the Hebrew.

2. The word here is *legadlām* which means literally 'to make them great'. The piel form occurs elsewhere in the context of bringing up children: cf. Isa. 1.2, 2 Kgs 10.6. Whether *gdl* in this case refers to physical growth or mental development is uncertain. Scholars are divided as to the term's precise meaning in this context. Some understand the word to connote physical growth and translate with the phrase 'to nourish them', e.g. S.R. Driver, *The Book of Daniel* (Cambridge: Cambridge University Press, 1905) 7; J. Slotki, *Daniel, Ezra, and Nehemiah* (London: Soncino, 1951) 3. This translation

closely attaches the term to the preceding assignment of food and wine. Others translate the term 'to educate', e.g. J.A. Montgomery, *The Book of Daniel* (Edinburgh: T. & T. Clark, 1927, 1950) 128; Delcor, 62; O. Plöger, *Das Buch Daniel* (Gütersloh: Gütersloher Verlagshaus/Gerd Mohn, 1965) 35 ('ausbilden'); Hartman and DiLella, 127 ('training'); J. Collins, *Daniel, First Maccabees, Second Maccabees* (Wilmington, Delaware: Michael Glazier, 1981) 21; N. Porteous, *Daniel* (London: SCM, 1965) 23. This translation connects the term to the preceding order 'to teach them the letters and the language of the Chaldeans'. Yet other scholars retain the sense 'to bring up children' in their translations, e.g. A. Lacocque, 20 ('to raise them'); A. Bentzen, *Daniel* (Tübingen: J.C.B. Mohr, 1937) 2 ('zu erziehen'). This translation captures both physical and mental development, but gives the impression that the selected Israelites are just children. Though the text calls the young men *yelādîm*, it does not specify their ages. Furthermore, Daniel's thoughts and actions can hardly be considered those of a child. R. Mosis ('*gdl*', *TDOT* II [Grand Rapids: William B. Eerdmans, 1977] 390-416) suggests a related, but not so limited meaning: 'to make something out of them', to let them become something' (p. 403). This sense allows for both nourishment and education and yet also points to the fact that the young men are being readied for a new role in life.

3. From the root *g'l* ('abhor') not *g'l* ('redeem'). The spelling is late. Its other occurrences refer to cultic defilement, cf. Isa. 59.3; Lam. 4.14; Mal. 1.7, 12; Ezra 2.62 = Neh. 7.64. A.R. Johnson has argued that *g'l* and *g'l* have a common root with the primary meaning 'to cover', see 'The Primary Meaning of *g'l*' (VTS 1; Leiden: E.J. Brill, 1953) 66-77. Others have found this relationship dubious, e.g. J. Blau, 'Über homonyme und angeblich homonyme Wurzeln', *VT* 6 (1956) 242-48, esp. 244.

4. The verb is passive in Hebrew.

5. The hiphil form of the verb as well as the grammatical construction of the sentence makes two readings possible: Either Daniel simply understands dreams and visions or God gives Daniel understanding.

6. Reading the Greek and Latin emendation. The MT reads 'the wisdom of understanding'.

7. Cf. Jer. 25.1 and 2 Chron. 36.21 as opposed to 2 Kings 24-25. We cannot depend upon our narrator for historical accuracy. See the discussion on the reader's legitimate expectations of fiction in the introduction.

8. Lacocque also sees this connection, but concludes from the analogy that the offices for which the young men are being prepared are also priestly in nature (p. 27). I see, rather, that the phrase 'without blemish' raises the thematic issue of sovereignty (god versus king) and plays with the notion of offering or sacrifice. Are these young men being 'sacrificed' to the king in the same sense that Jerusalem, King Jehoiakim, and the temple vessels have been given (sacrificed?) to Nebuchadnezzar? At the very least, the play on sacrifice foreshadows chs. 3 and 6.

9. Cf. Esther 2 where the young women who are chosen for the king also undergo an extensive period of preparation.

10. See Driver, 12-16.

11. Joyce Baldwin, *Daniel* (Downers Grove, Illinois: Intervarsity, 1978) 82-83.

12. See note 2.

13. According to Montgomery, these names reflect intentional perversions of names containing Bel, Marduk, and Nebo (pp. 129-30). If they are indeed such perversions, the narrator may here be sharing a joke with the reader behind the characters' backs.

14. See the germinal work of Arnold van Gennep, *Rites of Passage* (Chicago: University of Chicago, 1960) and the subsequent elaboration of passage ritual by Victor Turner, 'Betwixt and Between: The Liminal Period in *Rites de Passage*', in *The Forest of Symbols* (Ithaca: Cornell University, 1967) 93-111; *The Ritual Process* (Chicago: Aldine, 1969); 'Passages, Margins, and Poverty: Religious Symbols of Communitas', in *Dramas, Fields, and Metaphors* (Ithaca: Cornell University, 1974) 231-71.

15. Such is the reading reflected in H.L. Ginsberg's argument, based on Lev. 11.37-38, that the only food that would be beyond defilement is dried legumes, thus the reason for Daniel's later request for vegetables, 'seeds'. See 'The Composition of the Book of Daniel', *VT* 4 (1954) 246-75, esp. 256. The observation that ritual purity appears to be a prominent concern in the literature of the second temple period—cf. Jub. 22.16, Jdt 10.5, 2 Macc. 5.27, Tob. 1.10—also supports such an understanding of Daniel's situation, see Porteous's discussion, pp. 29-31.

16. Baldwin, 83.

17. See the excellent discussion of the political dimensions of the king's food by Davies, pp. 90-91.

18. According to Josephus, Daniel is a descendant of King Zedekiah (*Antiquities* 10.10.1).

19. See also Lacocque's observation that food is a symbol of one's culture. He compares Daniel's refusal of the king's food with the more modern situation of immigrants in American and French cities who insist on maintaining their national diet (p. 28).

20. Cf. Dan. 3.19. In fact, the term *mar'eh* is more often used to refer to a character's physical appearance as viewed by someone else, cf. its earlier use in Dan. 1.4.

21. BDB, 277.

22. The meaning of *melṣar*, here translated 'guardian', is uncertain, but according to Montgomery, it comes from the Akkadian maṣṣor meaning 'watch'. This meaning, 'one who watches', is corroborated by Syriac and Arabic translations. Montgomery critiques attempts to interpret this office to be that of a treasurer with the comment: '... such an identification ignores a

clever moment in the story, the appeal to a lower servant' (p. 134).

23. Obviously, his friends have been involved in his scheme from the beginning. Note the chief eunuch's use of the second masculine plural in v. 11.

24. On coda, see Berlin, 107-10.

Notes to Chapter 2: Daniel 2

1. My translation follows the MT which reads *nihyetāh*, a niph. 3fs pf. of *hyh*. BDB gives the meaning of this form as it occurs in Daniel (here and in 8.27) to be 'to be done, finished, gone' (p. 227). Since there are no clear parallels in the OT (although some commentators cite Prov. 13.19), this is the more difficult reading for this passage. The text may have originally read *šenātô nāddah* ('his sleep fled from him') as in 6.19. This is supported by the fact that *ndd* is a word sometimes used in the context of sleeplessness, e.g. Gen. 31.40, Esth. 6.1, Job 7.4 (noun). Whether one reads with the MT or makes the emendation, the sense of the sentence remains essentially the same: Nebuchadnezzar is deprived of his sleep.

2. This is an elliptical construction in which the subject of the infinitive is understood. See Ronald J. Williams, *Hebrew Syntax: An Outline*, 2nd edn (Toronto: University of Toronto, 1976), section 586.

3. Here the language of the text switches from Hebrew to Aramaic. Most likely, the phrase 'in Aramaic', which I have omitted from my translation, was originally a marginal note that simply indicated the language change in the text. Later scribes, perhaps understanding it to refer to the language of the Chaldeans, incorporated the phrase into the text itself.

4. Probably from the Akkadian root *nabalu*, 'destroy'. See E. Vogt, *Lexicon linguae aramaicae Veteris Testamenti documentis antiquis illustratum* (Rome: Biblical Institute, 1971) 110.

5. Literally, 'until the time has changed'. Vogt suggests that 'the time' refers to Nebuchadnezzar's reign: '"donec mutetur (presens) condicio temporis", prob. regnum meum' (p. 124).

6. 'Difficult' is derived from the basic meaning 'heavy'. Cf. Ps. 49.9 (Eng. 49.8). See Montgomery, 153.

7. On translating Aramaic infinitives without explicit subjects, see W.F. Stinespring, 'The Active Infinitive with Passive Meaning in Biblical Aramaic', *JBL* 81 (1962) 391-94.

8. See J.G. Williams, 'Critical Note on the Aramaic Indefinite Plural of the Verb', *JBL* 83 (1964) 180-82.

9. *bē'dayin* is a term often used to emphasize a change of subject or a new stage of narrative. BDB, 1078; Montgomery, 155.

10. *ṭe'ēm* literally means 'taste'. The phrase *hatîb ṭe'ēm* is a technical term in wisdom. See Bentzen, 'Hebr. *hešîb ṭa'am* ist der Weisheitsliteratur eigen

und bedeutet hier: "in entscheidender Stunde das rechte Worte finden", cf. Prov 26.16' (p. 6).

11. In the Targums and the Talmud, *ḥṣp* means 'to be without shame', 'hard of face'. However, the Arabic word *ḥaṣaba* means 'to go quickly'. Consequently, scholars are divided as to whether the term in this case (and in 3.22) should be rendered 'harsh' or 'hasty'. Cf. Montgomery, 156; Slotki, 11; Lacocque, 41; Plöger, 46; Driver, 23; Keil (*Biblischer Commentar über den Propheten Daniel* [Leipzig: Dörffling und Franke, 1869] 78-79). It is difficult to judge from the context in either this case or in 3.22 the exact sense of the term. The force of Daniel's question remains the same in either sense: He is asking 'Why the sentence?' He could credibly be stressing *either* the suddenness of the sentence *or* the severity of the sentence.

12. See note 9.

13. In the interests of smooth English, I have rendered the infinitive as a perfect in order to parallel 'and he made the matter known' in the preceding verse.

14. As Montgomery has noted, this term invariably refers to pottery ware or potsherds, never to raw clay (p. 167).

15. Literally, '(to) the earth from you'. In the context of the dream, hierarchy appears to be denotative of value.

16. In this context *pelîgāh* means 'diverse, composite' rather than 'divided' (Montgomery, 177).

17. Cf. Montgomery, 179.

18. All of these terms are commonly used in the context of cultic ritual. See Montgomery's notes, 181-82.

19. S. Niditch and R. Doran, 'The Success Story of the Wise Courtier: A Formal Approach', *JBL* 96 (1977) 179-93.

20. Type number 922 as designated by A. Aarne and S. Thompson in *The Types of Folktale*.

21. Niditch and Doran, 180.

22. Ibid., 181.

23. Ibid.

24. Ibid., 190.

25. Cf. Baldwin's discussion, 85-86, 92.

26. The temporal incongruity between chs. 1 and 2 has prompted the common observation that biblical authors and redactors are unconcerned with accurate synchronization. This might stem from a lack of 'genuine historical interest' (see Porteous, 39), or from a lack of care on the part of the redactor (see P.R. Davies, 'Daniel Chapter Two', *JTS* 27 [1976] 392-401, 394). The apparatus to the Massoretic text suggests that the phrase be emended to 'the tenth year', but there is no textual support for this change.

27. On this device as a folktelling technique, see V. Propp, *Morphology of a Folktale* (2nd edn, Austin: University of Texas, 1979) 74-75.

28. Montgomery notes the switch to a more respectful tone, 149, 151.

29. Cf. Baldwin, 87-88, and Lacocque, 38.

30. Cf. Bentzen, 225.

31. See note 5.

32. See Keegan, 100-102, 112-13.

33. For an explanation of this sentence from the perspective of redactional history, see Davies, 'Daniel Chapter Two'.

34. See Berlin, 47-50.

35. See the discussion of character types in the Introduction.

36. Davies points out the tension between Daniel's action in this instance and v. 25 where Daniel is introduced to the king as if for the first time ('Daniel Chapter Two', 393).

37. On suspense and curiosity, see the discussion in the Introduction.

38. Niditch and Doran, 190.

39. W.S. Towner has convincingly argued that, though Daniel's prayer is obviously a different genre, it is not obtrusive to the text and was most likely composed for this particular literary context ('Poetic Passages of Daniel 1–6', *CBQ* 31 [1969] 317-26, see esp. 318-20).

40. Preben Wernberg-Møller argues that *gebûrtā'* refers to intellectual strength, 'wondrous, mysterious wisdom' (*The Manual of Discipline* [Grand Rapids: Eerdmans, 1957] 74).

41. Cf. Baldwin, 91.

42. Daniel's verbosity in vv. 27-30 may technically be due, as Hartman and DiLella have suggested (p. 140), to the secondary addition of vv. 29-30. The drawing out of the explanation, however, is not necessarily out of place, but functions dramatically.

43. See Berlin's discussion of *hinneh* as an indicator of perceptual point of view (pp. 62-63).

44. See the discussion in ch. 1 concerning disparity between the king's point of view and the narrator's point of view.

45. See my discussion of Sternberg's understanding of the narrator in the Introduction.

46. The succession of kingdoms is an attested motif in ancient Near Eastern literature. See the discussions of D. Flusser, 'The Four Empires in the Fourth Sibyl and in the Book of Daniel', *Israel Oriental Studies* 2 (1972) 148-75; G.F. Hasel, 'The Four World Empires of Daniel 2 Against Its Near Eastern Environment', *JSOT* 12 (1979) 17-30; J.W. Swain, 'The Theory of the Four Monarchies: Opposition History under the Roman Empire', *Classical Philology* 35 (1940) 1-21. While most scholars commenting on Daniel 2 attempt to identify the various metals with a succession of kings, dynasties, or empires (and thus, in a manner of speaking, adopt Daniel's temporal interpretation), a few (though still historically oriented) have been drawn to a more synchronic understanding. See e.g. H.L. Ginsberg, 'Pre-

Epiphanian and Epiphanian Four-Monarchy Theories', in *Studies in Daniel* (New York: Jewish Theological Seminary of America, 1948) 5-23, esp. 8; and more recently, Baldwin, 92-94.

47. Cf. Lacocque's comment on the difference between the statue and the stone (p. 52).

48. Cf. the interpretation of E.F. Siegmann, 'The Stone Hewn from the Mountain', *CBQ* 18 (1956) 364-79.

49. Cf. Montgomery's comments on the distinction between the image and the stone: The image is '... the artificial figure of a human body... The metallic character of the Image deliberately stamps it as artificial and but heightens the truth of the symbol. For it is the man-made and hand-made construction of the kingdom of this world that the narrator would portray. The figure stands there stiff and stark, the product of human law and convention at their best and truest, but a lifeless creation. Over against this appears the mobile, supernaturally moving stone, coming how and whence none knows, which, as is true of the cosmic forces, crumples up that proud and complacent work of human art' (p. 187). 'The sphere of that Kingdom is that of its predecessors, only it possesses the everlasting endurance of the natural rock. The supernatural feature is that this Stone becomes a great Mountain. The artifice of men's hands has been replaced by the earthly type of eternity' (p. 191).

50. Hebrew narrators employ dreams as messages from the divine (see e.g. Genesis 21) which is much in keeping with a common ancient Near Eastern understanding of dreams (see A.L. Oppenheim's classic study, *The Interpretation of Dreams in the Ancient Near East* [Philadelphia: The American Philosophical Society, 1956]), but they also used dreams to indicate mental preoccupation. Joseph's dreams of the sheaves and the stars (Genesis 37), for example, are telling reflections of his pompous personality.

51. Cf. Baldwin's use of Jung in her reading of Daniel 2 (p. 92).

52. See note 18. 'Incense' and 'libation' are Montgomery's suggested translations (pp. 182-83). See also his comment 'There can be no question but that Neb. intended divine honors to Dan. in the true spirit of Paganism' (p. 180).

53. The discrepancy has often been explained by the appeal to redactional history. (See, again, the work of P.R. Davies, 'Daniel, Chapter Two'.) Daniel 1 and Daniel 2 represent two originally independent accounts of Daniel's introduction to the Babylonian court that have been secondarily fitted into a chronological framework. The process and the effect is much like that of the two creation stories at the beginning of Genesis—they function to tell the story of the beginning of the world, but they go about it in quite distinctive ways. Their present arrangement lures the reader into viewing them as sequential. (Cf. also the two stories of David's introduction into Saul's court.) Such an analysis may explain how the stories came together, but it does not explain the effect they have.

Notes to Chapter 3: Daniel 3.1-30

1. On these titles, see the discussions of Hartman and DiLella, 156-57; Lacocque, 56-57; Montgomery, 199-200. It appears that these officers are being listed from highest to lowest (Montgomery, 197; Hartman and DiLella, 156).

2. For a discussion of the identities of these instruments and how the mention of these instruments can and cannot be used to date this story, see T.C. Mitchell and R. Joyce, 'The Musical Instruments in Nebuchadrezzar's Orchestra', in D.J. Wiseman et al., *Notes on Some Problems in the Book of Daniel* (London: Tyndale, 1965) 19-27.

3. The *symphonia*, here translated 'bagpipes', has been omitted in this verse, most likely through scribal error.

4. Literally, 'ate the pieces'. On this idiom, see Montgomery, 204-205, and Lacocque, 61.

5. See Montgomery's discussion of this word (p. 207).

6. According to Massoretic punctuation, the three men impudently omit the royal title. The LXX, and other versions, however, punctuate the sentence to read, 'and they said to King Nebuchadnezzar'. Following the Massoretic reading, Lacocque comments, 'The words "King Nebuchadnezzar" moreover appear nine times in this chapter. The Masoretic editors would have certainly been sensitive to the unexpected change in construction' (p. 63).

7. According to Montgomery, 'to make answer' has a legal flavor, i.e. to make defense (p. 206).

8. As Lacocque points out (p. 63), *'îtay* is inseparable from the participle *yākil*. *'îtay* can be understood to be replacing the copula which is usually either left unexpressed in Biblical Aramaic or is represented by a personal pronoun (see Franz Rosenthal, *A Grammar of Biblical Aramaic* [Wiesbaden: Otto Harrassowitz, 1964] 41, section 95). Cf. Dan. 2.26, *ha'îtāyk kāhel*, 'are you able?' Consequently, I read the sentence as 'if he is able, our God whom we serve, to deliver us...' Cf. this translation with those of Montgomery (p. 206), and Lacocque (p. 62). Translations, like those of the RSV and KJV, which read something along the order of 'If it be so, our God... is able...' are guided less by grammar than by a theological bias against questioning God's ability. See P.W. Coxon, 'Daniel 3.17: A Linguistic and Theological Problem', *VT* 26 (1976) 400-405.

9. On the various pieces of clothing, see S.A. Cook 'The Articles of Dress in Dan. 3.21', *Journal of Philology* (1899) 306-13.

10. Following the suggested reading that *šlh* is an error for *šālū*. Cf. Montgomery's paraphrase (p. 216). See also his discussion of the alternative ways of reading this text (p. 219); and the recent work of Shalom M. Paul, 'Daniel 3.29: A Case Study of "Neglected" Blasphemy', *JNES* 42 (1983) 291-94.

11. The LXX, however, does have a temporal introductory clause, 'In his eighteenth year'. If this is, as Lacocque suggests (p. 56), borrowed from Jer. 52.29, the Greek version implies that Nebuchadnezzar's erection of the image is a commemoration of the destruction of Jerusalem and its temple. The work *ḥnk*, 'dedicated', also links the image with the temple (cf. 1 Kgs 8.63; 2 Chron. 7.5, 9; Ezra 6.16, 17) and the city (cf. Neh. 12.17).

12. This association was made as early as Hippolytus (ii, 15); see the discussion of Montgomery (p. 195).

13. Cf. Robert A. Anderson, *Signs and Wonders: A Commentary on the Book of Daniel* (Grand Rapids: Eerdmans, 1984) 29-30; and Baldwin, 99.

14. 'Fall down' and 'pay homage' are the words and acts of worship (cf. Dan. 2.46). *Sgd* appears only in contexts dealing with the worship of idols (cf. Isa. 44.15, 17, 19; 46.6). the noun itself, *ṣlm*, is often used in reference to idols (e.g. 2 Kgs 11.18; Ezek. 16.17; Num. 33.52), but its usage is not confined to this (cf. e.g. Pss. 39.7; 73.20). The nature of the 'image' in Daniel 2 is, of course, ambiguous. None of the characters in the story refer to the image as an idol, but the reader is aware that, at least on one level, the image represents the idol of human pride and power.

15. Cf. Lacocque's comment, 'The absence of any formal identification is not necessarily a weakness... In any case, the stele represents the empire and is the manifestation of a grotesque hubris' (59). Montgomery also (following Jephet Ibn 'Ali, *Commentary on Daniel*, 1889) regards the image as 'a symbol of allegiance to the empire' (p. 195).

16. Sternberg argues that repetitions can be varied in five ways: 1. expansion or addition, 2. truncation or ellipsis, 3. change of order, 4. grammatical transformation, 5. substitution (see pp. 390-93).

17. Although an attempt at historical reconstruction rather than a literary reading, cf. William Shea's interpretation of this story as the swearing of a loyalty oath after a rebellion during Nebuchadnezzar's reign, 'Daniel 3: Extra-Biblical Texts and the Convocation on the Plain of Dura', *AUSS* 20 (1982) 29-52.

18. Several scholars have seen the repetitions in this story to have a humorous and/or satirical function. Cf. Edwin Good, 'Apocalyptic as Comedy: The Book of Daniel', *Semeia* 32 (1984) 41-70, esp. 52; Towner, *Daniel*, 48; Baldwin, 102.

19. Sternberg, 422.

20. While the omission of Daniel is understandable from the standpoint of the story's transmission, Daniel's absence is, nonetheless, surprising to the final form reader (cf. Towner's puzzlement, *Daniel*, p. 47). One might assume that, since he passed the provincial post on to his friends (2.49), he was not among those summoned to the gathering and thus, was not confronted with the critical situation. Or one could suppose that the Chaldeans do not implicate Daniel because he is a favorite of the king.

Porteous notes ' . . . to bring Daniel into this chapter as worthy of punishment for loyalty to a God whom Nebuchadnezzar, according to the previous chapter, had acknowledged so handsomely, would have seemed very strange' (p. 55). Although Porteous is referring to the narrator's logic, one might see a slightly different version of his thought plausible in terms of Nebuchadnezzar's logic. If Nebuchadnezzar is, in the least, in awe of Daniel's rather superhuman ability as the end of ch. 2 suggests, would he require this quasi-divine figure to bow to an image, the significance of which (if this image can be associated with the image in the dream) Daniel himself had explained to the king to begin with? Of course, such a hypothesis leaves Daniel's character somewhat questionable since he does nothing to aid his friends. But, then, Shadrach, Meshach, and Abednego are not assertive characters either; they simply respond to the situation that is presented to them.

21. Lacocque writes, ' . . . in reality the accusation is based on facts. What is slanderous is presenting the Jews as poor administrators of the affairs of the kingdom' (p. 61).

22. Her speech takes the form of a reminder—she may or may not be making this up.

23. James Wharton ('Daniel 3.16-18', *Int* 39 [1985] 170-76) puts it nicely, ' . . . this unconditional affirmation of integrity asserts that no threat and no conceivable outcome can deter these witnesses from their commitment to the highest and best that they know. They cannot answer for God in this situation, but they can answer for themselves. From the human side, and *even if that were the only side there is*, they propose to stand their ground' (pp. 174-75).

24. See note 8.

25. Curt Kuhl, *Die drei Männer im Feuer* (Giessen: Alfred Töpelmann, 1930) 18.

26. Cf. the satirical treatment of idol worship in 2 Isaiah, particularly ch. 44.

27. Our expectation of death might also be controlled by genre. It has been argued that the story displays the characteristics of a martyr legend; see e.g. Collins, 55; Kuhl, 71-76; Porteous, 55-56. The only clear examples that we have of martyr legends, however, postdate this story. Perhaps it is more accurate to say that our expectations are guided by less formal elements, plot- and theme-oriented allusions and paradigms (see the discussion of allusion and paradigm in the Introduction) or even our common human experience.

28. Porteous, 59.

29. Lacocque, 66.

30. Lacocque also observes (p. 66) that, just as the ram is substituted for Isaac, so the executioners are substituted for the three Jews.

31. Kuhl, 39.

32. See the discussion of suspense in the Introduction (under 'Plot Structure' and the discussion in Sternberg (pp. 264-65).

33. The narrator also refers to both parties as 'these (or those) men' (see vv. 22 and 23).

34. Kuhl identifies this as a 'Märchenmotiv' (pp. 32-33).

35. Cf. Lacocque, 61-62.

36. The pause is indicated in the Massoretic text by a *pe*, the mark of an open paragraph. Furthermore, when our attention is returned to Nebuchadnezzar in v. 23, it is clear that we have experienced an implicit temporal ellipsis of at least a few minutes. (On implicit and explicit ellipses, see the discussion of narrative tempo in the Introduction and the discussion in Genette, pp. 106-109.) At some point a fourth man has joined the original three, the bonds have been loosened, and the men have begun walking around. This activity, however, is not reported, but is later understood to have taken place.

37. Kuhl, 38.

38. Ibid., 39.

39. Cf. Lacocque: ' . . . only the king sees the miracle (vv. 24-25); for the miracle is never seen except by the one whom it concerns. . . ' (p. 66).

40. On surprise, see the discussion of narrative interest under 'Plot Structure' in the Introduction, and the discussion in Sternberg, 256-60, 309-20.

41. Plöger, 63-64.

42. Of this Good writes 'the thought will not down that the list in v. 27 would have been complete had not some weary copyist decided, "Oh, to hell with it!"' ('Apocalyptic as Comedy', p. 52).

43. See Joseph Campbell, *A Hero with a Thousand Faces* (Princeton: Princeton University, 1949) and the discussion of rite of passage in Chapter 1.

44. Of course, the interpreter has the right to focus on the persecuted's point of view; see e.g. the provocative readings of James Wharton, 'Daniel 3.16-18', and Robert McAfee Brown, 'Furnaces and Faith: "But If Not. . ."' in *Unexpected News: Reading the Bible with Third World Eyes* (Philadelphia: Westminster, 1984) 142-56. However, the story itself clearly elevates the oppressor's point of view.

45. Sternberg argues that all biblical narratives are about the acquisition of knowledge about God (pp. 176-79).

46. Montgomery, 216.

47. Wharton, 171-72.

48. Lacocque, 66.

49. Lacocque sees this analogy in terms of aggadic development (p. 60).

50. This level of interpretation explains one of the mimetic problems of the story: Why were not other Jews brought up on similar charges?

51. This interpretation on metaphorical grounds is supported by the narrator's collective portrayal of Shadrach, Meshach, and Abednego. The fact that none of these three exhibits an independent personality makes their association with the Jewish nation more apparent.

52. This issue is also prominent in the story of Daniel 1.

53. Cf. the suffering servant songs of 2 Isaiah, 42:1-4; 49.1-6; 50.4-11; 52.13–53.12.

54. Lacocque, 66.

Notes to Chapter 4: Daniel 3.31–4.34

1. Referred to in this work as Daniel 4.

2. The root of *harhōrîn* is dubious. It may come, according to Montgomery (p. 227) from *hrh*, 'to conceive'. *harhar* seems to be used in later Rabbinic writings to refer to 'impure' dreams. Ibn Ezra speaks of 'a mental *harhor* without ejaculation'. The sexual connotations do not seem amiss to the post-Freudian reader when one considers the phallic image of the tree (cf. also the gold image in ch. 3!) and its subsequent castration. However one nuances the word, I think it consistent with the story to surmise that the 'imaginings' are rather unpleasant. For discussion and citations of this word, see Montgomery, pp. 226-27, and Lacocque, p. 72.

3. On identifying these four classes of sages, see Delcor, pp. 110-11. However one translates these titles, the emphasis here, as in ch. 2 and later in ch. 5, is on the variety of specialists who are of no help to the king. In other words, the listing magnifies Daniel's ability.

4. *'ānēs* occurs in the Hebrew Bible only in Esth. 1.8 in the sense of 'force' or 'compel'. It occurs in Rabbinic literature as 'force' or 'outrage'. Here the sense seems to be 'no mystery disturbs you', 'no mystery outrages (or is too outrageous for) you'. See Montgomery, p. 228.

5. Or a wakeful one.

6. Aramaic reads 'his hair grew long like eagles and his nails like birds'.

7. I have taken *dî* in this instance to be an indicator of direct speech, cf. Dan. 2.25; 5.7; 6.6, 8, 14. See Rosenthal, section 36. *dî*, of course, can also be translated here as a relative pronoun, 'whose', or as a causal connective, 'for'.

8. On the relation of this genre to Daniel 4, see Collins, *Daniel*, 61-62.

9. See my discussion in the Introduction as well as Genette (pp. 259-60), who would call this addressee the intradiegetic narratee who corresponds to the intradiegetic narrator (i.e. Nebuchadnezzar).

10. According to Genette (p. 260), this would be the extradiegetic narratee who is not to be confused with the fictive, i.e. intradiegetic, narratee.

11. Of course, Nebuchadnezzar does not actually break the frame of

artistic space, but the ambiguity of his addressee changes the borders, allowing the artistic space to be expanded. See Uspensky, pp. 137-40.

12. The Massoretic placement of this doxology with the preceding story rather than with Daniel 4 attests to its ambiguous relationship to its context.

13. On curiosity as opposed to suspense, see the discussion of narrative interest in the Introduction and in Sternberg, pp. 284-85.

14. See Deut. 13.1-2 (2-3); 28.46; Isa. 8.18; 20.3.

15. See Exod. 7.13; Deut. 4.34; 6.22; 7.19; 26.8; 29.3 (2); 34.11; Neh. 9.10; Pss. 78.43; 135.9; Jer. 32.20, 21.

16. Deut. 13.1 (2), 2 (3); Isa. 8.18; 20.3.

17. Or in Genette's terms (p. 260), an extradiegetic narrator.

18. Cf. Genesis 41, where the Pharaoh's crucial dreams are told to the reader at the moment Pharaoh dreams them.

19. Contra Humphreys, 'A Life-Style for Diaspora'.

20. Slotki (p. 30) observes this foreshadowing device. Peter Coxon makes an interesting suggestion on the basis of an Arabic etymology that the word is a *double-entendre* that plays upon both the meanings of 'flourishing, prosperous' and 'foolish', 'weakminded'. See 'The Great Tree of Daniel 4', in *A Word in Season: Essays in Honor of William McKane*, ed. J.D. Martin and P.R. Davies (JSOTSup 42; Sheffield: JSOT, 1986) 91-111, esp. 96-97.

21. One particular metaphor, Ps. 92.12-15 (Eng.), in which people are imaged as plants, casts a highly ironic light upon Nebuchadnezzar's statement in Dan. 4.1 (Eng. 4.4). In Psalm 92 the righteous 'flourish like the palm tree, and grow like a cedar in Lebanon. They are planted in the house of the Lord; they flourish in the courts of our God'. In direct contrast, Nebuchadnezzar, who, by Daniel's implication is unrighteous, flourishes in his own house, which, as we discover in 4.26-27 (Eng. 4.29-30), is more important to him than the house of any deity.

22. See Geo Widengren, *The King and the Tree of Life in Ancient Near Eastern Religion* (Uppsala: Lundequistska, 1951) and Mircea Eliade, *Patterns in Comparative Religion*, trans. Rosemary Sheed (New York: Sheed & Ward, 1958) 265-326.

23. Donald Gowan, *When Man Becomes God: Humanism and Hybris in the Old Testament* (PTMS 6; Pittsburgh: Pickwick, 1975) 110.

24. Heaton, 149; Louis F. Hartman, 'The Great Tree and Nabuchodonosor's Madness', *The Bible in Current Catholic Thought*, ed. John L. McKenzie (New York: Herder and Herder, 1962) 75-82, see 78-79; and the more extensive comparison of Alexander DiLella, 'Daniel 4.7-14: Poetic Analysis and Biblical Background', in *Mélanges bibliques et orientaux en l'honneur de M. Henri Cazelles*, ed. A. Caquot and M. Delcor (Alter Orient und Altes Testament 212; Neukirchen-Vluyn: Neukirchener Verlag, 1981) 247-58, esp. 255-58.

25. Or in Genette's terms, extradiegetical narrator.

26. Montgomery was, I think, the first to suggest that the change of person represents more than simply a lapse on the part of the author. He wrote, '. . . it has not been observed by the comm. that the same phenomenon appears in the book of Tobit, which begins with the ego of the hero and passes over into the 3d pers. at 3.7. . . The change of person in both stories is due to an unconscious dramatic sense. In Tobit the hero speaks in the first act, but when the drama passes to other scenes and characters, the ordinary narrative style of the 3d pers. is adopted. And so in our story, in which the alleged edict form sat lightly on the composer's mind, dramatically the account of the king's madness is told in the 3d pers., for of that he would not have been a sane witness; the change of person is anticipated somewhat too early in v. 16. The dramatic propriety involved appears from the fact that probably most readers do not stumble over the incongruity' (p. 223).

27. Cf. Montgomery's observation, 'The story is deftly told. The seer was Daniel to the Jewish readers, but Belteshazzar to the court' (p. 225). On naming as an indicator of perceptual point of view, see Berlin, pp. 59-61.

28. Gowan recalls that, according to Niebuhr, there are three types of pride: the pride of power, the pride of knowledge, and the pride of virtue. Gowan observes that the Old Testament is barely aware of the last two but is acutely conscious of the first (p. 20). I think one could legitimately question, however, if in this story (whether the narrator acknowledges it or not) Daniel is not dangerously close to the pride of knowledge. He, at least, now seems to be taking his wisdom for granted and he easily accepts (even divine) credit without disclaimer.

29. Cf. Lacocque's understated contrast of this passage to Dan. 3.16-18: '. . . there is a great distance between the polemic in 3.16-18 and Daniel's wish as expressed in 4.16' (p. 74).

30. This instance in which the character intends one thing, but God hears another, gives the reader the license of suspicion. We are not required to take Nebuchadnezzar's speech (at this point or any other) at face value.

31. Others have seen the connection between this story and Genesis 11. Cf. DiLella, 'Daniel 4.7-14', 255, 257-58; G.A.F. Knight, 'The Book of Daniel', in *The Interpreter's One-Volume Commentary on the Bible*, ed. C.M. Laymon (Nashville: Abingdon, 1971) 436-50, esp. 441; J. Steinmann, *Daniel: Texte français, introduction et commentaires* (Bruges: Desclée de Brouwer, 1961) cited by DiLella, no page number given.

32. This theme of dominion—the grasping of it and the loss of it—plays ironically on the theme of the Genesis 1 creation story. There humanity is given dominion over all the birds, fish and beasts. Here in Daniel 4, the one who has seized dominion is one who must become like a bird-beast over which other humans have dominion.

33. In a sense, the progression of Nebuchadnezzar's recognition of divine

sovereignty is very like the plagues and the hardening of Pharaoh's heart in the Exodus story. Not until God strikes the Pharaoh's household with the death of his firstborn son, does Pharaoh relent and allow the people to go.

34. As many scholars have recognized, both the first person narrative voice, as well as many of the motifs in Daniel 4, are reminiscent of the Nabonidus traditions. (The relationship between the Nabonidus material and the book of Daniel has been a major topic of interest in Daniel studies; see e.g. the work of W. Dommershausen, *Nabonid im Buche Daniel* [Mainz: Grünewald, 1964]; D.N. Freedman, 'The Prayer of Nabonidus', *BASOR* 145 [1957] 31-32; Martin McNamara, 'Nabonidus and the Book of Daniel', *ITQ* 37 [1970] 131-49; A. Mertens, *Das Buch Daniel im Lichte der Texte vom Toten Meer* [SBM 12; Stuttgart: Katholisches Bibelwerk, 1971]; W. von Soden, 'Eine babylonische Volksüberlieferung in den Danielerzählungen', *ZAW* 53 [1935] 81-89.) The Nabonidus literature often associated with Daniel 4 are the Harran inscriptions (published by C.J. Gadd, 'The Harran Inscriptions of Nabonidus', *Anatolian Studies* 8 [1958] 35-92; see also *ANET*, 562-63) and the 'Prayer of Nabonidus' (Nab or 4Q) found at Qumran (published by J.T. Milik, '"Prière de Nabonide" et autres écrits d'un cycle de Daniel', *RB* 63 [1956] 407-15). The king's extended absence from Babylon is described in the Harran inscriptions. In the Prayer of Nabonidus, the Most High afflicts the king with a disease that lasts seven years. The text implies that the disease is a result of sins that are remitted by a Jewish exorcist. Daniel 4 shares with the Nabonidus material some basic blocks of tradition, but the blocks, as they stand in Daniel 4, have been reshaped and repainted to produce a very different effect. The absence from Babylon is punishment, not a deity's act of protection. The disease is madness. The sin is hubris. The Jew involved is merely an interpreter not an exorcist. And, of course, the king is Nebuchadnezzar, not Nabonidus. (For a more detailed discussion of the contrasts, see A. Dupont-Sommer, *The Essene Writings from Qumran*, trans. G. Vermes [Cleveland: World, 1961] 321-25; and Collins, *Daniel*, 62-63.) The result is a story about sovereignty, knowledge, pride, and one of the more infamous kings in Jewish history. The similarities of Daniel 4 to the Nabonidus literature do not function as allusion (i.e. the reader is not expected to know the Nabonidus stories in order to fully appreciate Daniel 4), but rather, the similarities function to *displace* the Nabonidus material (cf. Lacocque, p. 75), much in the same way that David's slaying of Goliath attempts to displace Elkanan's slaying of the giant.

35. See the discussion of short story in the Introduction.

36. W. Shea, 'Further Literary Structures in Daniel 2-7: An Analysis of Daniel 4', *AUSS* 23 (1985) 193-202.

37. In terms of form, he connects character dialogue, bits of straight narration, and doxologies. In terms of content, he associates pieces of the story which have the same vocabulary, the same subject matter, and similar actions.

38. Taken with slight variation from Shea (p. 202). He enumerates the verses according to the English Bible.

39. See above, note 26; Montgomery, 223.

40. My punctuation suggests that he sings his doxology at the end of 'seven times'. See above, note 7.

41. Cf. R. Meyer, *Das Gebet des Nabonid* (Berlin: Akademie, 1962) 101-104, who compares the Prayer of Nabonidus with the framework of Job; and also J. Gammie, 'On the Intention and Sources of Daniel 1-6', 284-85.

42. It is impossible, in my estimation, to determine which is the older or younger text; consequently, if one assumes that allusion must be based upon a history of literature, there is no way to determine if Daniel 4 is actually alluding to Ecclesiastes 8. Ecclesiastes 8 could, quite possibly, represent a truism, a widely accepted picture of the world, and would, from earliest times, have been part of an audience's experience of Daniel 4. (On audiences' appropriations of pre-existing patterns in the world, see Rabinowitz, '"What's Hecuba to Us?", 252-56.) The similarity of scenario and vocabulary invites a reading of Ecclesiastes 8 as a companion text to Daniel 4, particularly because some of this vocabulary, e.g. 'rule' and 'sentence', occurs in few other places. When such an invitation is accepted, the reader discovers that the conversation between the two texts sets an ironic tone for the discussion of kingship.

43. The translation is basically that of the RSV although I have retranslated some portions to emphasize the common terms and to minimize the gender exclusive language of the text. In several instances the grammar has been altered slightly. The words and phrases that this text has in common with Daniel 4 are italicized.

44. Ps. 145:10-13a, RSV, altered by the author.

45. For a less caustic reading of Nebuchadnezzar's doxologies, see W.S. Towner, 'The Poetic Passages of Daniel 1-6'.

46. Cf. Towner, *Daniel*, 59.

47. Mary Daly, *Beyond God the Father* (Boxton: Beacon Press, 1973) 19.

48. This is the only occurrence of this term in biblical Aramaic; however, its kinship with the Hebrew term *g'h* suggests that its basic meaning has to do with height, and can be interpreted positively or negatively according to context.

49. Perhaps this indicates that the God of heaven is also uncomfortable with this ambiguous testimony of Nebuchadnezzar.

50. Chatman writes: 'In "unreliable narration" the narrator's account is at odds with the implied reader's surmises about the story's real intentions. The story undermines the discourse. We conclude, by "reading out", between the lines, that the events and existents could not have been "like that", and so we hold the narrator suspect... The implied author has established a secret

communication with the implied reader' (p. 233). Cf. also Booth, *The Rhetoric of Fiction*, 304-309, 432.

Because the character-narrator Nebuchadnezzar is built around the reputation of a historical personage, the effect of the story is dependent upon an unspoken familiarity with history on both the parts of the implied external narrator and the implied external narratee. The historical Nebuchadnezzar was never a convert to Israelite religion. If he worshipped a 'Most High', he certainly did not identify the deity with the god of the Jews. If the reader knows this, then what are we to make of this testimony? The reader faces the same situation in the book of Jonah, where the story describes the conversion and subsequent sparing of Nineveh, but the reader knows that Nineveh, as well as Jonah's precious Jerusalem temple, is eventually destroyed. In light of this information, how then does the reader interpret the role of God in the story of Jonah?

51. The irony of re-membering history parallels yet another dimension of the dream in Daniel 2: In a diachronic reading of the dream, the great image represents a chronological sequence of kings or kingdoms. The stone destroys all simultaneously—the 'first' are destroyed with the 'last' as if in attempt to exorcise a part of history that still troubled later readers. Here in Daniel 4 this part of history is not exorcised but substantially revised.

Notes to Chapter 5: Daniel 5

1. The word *ṭeʿēm* is an ambiguous word that can mean 'taste' (cf. Dan. 4.22 [Eng. 4.25], 29 [Eng. 4.32]; 5.21), 'counsel' (cf. Dan. 2.14; 6.1 [Eng. 5.31]) or 'decree' (cf. Dan 3.10, 29; 4.3 [Eng. 4.6]; 6.27 [Eng. 6.26]). In the context of consuming food or drink, it has the sense of 'taste'. However, the intoxicating effect of wine allows the other meanings to play as well. Consequently, the phrase might be rendered 'when he tasted the wine' or 'under the influence (i.e. the decree or the counsel) of the wine'.

2. Literally, 'the knots of his loins were loosened'. Cf. v. 12, where 'to loosen knots' is used of Daniel's ability to solve mysteries.

3. *taltî* (spelled *taltāʾ* in vv. 16, 29) might be an official title. The expression may mean to rule (or ruler) third in rank to the king, or to rule (or ruler of) a third of the kingdom. See Montgomery's discussion of this word and its difficulties, 256-57.

4. Here, the MT repeats 'your father the king'.

5. See note 2.

6. MT omits 'the days of'.

7. Or 'received'; *qabal* can mean either.

8. See the Excursus in Chapter 2.

9. The offering and conferring of a reward are elements found in Daniel 2 but not in Daniel 4.

10. Cf. Humphreys, 'A Life-Style for Diaspora'.

11. Cf. Collins, *Daniel*, 67.

12. Collins (pp. 67-68) observes that the main plot variation in Daniel 5 is Daniel's indictment of the king. We will find as we read the story that there are many other, perhaps more subtle, differences that are equally important to the story.

13. Stories that are at least loosely connected with one another (by chronology, characters, location, etc.)—and most of the narrative books in the Hebrew Bible are constructed in this manner—are usually linked by a *waw* if not by a transition or introductory phrase (e.g. 'after these things').

14. See the discussion on Daniel 3 concerning the ambiguity of the image.

15. We need not rely on historical information for this understanding, though historical information does support this. One need only read the introduction to the book in Dan. 1.1-2, Daniel's interpretations of Nebuchadnezzar's dreams in chs. 2 and 4, and Nebuchadnezzar's own words in Dan. 4.30, to see that the narrator has portrayed Nebuchadnezzar from the beginning as a king of great accomplishment. This will be further supported by Daniel's speech later in Daniel 5.

16. Indeed, the character Belshazzar son of Nebuchadnezzar stands in a tradition of weak sons of strong fathers, e.g. the sons of Eli, the sons of Samuel, the son of Solomon.

17. There were, after all, supposedly no divine images in the Jerusalem temple. From a pagan point of view, the vessels might be considered substitutive.

18. The narrator expects the implied reader—a reader with a knowledge of and an investment in the larger story of Israel—to have an interest in the temple vessels; see Dan. 1.2.

19. Cf. Towner, *Daniel*, 72.

20. Lacocque, 94.

21. The question here is one of motivation. Although Belshazzar's action is later interpreted by Daniel (and implicitly so by God, the narrator, and the reader) to be a direct affront to the lord of heaven, we are not justified in assuming that Belshazzar intends his act to be such. There is no evidence in the text at this point in the story to suggest that Belshazzar is attempting to challenge directly the god of Jerusalem or the god of heaven. If that were his intention, then he should not be surprised at the divine response. We have seen thus far in Daniel other examples of the difference between a character's intention and how God, the narrator and the reader interpret the character's action or speech. In Daniel 3 Nebuchadnezzar asks Shadrach, Meshach, and Abednego, 'Who is the god who will deliver you from my hands?' His intention is to challenge the three men who stand before him, but in actuality his question challenges the god whom they serve. Likewise,

in Daniel 4, when Nebuchadnezzar stands surveying Babylon and praises himself, he never intends to offend any deity. Nevertheless, the God of heaven interprets the comment to be offensive.

22. This depiction of what has happened to the temple vessels, as with the other traditions concerning the capture of the vessels (e.g. 2 Chron. 36.7, 18; Ezra 1.7-11; Isa. 52.11; Jer. 27.19-22) rather than their complete destruction (i.e. the melting down of the vessels for their elementary materials, e.g. 2 Kgs 24.13; 25.13-17) represents a theme of hope for and restoration of the exiles and their way of life. See Peter Ackroyd, 'The Temple Vessels—A Continuity Theme', *VTS* 23 (1972) 166-81. Like the ark of the Lord housed in the temple of Dagon (1 Samuel 5)—to the Philistines a symbol of their victory, but in fact a cloaked, divine power—the vessels represent to Nebuchadnezzar the defeat of the god of Jerusalem, but to the reader they represent Adonai's presence and ultimate victory.

23. In this sense, Lacocque's intuition concerning Belshazzar is correct (see above note) though I would rephrase his assessment slightly: Belshazzar is trying to reassure himself by degrading what intimidates him. However, what intimidates him is not the god of Jerusalem *per se*, but the reputation of his father.

24. One might also read this episode in a less Freudian vein as Belshazzar's attempt to assume some of Nebuchadnezzar's power and prestige by associating himself with the objects of his father's victory.

25. See note 1.

26. Contra Anderson, who characterizes Belshazzar's act as 'rash' (p. 53).

27. William Shea ('Further Literary Structures in Daniel 2-7: An Analysis of Daniel 5, and the Broader Relationships within Chapters 2-7', *AUSS* 23 [1985] 277-95) has pointed to the Nabonidus Chronicle (*ANET*, 306) as evidence that this list of gods in Daniel 5 reflects an historical occurrence. According to the Chronicle, Nabonidus, in the last year of his reign, gathered numerous gods from other cities and transported them to Babylon, supposedly for the purpose of reinforcing the city's defenses. Based upon the Chronicle and excavational evidence at Babylon, Shea states (pp. 306-307), '. . . there was no shortage of gods for Belshazzar and his friends to praise. . . for a considerable number of gods had been added to those normally present in the city'. Shea's observations are helpful in that they point out that, in the ancient world, the stockpiling of gods could be equated with the stockpiling of power, an idea which is at work in the story of Daniel 5. The list in the context of Daniel 5 suggests that, for Belshazzar, more gods mean more favor, more success, more power. However, it is unfortunate that Shea does not distinguish between historical information and the information provided by the story. The story character Belshazzar expresses no concern for the defense of the city. The story does not mention that the gods are new

to Babylon. Perhaps the storyteller does borrow an historical motif, but rather than attempting to describe accurately what went on in Babylon on the eve of its destruction, the storyteller uses the list of deities as a reflection of Belshazzar's personal ambition.

28. For a similar description, cf. Nah. 2.11.

29. Cf. Ezek. 7.17; 21.12 (Eng. 21.7).

30. Driver observes the different wording here and comments: 'the king's alarm was reflected in the tones of his voice' (p. 63).

31. Either Belshazzar's mother or grandmother. Cf. Montgomery's discussion, pp. 257-58, and Lacocque, p. 97. We, of course, are only concerned with how she can be identified in the context of the story. Her historical identity is a moot point since, historically, Belshazzar was not Nebuchadnezzar's son.

32. Lacocque, 97.

33. See the discussion of character types in the Introduction and in Berlin (pp. 23-42).

34. The similarity in the names of the sage and king is striking. Both, we assume, reflect the name of Nebuchadnezzar's god. Is the queen flaunting to the king that Nebuchadnezzar thought, as evidenced in his naming his sage and his son almost identical names, as much of this sage as he did of his son?

35. Anderson, 57.

36. Lacocque, 97.

37. Is the name Belteshazzar, in the king's view, too close to his own name? See note 34.

38. Lacocque, 97.

39. Cf. O. Plöger, 87.

40. So Heaton, 160, and cf. Lacocque's comment concerning Heaton's interpretation, 98.

41. Contra Porteous, 80.

42. Lacocque, 101. I disagree, however, with Lacocque's interpretation that Belshazzar's promise of reward is an 'attempt to bribe the "divine" and to change a "fate"'.

43. Heaton, 160; also Hartman and DiLella, 189.

44. Towner, *Daniel*, 74.

45. Porteous, 80.

46. Most commentators have discussed the sternness of Daniel's response. Heaton (p. 160) indicates that the tone of Daniel's reply is surprising and stands in direct contrast to Daniel's earlier attitude toward Nebuchadnezzar in ch. 4. Porteous (pp. 80-81) admits that Daniel's refusal of reward is out of character and rather limply suggests that the refusal might be intended as a lesson to Jewish sages concerning their dealings with foreign rulers. Cf. also Anderson, 59. Some scholars have expressed no surprise at the tone of

Daniel's response; they have, nevertheless, attempted to justify Daniel's rudeness by magnifying Belshazzar's transgression, e.g. Lacocque, Hartman and DiLella.

47. Cf. Anderson, 59.

48. Heaton, 160.

49. Cf. Lacocque's response to this, 101.

50. Cf. Deut. 32.39; 1 Sam.2.7; Ps. 75.8; Job 5.11-16; Sir. 7.11; Tob. 4.19.

51. See Collins, *Daniel*, 68, on the genre of indictment speech.

52. Cf. Anderson, 59, Towner, *Daniel*, 74, Lacocque, 101.

53. None of the statements are subordinated to others; they are all connected by 'and'.

54. Nebuchadnezzar's strength is paralleled to God's in that, just as God raises and lowers 'whomever he pleases', so does Nebuchadnezzar.

55. Cf. the interpretations of H.L. Ginsberg, *Studies in Daniel*, 24-26; E.G.H. Kraeling, 'The Handwriting on the Wall', *JBL* 63 (1944) 11-18; D.N. Freedman, 'The Prayer of Nabonidus', *BASOR* 145 (1957) 31-32.

56. It should be noted that there are only three words, rendered with some degree of variation, in the LXX, the Vulgate, Theodotion, Josephus, and Jerome. For attempts to uncover the 'original' inscription and to justify the longer version in the Massoretic Text, cf. C.C. Torrey, 'Notes on the Aramaic Part of Daniel' in *Transactions of the Connecticut Academy of Arts and Sciences* 15 (1909) 241; A. Alt, 'Zur Menetekel-Inschrift', *VT* 4 (1954) 303-305; O. Eissfeldt, 'Die Menetekel-Inschrift und ihre Deutung', *ZAW* 63 (1951) 105-14; F. Zimmermann, 'Writing on the Wall: Daniel 5.25f', *JQR* 55 (1965) 201-207.

57. First argued by C. Clermont-Ganneau, *Recueil d'archéologie*, I (1886) 136-59.

58. Judging from some Qumran texts, e.g. the Habakkuk Scroll, and subsequent comparison of these texts with texts dealing with interpretation in Hebrew Scripture, playing upon words and embellishing the original texts seems to have been acceptable in the practice of *pesher* or interpretation. The clue to interpretation is often the double meaning of a word. See A. Finkel, 'The Pesher of Dreams and Scriptures', *RQ* 4 (1963) 357-70, particularly 360; Michael Fishbane, 'The Qumran Pesher and Traits of Ancient Hermeneutics', in *Proceedings of the Sixth World Congress of Jewish Studies* 1 (Jerusalem, 1977) 97-114; and L.H. Silberman, 'Unriddling the Riddle: A Study in the Scripture and Language of the Habakkuk Pesher', *RQ* 3 (1961) 323-64.

59. Lacocque's reading, that, because of Belshazzar's act, 'the Spirit is dislodged from the vases where it was hiding. . . then openly reveals itself on the whitewashed wall from whence it can never again be erased' (p. 95), is a little too melodramatic and simplistic to completely account for the severe judgment that falls upon the king.

60. Lacocque, 95.

61. Cf. Samuel's attitude in 1 Samuel 8.

62. Daniel's reading and interpreting the words on the wall is exemplary of the reading process itself: It is impossible to read with complete objectivity, without passing judgment, without becoming personally involved.

63. Cf. Hartman and DiLella, 190

64. Porteous, 81.

65. For example, Anderson's reading, 59, 62.

66. Hartman and DiLella, 190.

67. Cf. David M. Gunn's reading of the Exodus story, 'The "Hardening of Pharaoh's Heart": Plot, Character and Theology in Exodus 1–14', in *Art and Meaning: Rhetoric in Biblical Literature*, ed. D.J.A. Clines, D.M. Gunn, and A.J. Hauser (Sheffield: JSOT, 1982) 72-96, esp. 89.

68. And so security and presumption are issues that challenge the reader, the one interpreting, the one passing judgment upon the text. Do we, like the queen, think that once the interpretation is given, the meaning, and thus the problem, of the text is solved?

Notes to Chapter 6: Daniel 6 and Epilogue

1. Or, 'cannot be revoked'.

2. The meaning of the word is uncertain. It has been translated variously as musical instruments, food (Rashi: 'table'), concubines or female dancers. See Montgomery's discussion, 277-78. I have adopted his noncommittal word choice.

3. Literally, 'eaten the pieces', see Chapter 3, note 4.

4. See J. Collin's earlier classification of the stories in *The Apocalyptic Vision of the Book of Daniel* (Missoula: Scholars, 1977) 27-59, which P.R. Davies develops further in *Daniel*, 50-55.

5. Humphreys, 'A Life-Style for Diaspora'.

6. Daniel 6 has affinities with the other stories also, as we shall see in the course of our reading.

7. Montgomery writes (p. 272), 'Hardly a word in the O.T. has provoked more variety of interpretation than this (word) in its triple occurrence in the chap.'. For an excellent overview of the various translations and interpretations of *rgš*, see his discussion, pp. 272-73.

8. Cf. masculine noun form (Hebrew) in Ps. 55.14 (Eng. 55.15).

9. Cf. the Hebrew verb in Ps. 2.1 and the feminine noun in Ps. 64.3 (Eng. 64.2). In both cases, *rgš* parallels *sud* which seems to mean 'counsel together' or 'scheme'.

10. The Aramaic term *rgš* is used in the Targums to translate *hāmāh* ('to rage') in Ps. 46.7 (Eng. 46.6) and *šā'āh* ('to be in an uproar') in Isa. 17.12f. (See BDB, 921). Furthermore, *rgš* plays upon the word *rgz* which means to disturb, excite, enrage, rage.

11. As does Towner, *Daniel*, 81-82.

12. Cf. Edwin Good, *Irony in the Old Testament* (Philadelphia: Westminster, 1965; repr. Sheffield: Almond, 1981) 13-38.

13. On *iterative* narrative in which a singular narrative utterance describes an event that occurs more than once, see Genette, 115-60.

14. On the accusation as a subordinate genre in Daniel 6, see Collins, *Daniel*, 72.

15. For another case of the ambiguity of the direction of displeasure, cf. Judges 10, Jephthah's speech to his daughter.

16. The term employed is *zā'aq*, which usually means to cry for help or to cry in anguish, rather than *qārā'*, which can simply mean to call (loudly).

17. And perhaps also to the reader since these are the first words that we hear Daniel speak in the story.

18. The RSV translation 'I have done no wrong' unfortunately misses the word play and, in the context, suggests Daniel to be lying. 'Wrong' is relative. Daniel has defied the king's edict and has, according to the law, done 'wrong'. However, in doing 'wrong', Daniel has done nothing *harmful*. Just as the officials wanted the king to think that Daniel's defiance of the edict was injurious to the king himself, Daniel is saying that his defiance of the edict has nothing to do with his loyalty to the king.

19. The translation 'he was faithful to (or in the matter of)' is more appropriate than the RSV's 'he had trusted in' because the latter not only suggests passive belief, but also implies that Daniel is saved because he trusts in God's deliverance. The story clearly shows Daniel's faithfulness to be active. It is, according to the narrator, because of his active loyalty to God that God is actively loyal to him. The point of the story is not so much 'trust in' but 'fidelity to' both god and king.

20. Towner's pun, *Daniel*, 86.

21. Starting with the Septuagint translators, who confined the punishment to the two other prime ministers. See Porteous, p. 89. But, for the argument that the Septuagint is the older text, cf. Nathaniel Schmidt, 'Daniel and Androcles', *JAOS* 46 (1926) 1-7.

22. Porteous, 91.

23. This same motif of 'overkill' and the shadows that it casts on the characters involved can also be found in chs. 8 and 9 of Esther. The Esther narrative raises the question, when does defense become offense? Daniel 6 raises the question, when does punishment for wrongdoing become personal revenge? The book of Esther, of course, also shows other affinities with Daniel 6 in terms of form, theme, setting, and to some extent, characterization, e.g. of the king. In addition to Humphrey's work ('Life-style'), see Sandra Beth Berg, *The Book of Esther: Motifs, Themes and Structure* (Missoula, Montana: Scholars Press, 1979) 143-45; Ludwig A. Rosenthal, 'Die Josephsgeschichte mit den Büchern Ester und Daniel verglichen', *ZAW*

(1895) 278-84, and 'Nochmals der Vergleich Ester, Joseph–Daniel', *ZAW* 17 (1897) 125-28.

24. On the reconstitution of society as a comic device, see Good, 'Apocalyptic as Comedy', 55.

25. In other words, the motif of the 'irrevocable law of the Medes and Persians' contributes, as it does in the book of Esther, to the tension of the plot. The conflict produced by the irrevocable law, however, is a false construct. The reader cannot know this for sure until the end of the story, although Darius's struggle to rescue Daniel hints that this is the case. Consequently, Darius's decree at the end signals that the reader should back up and reinterpret what actually is at stake in the preceding situation.

26. Cf. the indictment of a certain king in Daniel 7, that he seeks 'to change the times and the *law*' (v. 25).

27. David M. Gunn ('The Anatomy of Divine Comedy: On Reading the Bible as Comedy and Tragedy', *Semeia* 32 [1984] 115-129) expresses it this way: ' . . . Yahweh, makes clear that to choose Yahweh, to "fear" Yahweh, to respond to Yahweh in faith, comes only by divine decree or out of human freedom. It cannot come by human decree. No one can secure God (it is a familiar theme!). The book is punctuated by decrees. The injunction to "worship the image" in chapter 3 gives place to "fear before the God of Daniel" in chapter 6. Against the irony of the king decreeing the worship of Yahweh (Daniel's god!) is set the irony of his unawareness that such is not his to decree. In humility he still plays God! Here is but the obverse of the tyrant who decrees worship of *other* gods. Both decrees are ultimately absurd. The irony, therefore, touches *all* who think to enforce religion—it is a message to Constantine, as it is to Antiochus' (p. 128).

28. Both kings also mention God's work in 'heaven and earth' but Nebuchadnezzar's use of this phrase comes in his later doxology (4.32 [Eng. 4.35]).

29. Tradition testifies to the uneasy placement of this hymn. The tradition reflected in the Massoretic text places the doxology at the end of ch. 3. Greek translators moved the material to the end of ch. 4 alongside vv. 34-35. Theodotion-Daniel moved the hymn back to its present place in the Aramaic text. Most modern English versions place the material at the beginning of ch. 4 because of the introductory nature of the formula and its consistency with the first person account that follows. On the different versions of Daniel, see Hartman and DiLella, 72-84, and Montgomery, 24-57.

30. Thus, in Humphrey's terms, 'a life-style for diaspora'.

31. Cf. ch. 9 and his question after the final vision in 12.6: 'How long shall it be till the end of these wonders?'

32. Gunn ('The Anatomy of Divine Comedy', 123), in stressing the importance of the Babylonian king's expanding knowledge of God, draws attention to the similarity with Pharaoh in Exodus 1–14. Gunn's line of thought on the theological significance (and irony) of divine recognition has

been germinal for this present reading of Daniel. See, for example, his comment ('The Hardening of Pharaoh's Heart', 83-84; and cf. p. 89): 'It is not only Egypt and the nations who will learn of God's power . . . Yahweh's demonstration of his power over the Egyptians is also bound up with his need to establish himself securely as Israel's God, the god of the covenantal promise, in the eyes of Israel . . . After all, what does it profit God if he "provides" but his people fail to identify their provider? It is a vulnerability of all gods! Yahweh needs Israel, just as Israel needs Yahweh. Thus by his signs and wonders Yahweh seeks to secure his identity.'

33. A helpful discussion of the names and nature of the 'god of Daniel' can be found in Davies, *Daniel*, 81-88.

34. The issue is being discussed in terms of epistemology—the knowledge of God. Why is recognition so important to God? Why is God so determined to gain the recognition of these kings? Can it be that epistemology casts a shadow on ontology—that God is not sovereign until God is recognized as sovereign?

35. The determinism that scholars have long recognized as characteristic of apocalyptic ideology, then, can be read in Daniel as an attempt to answer the irony of divine and human sovereignty that emerges from Daniel 1-6. Cf. Gunn, 'The Anatomy of Divine Comedy', 127-28.

36. The connection between lions and monarchs is playfully alluded to in the language used in 6.24, literally, 'the lions ruled over them'.

37. Ps 30.10 (Eng. 30.9).

WORKS CITED

Literary Criticism and Theory

General Works

Booth, Wayne C. *Critical Understanding: The Powers and Limits of Pluralism.* Chicago: University of Chicago, 1979.

—*The Rhetoric of Fiction.* Chicago: University of Chicago, 1961; reprint, 1983.

Chatman, Seymour. *Story and Discourse: Narrative Structure in Fiction and Film.* Ithaca: Cornell University, 1978.

Culler, Jonathan. *On Deconstruction: Theory and Criticism after Structuralism.* London: Routledge & Kegan Paul, 1983.

—*Structuralist Poetics: Structuralism, Linguistics, and the Study of Literature.* Ithaca, New York: Cornell University, 1975.

Eagleton, Terry. *Literary Theory: An Introduction.* Minneapolis: University of Minnesota, 1983.

Empson, William. *Seven Types of Ambiguity.* New York: New Directions, 1930; reprint, 1966.

Genette, Gerard. *Narrative Discourse: An Essay in Method.* Translated by J.E. Lewin. Ithaca: Cornell University, 1980.

Iser, Wolfgang. *The Act of Reading: A Theory of Aesthetic Response.* Baltimore: Johns Hopkins, 1978.

—*The Implied Reader: Patterns of Communication in Prose Fiction from Bunyan to Beckett.* Baltimore: Johns Hopkins University, 1974.

Jefferson, Ann and David Robey, eds. *Modern Literary Theory: A Comparative Introduction.* London: Batsford Academic and Educational Ltd, 1982.

Johnson, Barbara. 'The Critical Difference: BartheS/BalZac'. In *Contemporary Literary Criticism*, 439-46. Edited by Robert Con Davis. New York, London: Longman, 1986.

Kristeva, Julia. 'The Bounded Text'. In *Contemporary Literary Criticism: Modernism Through Post-Structuralism*, 448-66. Edited by Robert Con Davis. New York, London: Longman, 1986.

Miller, J. Hillis. 'The Critic as Host'. In *Deconstruction and Criticism*, 217-53. New York: Continuum, 1984.

Rabinowitz, Peter J. '"What's Hecuba to Us?" The Audience's Experience of Literary Borrowing'. In *The Reader in the Text: Essays on Audience and Interpretation*, 241-63. Edited by Susan R. Suleiman and Inge Crosman. Princeton: Princeton University, 1980.

Scholes, Robert and Robert Kellogg. *The Nature of Narrative.* Oxford: Oxford University, 1966.

Scholes, Robert. *Structuralism in Literature: An Introduction.* New Haven: Yale University, 1974.

Uspensky, Boris. *A Poetics of Composition: The Structure of the Artistic Text and Typology of a Compositional Form.* Translated by Valentina Zavarin and Susan Wittig. Berkeley: University of California, 1973.

Wellek, Rene and Austin Warren. *Theory of Literature*. New York: Harcourt, Brace & World, 1956.

Works Relating to Biblical Narrative

Alter, Robert. *The Art of Biblical Narrative*. New York: Basic Books, 1980.
Berlin, Adele. *Poetics and Interpretation of Biblical Narrative*. Sheffield: Almond, 1983
Jobling, David. 'Structuralism, Hermeneutics, and Exegesis: Three Recent Contributions to the Debate'. *USQR* 34 (1979): 135-47.
Keegan, Terence. *Interpreting the Bible: A Popular Introduction to Biblical Hermeneutics*. New York: Paulist, 1985.
Licht, Jacob. *Storytelling in the Bible*. Jerusalem: Magnes, Hebrew University, 1978.
McKnight, Edgar V. *The Bible and the Reader: An Introduction to Literary Criticism*. Philadelphia: Fortress, 1985.
Miscall, Peter. *The Workings of Old Testament Narrative*. Philadelphia: Fortress, 1983; Chico, California: Scholars, 1983.
Sternberg, Meir. *The Poetics of Biblical Narrative: Ideological Literature and the Drama of Reading*. Bloomington: Indiana University, 1985.

Comparative Religion and Literature

Aarne, A. and S. Thompson. *The Types of Folktale*. Folklore Fellows Communications 184. Helsinki: Suomalainen tiedeakatemia, 1964.
Campbell, Joseph. *A Hero with a Thousand Faces*. Princeton: Princeton University, 1949.
Eliade, Mircea. *Patterns in Comparative Religion*. Translated by Rosemary Sheed. New York: Sheed & Ward, 1958.
Gennep, Arnold van. *Rites of Passage*. Chicago: University of Chicago, 1960.
Propp, V. *Morphology of a Folktale*. 2nd edn, Austin: University of Texas, 1979.
Turner, Victor. *Dramas, Fields, and Metaphors*. Ithaca: Cornell University, 1974.
—*The Forest of Symbols*. Ithaca: Cornell University, 1967.
—*The Ritual Process*. Chicago: Aldine, 1969.
Widengren, Geo. *The King and the Tree of Life in Ancient Near Eastern Religion*. Uppsala: Lundequistska, 1951.

Biblical Studies

Ackroyd, Peter. 'The Temple Vessels—A Continuity Theme'. *VTS* 23 (1972): 166-81.
Alt, Albrecht. 'Zur Menetekel-Inschrift'. *VT* 4 (1954): 303-305.
Anderson, Robert A. *Signs and Wonders: A Commentary on the Book of Daniel*. Grand Rapids: Eerdmans, 1984.
Baldwin, Joyce. *Daniel*. Downers Grove, Illinois: Intervarsity, 1978.
Bentzen, Aage. *Daniel*. Tübingen: J.C.B. Mohr, 1937.
Berg, Sandra Beth. *The Book of Esther: Motifs, Themes and Structure*. Missoula, Montana: Scholars, 1979.
Blau, J. 'Über homonyme und angeblich homonyme Wurzeln'. *VT* 6 (1956): 242-48.

Brown, Francis, S.R. Driver and Charles A. Briggs. *The New Brown—Driver—Briggs—Gesenius Hebrew and English Lexicon with an Appendix containing the Biblical Aramaic*. Peabody, Massachusetts: Hendrickson 1979.

Brown, Robert McAfee. 'Furnaces and Faith: "But If Not . . . "'. In *Unexpected News: Reading the Bible With Third World Eyes*, 142-56. Philadelphia: Westminster, 1984.

Coats, George, ed. *Saga, Legend, Tale, Novella, Fable: Narrative Forms in Old Testament Literature*. JSOTSup 35. Sheffield: JSOT, 1985.

Collins, John J. *The Apocalyptic Vision of the Book of Daniel*. Missoula: Scholars, 1977.

—*Daniel, First Maccabees, Second Maccabees*. Wilmington, Delaware: Michael Glazier, 1981.

—*Daniel with an Introduction to Apocalyptic Literature*. FOTL 20. Grand Rapids: William B. Eerdmans, 1984.

Cook, S.A. 'The Articles of Dress in Dan. 3.21'. *Journal of Philology* (1899): 306-13.

Coxon, Peter W. 'Daniel 3.17: A Linguistic and Theological Problem'. *VT* 26 (1976): 400-405.

—'The Great Tree of Daniel 4'. In *A Word in Season: Essays in Honor of William McKane*, 91-111. Edited by J.D. Martin and P.R. Davies. JSOTSup 42. Sheffield: JSOT, 1986.

Davies, Philip R. *Daniel*. Sheffield: JSOT, 1985.

—'Daniel Chapter Two'. *JTS* 27 (1976): 392-401.

Delcor, M. *Le Livre de Daniel*. Paris: J. Gabalda, 1971.

Dexinger, Ferdinand. *Das Buch Daniel und seine Probleme*. SBS 36. Stuttgart: Katholisches Bibelwerk, 1969.

DiLella, Alexander. 'Daniel 4.7-14: Poetic Analysis and Biblical Background'. In *Mélanges bibliques et orientaux en l'honneur de M. Henri Cazelles*, 247-58. Edited by A. Caquot and M. Delcor. AOAT 212. Neukirchen-Vluyn: Neukirchener Verlag, 1981.

Dommershausen, W. *Nabonid im Buche Daniel*. Mainz: Grünewald, 1964.

Driver, S.R. *The Book of Daniel*. Cambridge: Cambridge University, 1905.

Dupont-Sommer, A. *The Essene Writings from Qumran*. Translated by G. Vermes. Cleveland: World, 1961.

Eissfeldt, Otto. 'Die Menetekel-Inschrift und ihre Deutung'. *ZAW* 63 (1951): 105-14.

Finkel, A. 'The Pesher of Dreams and Scriptures'. *RQ* 4 (1963): 357-70.

Fishbane, Michael. 'The Qumran Pesher and Traits of Ancient Hermeneutics'. *Proceedings of the Sixth World Congress of Jewish Studies* 1 (1977): 97-114.

Flusser, D. 'The Four Empires in the Fourth Sibyl and in the Book of Daniel'. *Israel Oriental Studies* 2 (1972): 148-75.

Freedman, David Noel. 'The Prayer of Nabonidus'. *BASOR* 145 (1957): 31-32.

Gadd, C.J. 'The Harran Inscriptions of Nabonidus'. *Anatolian Studies* 8 (1958): 35-92.

Gammie, John. 'On the Intention and Sources of Daniel 1-6'. *VT* 31 (1981): 282-92.

Ginsberg, H.L. 'The Composition of the Book of Daniel'. *VT* 4 (1954): 246-75.

—*Studies in Daniel*. New York: Jewish Theological Seminary of America, 1948.

Good, Edwin. 'Apocalyptic as Comedy: The Book of Daniel'. *Semeia* 32 (1984): 41-70.

—*Irony in the Old Testament*. Philadelphia: Westminster, 1965; repr. Sheffield: Almond, 1981.

Gowan, Donald. *When Man Becomes God: Humanism and Hybris in the Old Testament*. PTMS 6. Pittsburgh: Pickwick, 1975.

Gunn, David M. 'The "Hardening of Pharaoh's Heart": Plot, Character and Theology in Exodus 1-14'. In *Art and Meaning: Rhetoric in Biblical Literature*, 72-96. Edited by D.J.A. Clines, D.M. Gunn, and A.J. Hauser. Sheffield: JSOT, 1982.

—'The Anatomy of Divine Comedy: On Reading the Bible as Comedy and Tragedy', *Semeia* 32 (1984) 115-29.

Haag, Ernst. *Die Errettung Daniels aus der Löwengrube: Untersuchungen zum Ursprung der biblischen Danieltradition*. SBS 110. Stuttgart: Katholisches Bibelwerk, 1983.

Hals, Ronald M. 'Legend: A Case-Study in OT Form-Critical Terminology'. *CBQ* 34 (1972): 166-76.

Hartman, Louis. 'The Great Tree and Nabuchodonosor's Madness'. In *The Bible in Current Catholic Thought*, 75-82. Edited by John L. McKenzie. New York: Herder and Herder, 1962.

Hartman, Louis and Alexander A. DiLella. *The Book of Daniel*. Garden City, New York: Doubleday, 1978.

Hasel, G.F. 'The Four World Empires of Daniel 2 Against Its Near Eastern Environment'. *JSOT* 12 (1979): 17-30.

Heaton, E.W. *The Book of Daniel*. London: SCM, 1956.

Humphreys, W. Lee. 'A Life-Style for Diaspora: A Study of the Tales of Esther and Daniel'. *JBL* 92 (1973): 211-23.

—'Novella'. In *Saga, Legend, Tale, Novella, Fable*, 82-96. Edited by George Coats. JSOTSup 35. Sheffield: JSOT, 1985.

Johnson, A.R. 'The Primary Meaning of *g'l*. *VTS* 1 (1953): 66-77.

Keil, Carl Friedrich. *Biblischer Commentar über den Propheten Daniel*. Leipzig: Dörffling und Franke, 1869.

Knight, G.A.F. 'The Book of Daniel'. In *The Interpreter's One-Volume Commentary on the Bible*, 436-50. Edited by C.M. Laymon. Nashville: Abingdon, 1971.

Koch, Klaus (with T. Niewisch and J. Tubach). *Das Buch Daniel*. Darmstadt: Wissenschaftliche Buchgesellschaft, 1980.

Kraeling, E.G.H. 'The Handwriting on the Wall'. *JBL* 63 (1944): 11-18.

Kuhl, Curt. *Die drei Männer im Feuer*. Giessen: Alfred Töpelmann, 1930.

Lacocque, André. *The Book of Daniel*. Translated by David Pellauer. Atlanta: John Knox, 1979.

Lenglet, A. 'La structure littéraire de Daniel 2-7'. *Bib* 53 (1972): 169-90.

McNamara, Martin. 'Nabonidus and the Book of Daniel'. *ITQ* 37 (1970): 131-49.

Meinhold, A. 'Die Gattung der Josephgeschichte und des Estherbuches: Diasporanovelle, I, II'. *ZAW* 87 (1975): 306-24; *ZAW* 88 (1976): 79-93.

Mertens, A. *Das Buch Daniel im Lichte der Texte vom Toten Meer*. SBM 12. Stuttgart: Katholisches Bibelwerk, 1971.

Meyer, R. *Das Gebet des Nabonid*. Berlin: Akademie, 1962.

Milik, J.T. '"Prière de Nabonide" et autres écrits d'un cycle de Daniel'. *RB* 63 (1956): 407-15.

Mitchell, T.C. and R. Joyce. 'The Musical Instruments in Nebuchadrezzar's Orchestra'. In *Notes on Some Problems in the Book of Daniel*, 19-27. London: Tyndale, 1965.

Montgomery, J.A. *The Book of Daniel*. Edinburgh: T. & T. Clark, 1927; repr. 1950.

Mosis, R. '*gdl*'. *TDOT* II, 390-416. Grand Rapids: William B. Eerdmans, 1977.

Müller, H.-P. 'Märchen, Legende und Enderwartung: Zum Verständnis des Buches Daniel'. *VT* 26 (1976): 338-50.

Niditch, Susan and Robert Doran. 'The Success Story of the Wise Courtier: A Formal Approach'. *JBL* 96 (1977): 179-93.

Oppenheim, A.L. *The Interpretation of Dreams in the Ancient Near East*. Philadelphia: The American Philosophical Society, 1956.

Paul, Shalom M. 'Daniel 3.29: A Case Study of "Neglected" Blasphemy'. *JNES* 42 (1983): 291-94.

Plöger, Otto. *Das Buch Daniel*. Gütersloh: Gütersloher Verlagshaus/Gerd Mohn, 1965.

Porteous, Norman. *Daniel*. London: SCM, 1965.

Pritchard, James B., ed. *Ancient Near Eastern Texts Relating to the Old Testament*. 3rd edn with supplement. Princeton: Princeton University, 1969.

Rosenthal, Franz. *A Grammar of Biblical Aramaic*. Wiesbaden: Otto Harrassowitz, 1974.

Rosenthal, Ludwig A. 'Die Josephsgeschichte mit den Büchern Ester und Daniel verglichen'. *ZAW* 15 (1895): 278-84.

—'Nochmals der Vergleich Ester, Joseph–Daniel'. *ZAW* 17 (1897): 125-28.

Schmidt, Nathaniel. 'Daniel and Androcles'. *JAOS* 46 (1926): 1-7.

Shea, William. 'Daniel 3: Extra-Biblical Texts and the Convocation on the Plain of Dura'. *AUSS* 20 (1982): 29-52.

—'Further Literary Structures in Daniel 2-7: An Analysis of Daniel 4'. *AUSS* 23 (1985): 193-202.

—'Further Literary Structures in Daniel 2-7: An Analysis of Daniel 5, and the Broader Relationships within Chapters 2-7'. *AUSS* 23 (1985): 277-95.

Siegmann, E.F. 'The Stone Hewn from the Mountain'. *CBQ* 18 (1956): 364-79.

Silberman, L.H. 'Unriddling the Riddle: A Study in the Structure and Language of the Habakkuk Pesher'. *RQ* 3 (1961): 323-64.

Slotki, Judah. *Daniel, Ezra, and Nehemiah*. London: Soncino, 1951.

Soden, W. von. 'Eine babylonische Volksüberlieferung in den Danielerzählungen'. *ZAW* 53 (1935): 81-89.

Stinespring, W.F. 'The Active Infinitive with Passive Meaning in Biblical Aramaic'. *JBL* 81 (1962): 391-94.

Swain, J.W. 'The Theory of the Four Monarchies: Opposition History under the Roman Empire'. *Classical Philology* 35 (1940): 1-21.

Torrey, C.C. 'Notes on the Aramaic Part of Daniel'. In *Transactions of the Connecticut Academy of Arts and Sciences* 15 (1909): 241-82.

Towner, W. Sibley. *Daniel*. Atlanta: John Knox, 1984.

—'Poetic Passages of Daniel 1-6'. *CBQ* 31 (1969): 317-26.

Vogt, E. *Lexicon linguae aramaicae Veteris Testamenti documentis antiquis illustratum*. Rome: Biblical Institute, 1971.

Wernberg-Møller, Preben. *The Manual of Discipline*. Grand Rapids: Eerdmans, 1957.

Wharton, James. 'Daniel 3.16-18'. *Int* 39 (1985): 170-76.

Williams, J.G. 'Critical Note on the Aramaic Indefinite Plural of the Verb'. *JBL* 83 (1964): 180-82.

Williams, Ronald J. *Hebrew Syntax: An Outline*. 2nd edn. Toronto: University of Toronto, 1976.

Wright, A.G., *The Literary Genre Midrash*. Staten Island: Alba House, 1967.
Zimmermann, F. 'Writing on the Wall: Daniel 5.25f.'. *JQR* 55 (1965): 201-207.

INDEX

INDEX OF BIBLICAL AND OTHER ANCIENT REFERENCES

[Brackets ( ) indicate alternative verse numbering; italics indicate major discussions.]

INDEX OF AUTHORS